Toward
Manhood

Larry Pesavento

Toward
Manhood

Into the Wilderness of the Soul

Toward Manhood is published by
Christos: A Center for Men

The Center offers individual counseling,
group counseling, educational programs, men's
retreats, and structured initiatory experiences.
Information on these programs, additional
resources and contact information can be found
at www.ChristosCenter.com or via email at
larrpes@gmail.com.

ISBN-13: 978-0692692387

Table of Contents

Introduction   1

Chapter 1—Hardwired   5
Training Manual; A New Movement of Men; Men of the Movement; Sudden Brothers; Hardwired; Enter Psychology; Initiation; Modern Initiation

Chapter 2—The Problem of Pain   17
Separation; The Shame of Pain; Ordeal; Ordeal and Loss; Ordeal and Identity; Return; Toward Manhood

Chapter 3—The Great Separation   25
Hardwired Trigger; Good Mothering; Limbo; The Mother Complex; From Mother to Mother Object; Separation; Engulfment; Men Need Men

Chapter 4—Boundaries   39
Space and the Final Frontier; The Boy Within; Engulfment; Declaration of Independence; Walls; Boundary as Betrayal; The Warrior; The Warrior Within

Chapter 5—Addictions: Life Behind the Wall   51
The Desperate Boy; Rage; Pit Bulls; Deeper Retreat; Signs of Substance Addiction; Process Addictions; Sexual Addiction?; Pornography; Sexual Trauma; Acting In; A Way Out; Moving On

Chapter 6—The Age of the Father   71
Assistant Mothers; Masculine Energy; The Initiated Father; The Modern Age of the Father; The Father Wound; The Traditional Father; Creating a Father; The Competitive Father; The Sins of the Father; Identifying with the Dark Patriarchy

Chapter 7—The Vader Voice   85
The Father's World; Patriarchal Reality; The Father Inside; The Vader Voice; The Dark Father Outside; Facing the Voice; Star Wars

Chapter 8—Thank God It's Monday   99

Work as Initiation; Cal; The Religion of Business; Work and Father;
The Good News, The Bad News; Work vs. Job

Chapter 9—A Second Father   111

A Second Chance; Mentor; Pseudo-Initiation; Second Fathers;
Our Invisible Sons; Refathering; The Youngest Boy; The Middle Boy;
Dialogue; The Second Father: Obi Wan; The Adolescent

Chapter 10—Midlife Brothers   131

Midlife; Adolescent Unbidden; Midlife Adolescent; Healthy Adolescence;
Competition; Finding Brothers; The Mature Adolescent; Hans Solo;
Questions

Chapter 11—The Elder Within   145

The Elder; Yoda; The Elder Within; Enough; Facing the Bull

Chapter 12—Death   153

Loss; Modern Wilderness; Depression; Turning the Tragedy;
Dealing with Depression; Luke's Death; Wilderness

Chapter 13—Humility   167

Hubris; Ego; Ritual and Humility; Dark Humiliation; Humility and
Counsel; Vader and Humiliation; Beyond the Ego

Chapter 14—The Other Side   177

Men's Church; Standing Ground; Hurry Up And Wait; An Initiatory
Experience; Starting to See

Chapter 15—The Call   189

Manhood and Identity; Call; Soul and Spirit; Enthusiasm and
Passion; Intuition; Luke

Chapter 16—Return   199
Third Step; The Common Good; Work and the Father Wound; Work and Play; Nontraditional Work; The Twelfth Step

Chapter 17—Patriarch Light   209
The Return of the King; Separation; Return; The Enduring Elder;

Chapter 18—Pain and Purpose   217
Neurotic Pain; Legitimate Pain; Groundhog Day; Holy Teachers; Luke and Pain; The Wounded Healer

Chapter 19—Alone Together   225
Tomme; A Second Chance; If Only She'd; Separation; Recontracting; Household Stage; Recontracting in the Wilderness; Covenant

Chapter 20—Just Peace   239
Wisdom of the Ancestors; Peacemaker; Indigenous Justice; Indigenous Community; Equality; Gratitude; Why the Green Mother?; Elder Watch

Appendix—Damsels   253

Annotated Bibliography   265

About the Author   273

Acknowledgments

First, I owe a great debt of gratitude to my editor and great friend Howard Wells. His continued support, wise counsel, professional expertise and confidence in my vision has made this book possible.

I owe much to my wife and teacher of all things feminine. Mica Renes, my colleague and life partner, has given me so much in what it means for two people to be called to each other in love. I thank her for answering that call.

I thank those friends who have patiently listened to my confused birthing of new ideas and understandings including Robert Rack, Jay Owen-Smith, Sara Williams, Donald Walker, Jeff Bates, Tom King, and Jason DeBord (also for all his technical help).

I thank all the men who have entrusted me with their stories of struggle toward manhood. They have taught me so much.

Introduction

Sooner or later every man will be confronted by an intense, painful emotional crisis. No matter if a man is younger or older, gay or straight, or of any color of skin. You may now be in a crisis, emerged from one, or about to experience one. How a man handles this emotional crisis will reverberate through the rest of his life. This is a book for men in crisis.

There is a persistent notion that the Chinese character for crisis contains two symbols. One symbol represents danger, the other opportunity. This is linguistically inaccurate but the idea is a useful one. This book is about the danger that leads to opportunity. The opportunity is to reach a level of mature manhood that brings inner peace on a foundation of lived meaning and purpose.

A crisis is actually a big change, often unforeseen. Most men will be unprepared for this crisis because the culture has no place for it. This leaves a man like a deer in headlights, paralyzed by the shock. Even dictionaries define crisis as a disaster with synonyms such as catastrophe, calamity, and emergency. Obviously their emphasis is on the danger part of crisis.

Though emergency may be an apt definition I like the Greek word *krinein* that the word crisis is based on. This Greek word means separation. Separation also happens to be the first stage of the process that I talk about in this book. This separation feels like danger, even tragedy. Learning the truth of the process allows a man to negotiate this crisis and find the opportunity.

Most of the time men come into my office in the midst of crisis, in the midst of separation. This separation can be from a relationship, a job, financial security, from good health, the death of a loved one, from one's heartfelt dreams. I know how they feel because a major crisis led me to write this book.

What I tell men is that they are being given an opportunity to become the man they are called to be, the man that mirrors their true self. I say that I believe every man is personally called by a higher, wiser power that is known by many names. Finding this true self or soul self involves an inner journey into a man's psyche and soul. I call this a psychospiritual journey. This is the journey of opportunity. Separation triggers this opportunity. But separation must be embraced.

I model this process and journey on the archetypal stages of initiation. In this case puberty initiation, the transformation from boyhood to manhood, most mirrors this journey. Most men are stuck in a boy mentality and psychology because that is all they've been taught. Through no fault of our own we are boys walking around in men's bodies. The archetype of initiation from one stage of life to another holds a key to our transformation to inner manhood. Few of us have been given this key.

So this is a book for men who have the courage and strength to embark on this inner quest for their own true self. I am a psychotherapist, a pastoral counselor, and a man. (Some would say an old man.) Writing this book is a major part of my calling. I draw on my personal experience, my education working with men for over 35 years, my studies and research, and my inner life. My job as an Elder is to explain the process and hold an initiatory space. Each man must walk the journey alone. Each man supplies his own ending.

The journey will always bring a man to a time called Ordeal. Separation is the painful part. Ordeal is the fearful part. Just staying in this part takes courage. There is inevitably a different kind of depression from the loss of separation and the loss of emptiness. Here there is chaos. No order. No roads to follow. Here is the Void that holds all answers and may or may not give them up easily. The culture calls staying here masochism. A wise Elder who holds space calls this becoming a man.

This is not the man running corporations or running in commercials. This is a man who has stood in his pain to find what's inside. And it happens that what's inside is what his community needs. Indigenous peoples put boys through initiation to find men to give the tribe exactly the talents needed to create harmony and abundance for all. They knew that boys take but men give.

The third part of initiation is the return of the transformed boy to the community as a man of vision and talents and courage, ready to give, eager to serve. This is not an arrogant man who can't wait to wield power over the weaker ones. This is a humble man who uses his power to create a community that helps the weaker become stronger.

The process of any initiation in modern society is countercultural. Modernity could be defined as lacking true initiations. This book speaks to the psychospiritual inner process I believe both men and this culture desperately need. This is a dangerous book as seen from the top of the culture. It holds an opportunity for those who take their initiation seriously.

In our culture this transformation can happen at any age. Often this happens after a man is 35. This is a time when a man has the internal strength to move into initiation even though he has little guidance or mentoring. Another initiatory period seems to start when a man faces retirement age. Often these two initiations are amalgamated into an extra intensive process.

The process is boy to man to healthy patriarch. This patriarch is the mature man with an even larger mission. A later initiation is to Elder. The lesson here is that major and minor transitional crises, initiations, happen throughout life for our own good and for the good of our community. When the process of initiation is experienced and learned the transitions that life and Spirit hold for us can be negotiated more and more effectively and successfully.

Chapter 1
Hardwired

Most men today are burnt out and don't know it. Whether a success or a failure most men suffer from some symptoms of burnout: depression, anxiety, lack of motivation, chronic physical ailments, fatigue from overwork, addiction to alcohol, compulsive sexual activity, regular bouts of anger at home or at work. We don't acknowledge these symptoms to ourselves because we, men, have been taught to numb our feelings as warriors must do. For first of all we are taught to be warriors. We are taught to be warriors until we die, gloriously, anonymously, or somewhere in between. We are taught that the mission is more important than our life, than life itself.

In fact, men do need a mission. We have been taught to be warriors with missions over the span of thousands of years. We have been bred and trained to be focused, intrepid, vigilant, goal directed. We are good at getting things done no matter the cost. We have been taught to ignore our well-being for the well-being of others.

We are also good at taking orders and being trained by older men. We are willing to fulfill the mission statements of our companies, organizations, communities because we are following a deeper programming. We are taught to give up our lives for the greater good of our community as ordered by older men. We are taught that the ideal we are fighting for is the protection of our beleaguered family and society. We are taught that as a warrior we are protecting by providing.

In our society becoming a man is becoming a warrior. Being a good man is being an intrepid yet numb warrior. In a real sense men are on a war footing emotionally most of their lives.

Training Manual

The truth is that we have been unknowingly betrayed by the very men who have trained us, our bosses and generals, our political and spiritual leaders. The modern way of achieving manhood is not working for us. We have been given a training manual for warriors assuming that it leads to manhood. But this manual is out of date and incomplete. Being a complete warrior does not make a mature man. Our training has been inappropriate for us men and for our society. Our mission of protection entails much more than providing. Men are burnt out by following the manual and the mission. Burnout is modern battle fatigue. And we are suffering a pain that our mission of protecting by providing won't allow us to admit.

Some men feel the pain as the "failure of success." They have done everything right—accomplished the mission—only to find themselves unsatisfied and vaguely frustrated. They find themselves king of a non-strategic hill.

Other men only partially fulfill their mission, but courageously keep trying while questioning their own skill and integrity. They are not gifted in their assigned training yet never question where that training manual came from. They are taught not to question the mission, only themselves. They are frustrated men, angry at themselves, sometimes taking it out on the loved ones whose welfare they are supposed to protect.

Still other men just give up and leave their manhood and self-respect behind. These are the casualties of this nonsensical mission.

The most compelling evidence for the depth of this unacknowledged burnout is in men's health statistics. The human psyche works in such a way that emotional pain that is not consciously dealt with goes deep into the unconscious. If the pain is driven deep enough it ends up in our bodies.

Herbert Benson, a physician and founder of Harvard's Mind/Body Medical Institute, estimates that 60-90% of all physician office visits in the United States stem from stress-related conditions. Psychic pain often leads to physical breakdown and men's bodies are riddled with deeply driven psychic pain. As a result men, today, live 5.3 years less than women on average.

Men also lead women in 8 of the top 10 causes of death. In what is called gender paradox men of all ages are four times more likely to commit suicide than women. Men's suicide rates increase with age as men suffer more burnout and have less capacity for joy and spontaneity.

After retirement, the suicide rate skyrockets for men, but not for women. Between the ages of 65-74 the rate is 6.3 times higher for males. Between the ages of 75-84, the suicide rate is 7 times higher. And for those over 85, it is nearly 18 times higher for men than it is for women. Suicide is the ultimate symbol of burying our pain.

Health statistics also show other symptoms of burnout. Men are 3 times as likely as women to have a drug or alcohol problem which may explain why men are more than twice as likely as women to have chronic liver disease. Addictions are a major sign of a man struggling with the pain of burnout. As we will see, addictions are also a major way men treat the most significant sign of burnout—an under the radar, low level depression that slowly drains a man of any natural, good feeling.

Only in the past few years have men stepped forward to point out the fact of burnout and to question its cause. Men with backgrounds as diverse as sociology, theology, philosophy, anthropology, psychology and even poetry have started to speak out on the problems of our manhood training manual.

A New Movement of Men

Answers are now emerging that address the problem of widespread male burnout. A movement has formed, though it is more like a guerrilla movement. Uprisings are happening spontaneously as men in small and larger groups start to question their mission and their trainers. To be sure this movement has come about 30 years after the start of the feminist movement. But this movement is much more pervasive and advanced than many men realize.

Men have started meeting together to share their frustration and pain. The movement shows up in men's councils, men's groups, and men's weekend workshops. (It also shows up in ongoing male gatherings such as the Mankind Project and Breakthrough.) It shows up in the growing amount of men's literature that I hope to acquaint you with. It even manages to creep into the fabric of our society with jokes about "drums and spears" and men "going native in the woods."

Common to the whole men's movement is the questioning of the modern cultural meaning of manhood. Along with this questioning is a deep searching for new rules of conduct that embody healthier standards of male behavior. Burnout shows the inner conflict most men have. This movement is starting to show that the problem is not the man but the mission.

Men of the Movement

In the men's movement there are many different perspectives on men's growth and behavior. Men like Sam Keen, David Gerzon, Warren Farrell, and David Gilmore write from a political and social perspective. They are looking at the big political picture and the social training men are given. They then look at the political, social, and environmental effects of a power structure controlled by these kinds of socialized men.

There are also men like Robert Bly, Michael Meade, Aaron Kipnis, Malidoma Some, and James Hillman who come more from the mythopoetic tradition which has an anthropological as well as literary base. These men write about the basis of culture itself, its underlying beliefs embodied in cultural myths. They believe we need to create new, healthier mythic ideals for our Western culture. They are looking for new paradigms of manhood that go far deeper than changing the power structure.

I will be drawing heavily on both these branches of the men's movement. However, I will be adding a psychological and spiritual perspective from my background as a psychotherapist and pastoral counselor working with men for over 35 years. This perspective describes the inner dynamics of men's growth. I will be describing a developmental and existential psychology that emphasizes the healthy stages of psychospiritual growth men must go through. From this perspective I will share the thoughts of men such as Carl Jung, Robert Johnson, Robert Moore and David Gillette, Scott Peck, Terrence Real, William Pollack and even Sigmund Freud.

All these men and others will be presented in this book. They are the pioneers. We owe them a great deal of gratitude. They are the modern guerrilla leaders fighting with healthy warrior energy for all of us. I feel like I am standing on the shoulders of giants in writing this book.

My own eyes were opened at a weekend workshop led by Michael Meade and Malidoma Some. They easily recruited me once I heard what they had to say. They touched something in my heart that I knew was true but had no words for. Their message changed my life. I can only wish the same to those who read on.

Sudden Brothers

One common tenet of the men's movement is that men need each other in order to grow. Some men talk of this need manifesting in father hunger. Others talk of each man's need for relatedness. Still others talk of the brotherhood that emerges in times of good teamwork and shoulder to shoulder intimacy.

No man can do it alone. We're not weak or cowardly in accepting this fact. Men are not made that way, even though that flawed training manual says differently. The self-made man is a myth. Men are made to grow with other men. Men are made by other men.

Men need brothers and close friends, fathers and mentors, Elders and wise male counsel in order to find their true manhood. I can remember when I first started attending men's workshops and meetings. When men started sharing their frustration instead of their elation, their failures instead of successes, I relaxed and had the strongest feeling of coming home. I felt like I had unexpectedly come to a place where I was deeply understood and accepted. I felt like I belonged. I felt totally supported in my broken manhood. I knew I needed more of this in order to survive and grow.

There is a term in the movement called "sudden brothers." This term was coined because many men experience a feeling similar to mine. This feeling has been reported in meeting after meeting where men who were strangers have come together, feeling and describing an instant, special bond toward each other. I now understand that term in my gut. And I understand how that feeling can have a profound effect on men's motivation to do men's work.

Men have been raised with positive male images that only sanction either standing alone or standing together as a team. Men coming together to share brokenness instead of victory is deemed unmanly. Sports or corporate teams, to fulfill the approved male mission, are the only ways of male connection. Men are left to share their full range of feelings only with women, usually mothers or wives or girlfriends, if they're shared at all. Too many men look to women for what they need from brothers.

We are cut off from relating to other men in meaningful ways. There's no room for shared feeling or true brotherhood in the modern male manual. There's no room for sharing what men need to share in order to mature. As we will see, brothers and Elders are crucial to our hopes of becoming men. We are cut off from our brothers and the family of men. We are cut off from the source of our own manhood.

Hardwired

All men have a deep yearning and need for this feeling of brotherhood. This need is so strong because it runs so deep, deeper than any one of us realizes. It goes deeper than our recent experiences or even our lifetime experience. It is as if we are experiencing some of what men have experienced since fathers had sons, and brothers wrestled with brothers.

This yearning for brotherhood is one example of the deep feelings that men have when they first come out of their goal-oriented numbness. Fr. Richard Rohr, a Franciscan priest who studies men's spiritual growth, emphasizes that what he is saying about these issues, men already know in their souls. Men are not surprised by what is said in many men's gathering because they already have a sense of the rightness of it.

Both Robert Moore and Sam Keen talk of this knowledge being in the hardware of every man. They talk of men being wired in specific masculine ways. We are wired to need brothers. We are wired to need older men. We are wired to yearn for a manhood we have not found in modern society.

Men accused of numbness take note. Men who feel numb take note. The numbness is in the software. We are hardwired to feel strongly. The deep, passionate aliveness is in there. There is a powerfully strong inner life of compassion and conviction in every man. The problem is in the program. Men are yearning to feel this aliveness and passion. Women who accuse men of numbness yearn to feel that emotion in their men.

Enter Psychology

These hardwired feelings can be explained psychologically by the theories of Carl Jung, Freud's contemporary and main early disciple. Jung broke with Freud's theories on some important points. One of those points had to do with the sudden brother feelings. Jung theorized after exhaustive research that there is a part of our psyche that is not immediately available to our awareness or experience. This unconscious part of ourselves is formed not only by our personal experiences, a personal unconscious, which was Freud's insight, but also by the accumulated experience of humanity as a whole. With this universal part of our psyche we can personally experience the essence of what every man and woman has experienced who has lived before us. Jung called this the collective unconscious.

In the case of men, we feel so strongly about connecting to other men because connecting with other men in meaningful ways, both our peers and older men, has been a primal need in the mystery of manhood since the beginning of humanity. This hardwired need resides in our collective unconscious.

Software or programming resides in our personal unconscious, our personal history and training. In the case of modern man, faulty software is a product of the modern training manual. Garbage in, garbage out. The important point here is that the software can be changed in a lifetime or in an intense time in life unlike the hardware of the collective unconscious which changes at glacial, millennial speed.

Jung posited that there were certain universal, human experiences that repeated themselves so often throughout history that we deeply yearn for these familiar patterns in our lives. He called these patterns archetypes of experience. For example, why are our social structures often developed around a single, male figure at the top of a hierarchy? These may be kings, presidents, bosses, coaches, gang leaders. We often refer to them as father figures. The archetypal experience of having a father as head of a family or clan is lived out in these structures. We react to a deep need for a father archetype when we react to a male leader figure.

Because men archetypally search for an experience of father, and have also had the historic political power to create social structure, many of our political structures are based on a patriarchal or father model. This is the man at the top model and most men react archetypally with unquestioning loyalty and obedience to that top man. Men have an archetypal yearning for male leaders that will give society direction just as they have a deep yearning for a father who will give them personal direction. If women had the political power, there is a good chance they would create a political structure based on a different archetypal experience.

Another example of an archetypal experience relates to why men react so strongly to the assignment of a mission. We have the warrior archetype in our psyches as a result of thousands of years of training and participation in war. For thousands of years warriors have been taught strict, unquestioning obedience. Leaders who understand this hardwired warrior personality can motivate us to their own ends by appealing to our martial instincts, as well as our needs for father. By installing and manipulating our software they can control the warrior in each of us and thus our behavior and mission. Good warriors don't question the mission. Many men felt manipulated by their leaders in this way in their Vietnam experience.

This warrior archetype is probably built on an even deeper archetype, that of the hunter. Hunters especially ancient ones, had to work in teams, be extremely focused, put emotions aside, and work silently and give signals in order to accomplish their goals.

Warrior and hunter, protector and provider. These are deeply hardwired roles that every man feels at some level. They are good and useful to society. For many men the problem resides in how the software, installed by modern patriarchs, affects those roles.

Archetypal experiences reside in our collective unconscious. They can come out in different ways in our behavior and attitudes. These archetypes affect us like independent personalities inside that can take over our attitudes and behaviors if we are not aware of our inner life and motivations. Some psychologists call these archetypal personalities sub-personalities. Others call them ego states or complexes. No, this is not the same as multiple personalities. The secret here is to be aware of how we use different archetypal energies.

It is not necessary to understand this theory of archetypes as much as it is necessary to be aware of how we are affected by them. If we start looking at human behavior from an archetypal viewpoint it is not as random as we might believe. There are many archetypes that affect us intimately every day. If we don't realize their existence and power we are not really free men. We end up reacting to powers we don't understand and going on missions we haven't freely chosen.

Initiation

Another archetype Jung named was the archetype of the initiate. The initiation experience has formed men over tens of thousands of years. Rites of male puberty initiation have been performed throughout most cultures for most of history. These rites were the formal process of a boy becoming a man. Adolescent boys for millennia have universally yearned for manhood through these rites. Tribal Elders in countless cultures have realized their duty to guide boys into finding their manhood through their initiatory traditions.

For thousands of years—even until today in some cultures—the process of undergoing these rites was as significant as anything the man would do in his whole life. The result of the rites was the possession of his full manhood. Manhood meant full and equal participation in the life of the community, with access to all the values and the power that community had to give. This manhood also included a sacred trust, the responsibility of carrying on the values to the next generation. Most importantly these rites gave, and still give in some cultures, what many men yearn for. They gave a sense of integrity and rightness to a man's life

Mircea Eliade, author of the book *Rites and Symbols of Initiation,* writes that "to gain the right to be admitted among adults, the adolescent has to pass through a series of initiatory Ordeals: it is by virtue of these rites, and of the revelations they entail, that he will be recognized as a responsible member of the society." He goes on to say that for indigenous peoples "a man is made—he does not make himself all by himself." He cannot do it alone.

My strong reaction to the workshop experiences mentioned earlier makes sense archetypally. Coming to a workshop with other men and wanting to learn about serious issues of manhood can trigger the archetype of the initiate. I felt just like other young, frightened but eager adolescents as they went in groups to start the rites of their own manhood. Most men at the workshop felt that same yearning and call.

Modern Initiation

We have no rites that truly give us a sense of manhood today. We are deprived of an authentic manhood training manual. We do have rituals that have some archetypal flavor to them. Getting a driver's license is one. Being old enough to drink is another. Graduating from high school or college has some sense of accomplishment, and graduation gives us some new social rights in the job market. Marriage is another. The closest is to an actual initiation is probably boot camp in the military. Yet we will see how that rite, as well as the others, leaves so much to be desired as a rite of manhood.

How about cigarette smoking and manhood? A 1995 *New York Times* article about the marketing of cigarettes quotes a marketing guru, who talks of the cowboy as the modern warrior and the Marlboro man as the ultimate man. Alan Brody goes on to say that "we as a society have abandoned tribal initiation rites and cigarettes are a substitute; kids want to prove themselves and play the role of adults. When you rob people of something they want, marketers find a way to give it to them."

How about sports and manhood? It is clear that our society believes that what a boy learns in sports will prepare him for manhood. And so many successful business executives use sports analogies in talking of their business plans. They make "end runs" around their competitors, "slam dunk" a sale, hit a "home run" strategy in order to be "winners." Our cultural models of manhood reside in the NBA and the NFL. Unfortunately our cultural models of manhood are boys, not Elders, who have no idea of what manhood is about. Yet many other young boys, and many older ones, satisfy their yearning for manhood by idolizing them.

So how do we become men today without any rite of initiation? Is this lack of a true rite the reason men are burnt out? How do we become mature men inside? These are the questions to be addressed in this book. And they take us into the modern realm of psychology as well as the ancient realm of ritual and spirituality.

I believe the initiation archetype, and the yearnings of the initiate, still hold a key to a modern understanding of a man's path to maturity. There is something hardwired in all of us that motivates us to find something more about being a man. There is something that tells us we haven't gotten it yet.

Ancient Elders still have something to tell us. Their teachings are so powerful because they are part of our own deep history. Because they are archetypal these teachings also keep recurring in our history in the words of modern Elders. The heart of the teaching is unchanged throughout the centuries but the teachings of ancient and modern Elders are often in a form that goes unnoticed in a society of uninitiated men. Fortunately, Elders are still there waiting to teach.

This book will describe a modern psychospiritual process of becoming a man based on clues from ancient and modern Elders. It describes a modern process of initiation. This book is not meant to be a self-help manual but an invitation to initiatory Ordeal. As I describe the process of the initiatory Ordeal I hope you will feel a deep connection. From that connection I hope you find the motivation to go through your own initiations.

Any initiation ritual puts one's whole life on the line. This is serious business. Initiates throughout history have faced the real possibility of death, and some did die. Manhood does not come easily. The issues brought up in this book are painful, difficult issues. But the rewards are great.

Chapter 2
The Problem of Pain

In the last chapter I talked about how men bury emotional pain in their bodies and the burnout that occurs when men numb themselves in the pursuit of someone else's mission. The burnout comes because men have been taught to ignore psychological and spiritual pain—to numb it, rather than deal with it.

The problem of achieving manhood in any culture always leads to the problem of pain. The healthy initiatory journey of manhood starts with the conscious choice to face emotional pain in our lives, the necessary inner pain that comes with finding one's own unique mission. The archetypal experience of initiation gives a man the motivation to face that pain.

Separation

Let me give you an example. The first stage of archetypal initiation is always separation. For thousands of years initiates in their early teens were suddenly separated from all that was familiar in village life and taken by Elders to a mysterious place outside the village. This sudden separation was a very painful emotional experience. The initiate was exiled for an indeterminate period of time to an inhospitable place to face unknown challenges. Yet the boy knew from early in his life to expect this painful separation. He had seen his brothers or other older boys disappear. He knew this disappearance had to do with boys coming back as men. He knew it would be painful. He had faith that his Elders would teach him what to do with the pain. He also knew that this was the way to his manhood.

Today, men inevitably face a similar sudden, forceful separation, an unexpected depressing crisis. Some are separated from their jobs by layoff or firing. Other men find themselves involuntarily in the pain of a divorce, or the abrupt termination of a significant relationship. Some men are suddenly separated from a former lifestyle because of serious illness or accident. Archetypal separations continue to occur in our lives.

Most men neither expect these separations nor have any clue as to how to handle the pain. This pain is too hard to ignore or bury. This pain is not the physical pain of a backbreaking job, or the pain of long work hours, or the pain of financial burden that men have been taught to endure. This confusing pain is not covered in the training manual.

Statistics show that a man who is rejected by a wife or suffers the rejection of job loss, even if he is not economically suffering, will face a high chance of hospitalization in the following year. In men this kind of separation stress most often leads to heart disease and stroke. Without the proper training, the emotional pain of separation gets dumped into the body, into the area of physical pain that men have been taught to endure.

Separation is always the first step in the initiatory process. Separation is also an inevitable life experience. It forces a man to confront a kind of pain he knows nothing about. The problem of pain in our society is that men are taught to handle physical pain as a badge of courage, like the bad knees of a star football player. Like good warriors we are taught to play through the pain not gain from it. The initiatory emotional pain is another matter. Admission of emotional pain, such as confusion, depression, discouragement, anxiety is seen as disgraceful. Shame causes the lessons of separation and initiation to be lost. Crisis becomes tragedy rather than opportunity.

The Shame of Pain

Most men come into my office feeling two things. One is a kind and intensity of emotional pain they have never felt before. The other is a deep shame that they are feeling this pain at all.

One of my clients going through a divorce had a long history of hard drinking and bar fighting. He was very familiar with physical pain and long recoveries. He was also very familiar with the stress of running a very successful business. He was a very successful warrior.

He was also very much in love with his wife who didn't reciprocate. In my men's group he trusted enough to admit of his sleepless nights and aimless days and lost business opportunities. He often repeated that the pain of his divorce was worse than any beating he ever had. He slowly started to realize he was going through initiatory pain.

The separated man, like the initiate who is taken away from the village, feels miserable, lonely, confused, and afraid—a normal reaction if looked at from an initiatory perspective. However, from the perspective of modern male culture these feelings are grossly unmanly. Admitting to them is the ultimate embarrassment. In the modern flawed training manual men are taught that emotional pain is a signal that something is wrong with their manhood. As one man told me, "I'm a wuss if I'm depressed."

This situation is similar to World War I, where the military training manual literally taught that to feel fear meant cowardice. Young men were told that good soldiers didn't feel fear. So, when men did feel the natural fear in war they knew to bury it or feel shame. Many became paralyzed by the shame of feeling fear, their fighting efficiency diminished greatly not by cowardice but by shame. Some died, emasculated by their shame. Others lived lives paralyzed by shell shock, their word for Post-Traumatic Stress. The Army couldn't understand why they did not have more effective fighters. The Military didn't realize the flaw in their manual.

It wasn't until World War II that the Army was forced to change their training dogma to properly prepare men for battle, by teaching that feeling fear, even terror, was normal. A good fighting man performed in the presence of his fear and in spite of it. World War II soldiers were able to be very effective fighting men, in part, because of this change in training.

In a sense most men today are taught the World War I mind set regarding emotional pain—real men don't have fear or anxiety or depression. Real men don't react to separation, don't even acknowledge it. Emotional pain is a sign of cowardice and weakness.

Most often, when men come in to counseling, they are trying to get rid of the pain, to get rid of their shame as well as their discomfort. This need to get rid of the pain is a predictable sign to me of the uninitiated immature man but the fact that he is in my office is a sign that he is a person of sincerity and courage.

My job as a counselor is first to help the man consciously understand his pain and what is happening to him. My job is to help him look past the feelings of confusion and shame by showing him that his separation feelings are a natural part of a different road to maturity, different from what he has been taught. I explain that he can show his true courage by consciously moving into the very pain he is ashamed of.

I explain to a man that he is unconsciously in the first stage of initiation, the stage of separation. I explain that it will take a while to negotiate this stage and it will be painful. I often give a man the first chapters of this book to help him understand what he is going through. The first half of this book talks about the complexity of this first stage and the trials of healthy separation. I tell him that he is going in the right direction and hope that he feels the rightness of what I am saying. Then I talk briefly about the further stages in his new mission.

Ordeal

The second broad step in the initiation journey is submission to Ordeal, to the pain of being changed. This is the time of the emerging man's life and the loss of the comforts of the boy's life. Ordeal is a time to discover a personal and unique definition of manhood and how to live out that definition. It is a time of looking inward, humbly waiting for an epiphany. It is a voluntary stay in the midst of pain, in the middle of crisis. It is a time of either tragedy or transformation. Ordeal is a time to be taught important lessons about one's life and life direction. Most men in our society are unprepared for this painful but necessary teaching. The opportunity of Ordeal then turns to tragedy. Indigenous men expected Ordeal. Indigenous men were prepared for the pain of transformation.

The boy in indigenous tribes went into Ordeal after being separated from the village. When the indigenous boy went into the Ordeal he was subjected to many tests that forced him to draw on his inner strength. He was taken away from all that was familiar to him by men he knew only by sight. He was forced to endure ritual pain even though he instinctively looked for someone to take it away. Much of the pain was physical: the shedding of blood, scourging, knocking out of teeth, circumcision and other rituals that I will explain throughout the book. Some anthropologists see this pain purely as basic warrior training, forming a man to endure the hardships of war as protection for the tribe. For some indigenous cultures this superficial training was and is the case. However for many cultures for thousands of years this Ordeal had much deeper spiritual and psychological aspects.

I understand the initiatory physical pain as a part of a larger psychospiritual pain. The Ordeal for most indigenous people was primarily an emotional and spiritual Ordeal. This is where deep change was supposed to happen, where manhood was formed. Mircea Eliade explains that a "novice emerges from his Ordeal endowed with a totally different being from that which he possessed before his initiation." Wise Elders have always said that emotional and spiritual pain is the necessary precondition for that change of inner being to take place.

Not all initiatory rituals were healthy. Some cultures disintegrated into violent, destructive forms of initiation. These cultures created warriors only to bring riches and status to the village. The temptation for older men to use younger men for selfish, power-seeking purposes has always been present in human culture.

However, the heart of the best initiatory rituals carries the ideal of transforming the pain of Ordeal into a new perception of what is most important to a man and to his community. A transformative Ordeal is a way for a man to find his deepest values and to live them out in service to those he loves. One of the most important values the Ordeal teaches is that the measure of a man is not how much pain he can inflict, as a warrior, but how much pain he can consciously endure and transform for a higher purpose.

Ordeal and Loss

The Ordeal is first meant to teach new ways to look at pain, especially the pain of loss. Separation brings loss. Initiatory Ordeal teaches how to handle loss. In the puberty initiations this is the loss of boyhood and its pleasures. The boy loses the entitled sense of being nurtured and protected by powerful adult figures. He loses his old, carefree lifestyle. He loses the illusion that he can indefinitely keep all his options open. He loses the illusion that he can take without giving back.

Robert Bly says that the key to a modern man's growth lies in his grief. If a man is willing to recognize and grieve all the losses in his life, he is well on his way to maturity. If he is willing to accept the losses as part of his initiation he will find his manhood. As we will see, today, the loss is related to what we were all taught manhood was about, especially by our fathers. It is the loss of old training habits as well as the loss of outworn missions.

It is the loss of most of what we were told would make us happy.

Many men come into my office and immediately start to cry, sometimes uncontrollably. They then immediately try to shut off the crying or hide their tears. They are ashamed of a natural reaction to their Ordeal. They are ashamed of their own grief. They try to stop the very process that leads to healing. It is my job to help them willingly stay in their Ordeal and ultimately be proud of their courage and their tears.

Ordeal and Identity

The Ordeal also teaches new ways to look at life. In the wilderness, in the middle of his pain, an initiate finds his calling. It is within the Ordeal that a man finds his new and truer identity. Within the Ordeal a man finds a deeper purpose in his life that completes his yearning for manhood. This is his epiphany. This is the core of initiation.

In the Ordeal a man must lose the expectations of others. Expectations of how he should fulfill his manhood. Expectations that have become a comfort. He must lose the expectation that parents, bosses, and friends can provide a secure direction. He must lose the notion that there is no need to leave the safety and boyhood rules of the village.

In Ordeal the boy struggles with finding his own purpose in a gray world. He must somehow find answers deep inside himself and deep inside the wilderness. The transformation happens in the wilderness of his own soul, where answers are much harder to come by than in the rules of society.

Most of the second half of the book talks of the Ordeal: both the pain and the promise of the Ordeal. It talks of what happens on the "other side," the indigenous people's words for the wilderness and of what men have found on the other side of their pain.

Return

The other side of Ordeal leads to the third step of the initiatory process, reintegration or return. The return explains the why of the pain, the why of the initiatory journey. It is upon return that the pain makes sense.

The explanation of the third step of initiation is also a typical mythical, as well as religious, theme. In the heroic journey the hero always returns from his Ordeals with a gift, often called a boon. In the hero myth there is always a critical piece of salvation that only the hero has. The boon is critical for the spiritual survival of the hero's community. So the pain of Ordeal, according to the heroic myth and the initiatory journey, is not only for a man's personal peace but for the good of all those he is intimately connected with. The boon always reinvigorates a dying community.

So the lonely initiatory journey is for the good of all those we love and touch. The Buddhist belief in the Bodhisattva is an example of the return of a mature man. The Bodhisattva is one who, on the very threshold of enlightenment, turns around to reenter the world to share and teach, and vows that he will not enter Nirvana until all other humans have entered before him. He reenters the world of pain for the sake of others.

A Christian core teaching is that God so loved the world that he took on the pain of the world in order to teach all people the meaning of conscious, voluntary suffering for the purpose of saving the community of all people. Out of Christ's pain came his own direction and the salvation of the human community.

The return stage is when a man steps toward being an Elder. He makes himself responsible for the emotional and spiritual well-being of the generation to come, as well as his whole village. He goes out of his way to give young men a chance for their own manhood. He is an active witness to the values he has found in his Ordeal.

The paradox here is that in a dying culture, a culture that has lost its deepest values, the man as hero and Elder is not embraced. A mature man is always an enemy to the status quo. He brings new life to a society that has lost its power of change and transformation. He brings a renewed and updated sense of values to a society that has lost sight of what is most important, what really matters. So a mature man most often has to use his lessons of pain not only to endure the rejection of the community but to be a witness to hope through change. Often, it is the witness of his endurance of pain for a higher purpose that is most transformative to the community.

When we talk of this deep personal change, we are as much in the world of spirituality as psychology. We are in the area of mystics and Zen masters as much as mature men and Elders. The psychological journey and the spiritual journey are closely tied together. That is why I will be talking of a psychospiritual evolution.

Toward Manhood

So the structure of traditional initiation can be seen as three large stages: Separation, Ordeal, and Return. Initiation is always a paradigm of some dramatic, painful change. To indigenous people it meant a significant change of status in the community and ongoing vibrant leadership for the tribe. Today this change has more to do with moving from one internal stage of growth to another. In other words the initiation archetype helps us learn how to grow through the stages of male psychospiritual development: from boy to adolescent, from adolescent to man, from man to healthy patriarch, from man to Elder. Hopefully if enough men go through this transformation we can again have a wise, Elder society instead of a modern, Elderless one.

I have found that when men know what to do with their emotional pain they show remarkable courage and insight. They take the goodness and strength of the warrior archetype and use it in their inner Ordeal. They then use that hardwired sense of purpose for something truly meaningful.

The rest of this book talks about the three initiatory steps, performed in the wilderness of our interior lives. It talks of the pitfalls in each step as well as the opportunities on the journey toward manhood.

Chapter 3
The Great Separation

The indigenous initiation experience has a lot to say about the healthy growth of men today. Modern psychology is one key in translating the ancient initiation experience into contemporary terms. Certain mystical spiritual traditions still hold keys to an authentic path to manhood. Both modern and ancient traditions can give answers to the perennial problem of the meaning of pain.

Puberty initiation prepared boys for the inevitable human pain of both growth and frustration, the pain of yearning and loss, the pain of both tragedy and transformation. Growth involves going through the pain of change. But there is also pain in resisting change. Elders knew there was no way around the pain of being human. Elders also knew that change always involves the pain of loss, and loss involves separation from something valued but no longer needed. The separation lesson was the first step toward manhood that Elders taught. It is no coincidence that unexpected, abrupt separation is what brings most men into counseling.

Hardwired Trigger

Separation always triggers the initiatory process. But what is initiatory separation in our modern lives? Separation from what? How does a man consciously know which turns to make once he is separated? How do we get in the way of separation? What crises are really opportunities?

Here is an excerpt from *Parabola* magazine, Fall, 1993, written by an African man, Nouk Bassomb, from his own contemporary initiatory experience:

> *Soon after a boy has been initiated, that is, soon after he has been allowed into the society of adults, African Bassa people put him to a*

test. Seven to nine Elders materialize one morning, at around five o'clock, outside his father's compound.

"Step outside, boy!" they shout.

The boy comes out. The Elders place themselves between him and the door.

"It's time for you to depart, boy. Go! Now!"

The morning this happened to me, I had only a little piece of cloth called sarja around my waist. I turned my back and left.

My mom ran after me, but the Elders who were behind me to make sure that I would cross the boundaries of our village kept her from hugging me.

"Go away, woman!" I heard the Elders say. "For the next eighteen 'moons' minimum, this boy has nothing, and we mean nothing, to do with the people of this village. That's the law. Let him go."

I did not even have the right to look back. I kept going. I had to show that I was a man, a little man, who one day would be a man, a grown man, an adult. A firm, upright support for the entire village. I was thirteen...

To undergo the transition from being a boy to becoming a man, male children spend ninety days in the deep forest. It is required. They must learn to survive in a dangerous and hostile environment, to find their food, cook it, and share it with their fellow comrades. There are no females around. In my age group, there were twenty-seven of us.

As you can see, these rites continue today as they have been for 10,000 years. In this case the separation process goes on for almost two years. The Ordeal lasts for 90 days.

In puberty initiation rites from earliest times the first step is the forcible abduction of an adolescent boy by the village Elders. These Elders decide when individual boys are ready to be taken from the village by discerning when a young boy is strong enough to go through the grueling cultural and spiritual transformation ritual. They hope they are correct in knowing the best time, as boys sometimes do not survive the initiation process.

In these rites the boy is forcefully separated from mother, father, grandparents, village—all that is familiar and nurturing. The separation is sudden and intense. It is an experience a boy will never forget. He will never see his mother or father or the village in the same way again.

In this chapter I will talk primarily about the psychological and symbolic meaning of separation from mother. This separation starts the initiatory process for most men, and is the place in our culture it often founders. If a man is able to negotiate this separation from mother he must then separate from the father. Both separations must happen if the boy is to become a man. The separation from mother I call the Great Separation for it is the first and most difficult one.

In the excerpt, Nouk said, "The Elders...kept her from hugging me." This forceful separation sounds rather harsh to our ears. Why not at least a last hug upon leaving? How can a mother's show of love hurt? Don't we all need some encouragement from loved ones to get along in life? Don't we all need human touch, especially from a woman? Where is the wisdom here, or the manhood?

If a boy stayed in the village near his mother's hut, he could not experience the Ordeal in the wilderness. Elders instinctively knew that overstaying in the village, especially by his mother's hut, softened a boy and robbed him of the courage and motivation for Ordeal, even though individual mothers knew and respected the importance of initiation. Elders realized that the world of comfort and physical nurturance, the maternal world of village life, could be dangerous and regressive to a boy's spirit as he approached puberty. The possibility of a mother's comfort would always be a temptation for a boy to never leave the village. The Elders and mothers realized that overstaying would be harmful to both the viability of the community and the spiritual maturity of the boy himself.

Good Mothering

Hugging is symbolic of all that is nurturing, that protects a boy from harm, that tells the boy he is loved, that says he is important. In his infancy and early years that kind of nurturing and comforting is essential. A young boy's ability to meet his own needs is minimal. The feminine motivation to incorporate the needs of a child as her own, greater than her own, is profound. Good mothering intuits a child's needs because a mother revolves her whole life around that child's well-being.

The result of this good mothering is a deep sense of trust in the boy. The boy trusts that somehow his needs will be met. He learns to trust that the universe is not an impersonal enemy and that he holds an important part in his world. Nurturing mother energy is probably the ultimate energy that enables a man to keep going in a sometimes painful life with a sense of hope. Mothering energy, symbolized as unconditional love, is the foundation of the initiatory journey.

Especially in the first two or three years of a child's life, mothering energy is vital to protecting the child from being overwhelmed with the pain and frustration of not getting its needs met. Starting at infancy the child is helpless in meeting even primitive biological needs. The mother, or anyone bringing the mother energy, then starts one of the most complex dances in the natural world. At once, she protects the infant from too much deprivation and overwhelming pain while gradually teaching the young child to soothe itself in the midst of pain and learning. This crucial dance requires much balance and finesse. Good mothering results in a boy learning to gradually comfort himself in the same way he was comforted. In effect he will carry good mothering energy inside himself.

The mother who knows that her boy child needs to grow into a man also knows the difference between comforting and nurturing. She knows instinctively that nurturing provides a protected space where a child learns, mostly by experimentation, by trial and error. The gradual letting go of the child to learn on his own is a precursor of the initiatory separation from mother at puberty. Nurturing provides the space for learning, eventually leading to the Elder space of Ordeal. This healthy mother nurturing is a kind of early and healthy tough love.

Comforting involves wisely creating a space that is not beyond a child's capacity to learn and grow. When a child does get overwhelmed from lack of strength or experience, mother comfort becomes a safety net repairing any trauma so a child does not gradually lose hope and confidence.

Limbo

Most men in our society have had good enough emotional mothering. Their flesh and blood mothers have given them what they need to move on to the next stage of development. The problem for men is that our society does not know how to properly integrate this mothering energy. Our culture does not understand that separation from the world of the mother is the first step toward initiation while at the same time respecting mothering as a form of feminine energy.

Elders know when a boy is ready for initiation. They are initiated men themselves who have lived their manhood for many years. They know that the movement into the wilderness is a movement into the life of the soul. Though the direction is away from the village, the movement is an interior one. Elders know that the gateway to initiation is ultimately within the emotional, intuitive, and spiritual life.

The modern patriarchal culture is a culture of biological fathers who have not been initiated. Their training manual is faulty. They have not been taught by initiated Elders. Consequently, this culture creates a situation where young boys are both taken too early from their mothers and taken in the wrong direction. So young boys are not only traumatized by premature physical and cultural separation, but are led away from the healthy path of initiation. The movement within, into emotions toward soul life, is seen as feminine or sissy. The path to initiation is blocked by the patriarchy.

Early on boys are taught not to cry, to take it like a man. Dolls are taken from boys, replaced by cars. Later boys are lauded for their sports prowess where winning euphoria is the only feeling allowed while boys in the arts are mostly seen as feminine or gay. These are just some examples of boys being culturally cut off from an inner life seen as unmanly.

Modern men are caught in a limbo, barred from the path of initiation, led to a world that promises an initiation but does not deliver true manhood. The result is widespread burnout and a pandemic of under the radar depression that men themselves don't recognize. This is primarily an existential depression that results from men stuck in limbo, neither nurtured by a healthy mother or an initiated father.

Many in the men's movement see the trauma of premature separation as the primary reason for men's depression. The patriarchy teaches boys to be men on the outside, starting very early. They are taught to act like warrior men even though they don't feel like them. Most men have been told by society to be tough and not a mama's boy. Studies show that even from the moment of birth, boys are spoken to less than girls, comforted less, nurtured less. This is what William Pollack calls the Boy Code. The lack of nurturing, as well as emotional trauma, at this early an age can have the affect of creating an unconscious sense of hopelessness, a pained withdrawal from natural compassionate emotion.

This premature separation by patriarchal enforcement has the first and most powerful effect of cutting off a boy's access to his inner life. At such an age a boy experiences few of the emotions that give richness to life. He is often just left with the feelings of anger; shame; and, we will see, addictive elation. Kindlon and Thompson believe that "boys, beginning at a young age, are systematically steered away from their emotional lives toward silence, solitude, and distrust." As a boy grows into a man's body this becomes his Achilles heel.

The problem for men today is that society leaves us in the village, emotionally needy yet taught to ignore our emotions. We are unconsciously looking to be emotionally taken care of while being taught to act like caretakers. Even though there is a cultural separation from mothering, the patriarchal society doesn't recognize the buried emotional needs of men, still alive but forced underground. So the patriarchal society leaves men out on a limb, separated but needy, with no guidance toward a healthy initiation. The only avenue it gives for emotional connection is to hearken back to the mother's arms, most often into unhealthy sexual and emotional relationships with women.

Indigenous tribes knew the power of a boy's psychological needs and realized it could be regressive for a man to continue to meet those needs through external mothering energy. This connection would be harmful to the individual as well as the community. For the tribe needed men to carry on its work and its existence. It also needed mature men to carry on its spiritual tradition. Indigenous tribes did not leave a man hanging in emotional limbo or with a truncated emotional life. They realized the cultural threat of regression. They also realized that mother regression was a threat to their spiritual tradition. Gilmore points out that regression to "fantasy as a blissful experience of oneness with the mother" is a cultural threat to a society that needs adult men to protect and support it.

Upon separation Elders plunged a man deeply into his inner world. They gave men a whole new world, the world of mature masculine feeling, to enable him to separate from the mother's hut. Yet they knew a man had to find and connect with a new form of feminine energy as well. They introduced men to the other side, a place of connection and emotional fulfillment where their true identity and their spiritual tradition resided. I call this place the wilderness of the soul.

The Mother Complex

Because modern culture has no healthy initiatory feeling to offer men, most men are stuck in a place that is neither nurturing nor genuinely masculine. The result is a place of no feeling. This numbness is regularly punctuated by childlike anger whenever a man suffers the discomfort of frustration or loss. This is the reaction of a boy stuck in the village because of a lack of Elders. Numbness and anger are the signs of men in limbo.

The pandemic of numbness is part of the low level depression that most men are left with in limbo. Any natural feelings will break through the depression as unhappy frustration, the result of not having the emotional tools to handle the ups and downs of life. It is either numbness or emotional discomfort that causes most men to look back to lost mothering for some good feeling. This is the time that the mother complex appears in a man's psyche. She is called in by a man's desperate need for relief from frustration and emptiness.

On the archetypal level this regressive mother need, the need for escapist wishes in every man, is a mother complex. Others call this complex the dark mother. It could just as easily be called a mothering complex since it triggers a man's regressive desire for mothering. The complex causes a man to look for personal, nurturing mothering as a way to find some comfort in his arid no man's land inside. This complex tempts a man to act like a boy emotionally, like a boy stuck in the village. It is important to remember that this need, and this complex, resides in the man.

In his book, *Lying With The Heavenly Woman*, Robert Johnson describes the mother complex as a man's "wish to regress to infancy again and be taken care of, to crawl into bed and pull the covers over his head, to evade some responsibility that faces him." As such Johnson remarks that this complex "will destroy his life more quickly than any other single element in his psychology."

When the boy is ready to move beyond the village the dark mother will always emerge in a man's psyche. The male mother complex emerges as a secret need to be smothered, to be adored, adulated, propped up even if not warranted, to always be understood. She comes as the desire to be told it wasn't our fault, that the other guy has the problem, that we are a victim of tough breaks, that our mistakes are totally understandable. In a word we all want someone to cover for us and think we're wonderful and manly, even when we're not. Men who unconsciously look for this type of love in the real world are in the grip of the mother complex and unknowingly stuck in the village.

Sam Keen gets this idea of archetypal energy across in his fine book *Fire In The Belly*. He speaks of WOMAN in a man's life residing in his psyche. WOMAN encompasses the Great Mother and the Dark Mother. He talks of men having a WOMAN need, bigger than life and ready to meet all needs. This is the dark WOMAN, the mother full of comfort but lacking in wise nurturing. We are often attracted to this WOMAN in our women, the pleasure-giving, comforting, understanding, possessive side. We are frustrated to the point of irrational anger when our woman partner is not this comforting, yet regressive, WOMAN.

From Mother To Mother Object

Most men will unconsciously turn a wife or a lover (including another man in a gay relationship) into a mother through a psychological process called transference. In this situation transference allows us to find mother substitutes in other people, or even other things. In counseling I have to make mother transference clear to most men because they believe they separated from their mother when they left home. They believe that cultural separation is psychological separation. They don't realize they have taken their mother with them, in the form of their needs and dreams, only to later transfer her to another beloved woman.

We are often connected through the mother complex inside to the woman we love. When a man says he is looking for unconditional love from his wife he is really saying he wants his wife to be his emotional mother. When a man says he is looking for the right woman to make him happy he is usually fantasizing about a mother who makes him feel right. When a man spends most of his time fantasizing about women he is emotionally stuck in the village, close to his mother's hut.

When we project our mother complex needs onto another woman we turn her into a mother. Most every relationship a man has with a woman in our society is contaminated by this dynamic. Even though our society tells a man not to be a wimp or a mama's boy, it also teaches him that his ultimate happiness resides in a woman. This is the woman of the mother complex.

The beloved woman then becomes a mother object. Mother object is another psychological term that I will use often in this book. The word "object" conveys the reality that the man is reacting to his own transferred complex, a mother fantasy object, not a person. Object also conveys the meaning that the woman is not literally the man's mother. Through transference a woman loses her own personality and becomes a mother to the boy inside. A woman referred to as a "sex object" comes from this same psychological situation of impersonal attraction.

Unfortunately, women are taught an unconscious part in this drama, too, and are just as oppressed psychologically as men. In our traditional society the woman is taught that she must take care of her man. She is taught to identify closely with the mother archetype and goes about trying to please and pleasure her man as a sign of her womanhood. So a man is taught to find a mother object and a woman is taught to act as a mother. They treat each other as objects and lose intimacy in the process. The man stays a boy emotionally. The woman unknowingly keeps her man a boy while yearning for a man.

A man who can't find mother in another person is forced to look elsewhere or face the pain of his initiatory discomfort and loneliness. He often chooses to find his mother comfort in an addiction. In this case a substance becomes a mother object, giving him instant, on-demand comfort. The substance can be alcohol, hard drugs such as cocaine, or soft drugs such as nicotine. He gets hooked on the mother object because it consistently takes away the pain while giving him some elated feeling to relieve his depression. The inner regressive yearning is temporarily satisfied.

Addiction is winked at in the village. It is even seen as manly. Getting roaring drunk for the first time is an example of an empty initiation ritual for young adolescents that is accepted, even encouraged. Addictive highs are seen as a pleasurable rewards for hard work or as a manly way to drown sorrows. As we shall see in a following chapter, addictions are a normal part of village life in our society and a primary way that men get stuck by the mother. Addictions are one of the strongest weapons of the mother complex.

Separation

Just as there is a mother complex within pulling every man back to the village, there is the initiatory archetype in him pushing him toward the wilderness. This initiation archetype will surface first in a separation experience. As I have mentioned a contemporary man will most often experience the start of initiatory separation as an abandonment and betrayal brought on by the withdrawal of a loved one. This loved one will most often be a wife or lover who is a mother object. And the uninitiated man will be devastated by the experience of abandonment.

Separation often comes suddenly, like Elders in the middle of the night. A man's wife may tell him she has had enough and wants him out of the home. A man's lover, whom he has dated for years, says he/she has found someone else. A spouse is no longer interested sexually and is becoming distant.

The man will be surprised by the strength of feeling he didn't know he had. He will be shocked by the depth of his pain at feeling alone, abandoned, and helpless. He will not have realized how much he counted on his loved one, a loved one he had taken for granted. He will be shocked at the depth of his emotional yearning.

The separation is triggering his initiation but he doesn't realize it. Instead, the man sees himself in a crisis of deep pain. He doesn't realize that he is being separated unwillingly from his mother's hut, represented by his wife or family. All he knows is that his world is turned upside down and he is terrified. His first words are usually, "how can I get her back?" Like the young, startled boy he would give anything just for a hug from her.

The deep pain in the man comes from the uninitiated boy inside who suddenly realizes that he is disconnected from the source of his pleasure and security. Suddenly the man feels very empty and uncomfortable. Often, in the privacy of my office, he cries for the first time since childhood. Sitting before him I sometimes image a desperate 6 year old child who realizes that he can't find his mother to comfort him. This helps me see the genuine pain the man is in. The boy in the man's body, the *puer*, has taken over all feelings. The boy's only goal is to reunite with the bearer of his maternal solace or to keep her from leaving. I understand the boy's pain because my boy inside has suffered the same pain.

I know that a man hasn't had initiatory separation when he talks of being afraid to be alone. He will usually describe a history where he felt he could count on his wife or lover to be at home when he called or returned even if he no longer feels love for her. When he pictures his home without a woman's presence he becomes extremely agitated. He will not be able to be at his house alone. If he is home after separation he will be continually on the phone talking to friends about the woman who left. He will either continue to try for a reconciliation or he will very soon try to find another mother object to take her place. He will talk of being unable to imagine even a short period of time without a relationship with someone.

At this point it is not helpful for me to show my understanding and tell the desperate and hurting man that he is experiencing a great and crucial opportunity, that he is experiencing the Great Separation as an initiatory event. What I do make clear, though, from the beginning is that I am not the person to come to if he just wants to feel better. If that is his goal I can't help. I would be doing a disservice to him if I, too, identified with the mother archetype and protected him from his initiatory pain just to make him feel better.

I tell him that his pain is nothing to be ashamed of, that it is not a sign of weakness or lack of courage but is actually a sign that he is ready to do the work of manhood. I also tell him that I will be there with him through the process of facing the pain, because men need other men to go through these crises. I appeal to the warrior in him to summon the energy of separation and look toward the possibility of consciously continuing his crucial journey.

Engulfment

A man becomes numb because he has not lived his own life. Most often the uninitiated man, left without direction from his interior life, turns to his mother object for direction. To a great extent he looks to a mother object to initiate him, to look up to him, to praise him, to convince him of his manliness. He needs a woman to recognize his sexual prowess or his patriarchal power to feel like a man. He may need a trophy wife, or a woman to praise him for his trophies. Or he may need a woman to excuse him for an empty trophy case.

Much of the power of infatuation comes from this pseudo-initiation by a mother object. Suddenly a man feels manly. He has been given importance by her attention alone. If she treats him like a man he must be one. This is quick and easy manliness, shake and bake initiation. This is the ephemeral honeymoon of relationships.

But then an unfortunate thing happens. These superficial feelings of manliness inevitably fade. Since there is no initiation in the village, no initiation by mothers, the man starts to feel like a boy again. The mother complex exerts control and turns on him. For the dark mother ultimately wants control. A man starts to feel controlled by the very woman who supposedly freed him. This man feels engulfed. His life feels circumscribed by a controlling mother. He feels cramped, claustrophobic. She becomes the ball and chain. He starts wanting space. He doesn't realize that it is his connection that keeps him a frightened boy. He puts the blame on this mother object when it is his own mother need that is to blame. Eventually he expands the habit to blaming everyone but himself for his unhappiness.

At this point a man becomes paralyzed between his fear of being engulfed and controlled and his fear of abandonment and separation. He lives out the unfortunate saying, "you can't live with them and you can't live without them." He doesn't realize that he is imprisoned by his own dependence. He also doesn't realize how much he counts on the very person he feels controlled by. Nor does he realize that his fears of engulfment arise out of a healthy need for initiation. He doesn't realize how much he needs an Elder.

Most men are stuck in the limbo between regressive connection and separation wanting both security and adventure. A man in this situation ends up feeling neither good about himself or good about his partner. He is depressed about the possibility of feeling deprived of a mother object yet he is depressed about not feeling the aliveness of the initiatory journey. Numbness is a two-edged sword. It cuts off pain. It also cuts off feeling and the way to a man's soul.

Men Need Men

The man experiencing separation needs balancing masculine energy to move on developmentally. He first needs the masculine energy of the healthy, not patriarchal, father archetype and then the masculine energy of the Elder archetype. Masculine energy fuels the way for a man to move on. It is also the way for a man to satisfy his deepest yearnings, while bringing his regressive mother needs to closure.

As we will talk about in a following chapter masculine energy is separating energy. It is a hard energy, but it is the next step for the boy. Masculine energy stands between the boy and the door of his hut, not allowing him to go back. Masculine energy, first in the form of a good father, tells the mother very forcefully to "leave the boy to me." This energy gives a boy the courage and strength to face his pain. Masculine energy, in the form of the Elder, then leads a boy to the wilderness of his soul. It is only an Elder society that can teach a man how to be in right relationship to the mother archetype throughout his lifetime.

Men need to relate more to men, or the masculine experience, for healing. Wiser men are best equipped to lead a man away from the mother's hut and his own mother complex. Men are hardwired to respond at a certain time in their growth to fathers and Elders. Men are stuck because there are no men to lead them into the wilderness.

Most men come into counseling in great pain in the middle of an involuntary separation. They are desperate, understandably so. Their mother dependence comes out as the need to please or appease in order to avert a separation. They have come upon overwhelming painful feelings they never knew existed. They are like a wild animal suddenly caught in a vice-like trap. They look desperately to me to take away the pain.

Then a strange thing often happens. In the midst of terrible pain and confusion a man will hear my words of necessary separation and additional pain. After getting angry at my message, he will hesitate. Even in the middle of his negative whirlpool of feeling he will know that what I am saying is true. That hardwired knowledge seems to show up in the crisis. And he will often, very courageously, tell me to keep talking and tell him the next steps.

We then start talking about boundaries. Boundaries are conscious emotional separations for a higher purpose. At this point they are the psychological equivalents of completing separation from mother objects. Here is where positive warrior energy is needed. Here is where men's innate courage shows up. Men have little training in psychological boundary setting since they are taught they have already separated. It is their most important work at the beginning of therapy. Boundaries are what I always work on first when a man gives me the signal to go on.

Chapter 4
Boundaries

Most men come in to counseling because they have experienced an involuntary and sudden separation from a mother object. They are in the middle of a crisis, thrown prematurely into Ordeal without preparation. Only a catastrophic crisis will lead these men to counseling. Since most men have no Elders around to guide and interpret this separation experience they will usually squander another opportunity to be initiated. My job in this situation is to be an Elder, to educate about initiation and then to act as a boundary cop encouraging a man to hold his ground.

Other men seem to be living a life of quiet desperation, a crisis ready to happen. Frequently they remain in a stuck depression, feeling the powerless victim of fate, feeling numb. The separation crisis has not yet hit them. They don't realize they are in a chronic, low-level crisis. They are in the clutches of the dark mother. They are unaware of their latent abandonment fears. All they know is they feel lousy. They are good men trying to do the right thing for their family and community, not realizing that the right thing is wrong for them. They are less likely to come for counseling. When they do I must educate them about initiation and then talk of boundaries. A healthy response to these feelings of engulfment involves the learning of psychological boundaries.

Space And The Final Frontier
The term boundary is popular because of the family systems theory explanation of human behavior. Much of addiction literature, especially the adult children of alcoholics movement, stresses the need for boundary setting in relationships. Boundary issues emerge in the initial growth conflict between the needs of the community and the need of personal initiation. The rule is that wherever two or three are gathered together in community there are boundary problems in the midst of them. Families are

most people's first and most powerful experience with community and the need for boundaries.

When a family or community has loose boundaries or no boundaries then "everyone lives in each other's pockets," and nobody is allowed to leave those pockets. Nothing is allowed to be personal and private. Being different or not agreeing with family attitudes is seen as a threat to the family existence. In this type of family there is no way to separate and grow personally.

In any family without boundaries separation is seen as betrayal. The only safety is seen in the connection with other family members. Moving toward a personal life path is seen as endangering the whole family. Following a personal path is seen as a repudiation of the family direction and expectations. A man's feeling of engulfment is often a consequence of growing up in this kind of family. For men coming out of this family any subsequent relationship feels like a life sentence.

Often when a man is in a relationship he feels smothered after the infatuation period. He feels engulfed. He doesn't know why, but he feels he needs space. Space is often an unconscious code word for boundaries. The man is really incoherently yearning for an initiatory separation, a movement away from the mother complex. He is experiencing the pull of the dark mother. Here is the start of the pull toward initiation. Here is the initiation archetype stirring within. This man is unknowingly yearning for the wilderness.

However, if a man is not guided by Elders he will invariably succumb to his abandonment fears once he takes or is given his space. He will feel pain when he thought he would feel liberated. With no clear life path he will feel lost and disoriented and very alone. Because of either abandonment or disillusion he will fearfully give up his boundary. He will flee his separation experience with no Elders there to block his way back.

Boundaries are psychological lines denoting what is personal. They are there to protect a man's personal life path. Psychological boundaries are conscious emotional separations for a higher purpose. They sever unhealthy emotional dependencies that keep a man a boy in the village. Boundaries help a man stand up for himself, not in a macho adolescent way, but in a way that announces what he stands for. Boundaries create that space for the realization of a higher personal purpose that will ultimately serve the community in a profound way. An uninitiated family or community will not understand any of this.

The Boy Within

An uninitiated man will react to separation abandonment by desperately trying anything to keep his partner close. He will restore his passionate dating behaviors, give uncharacteristic attention and support, promise anything. He will forget his own needs, values, and life direction in order to keep connected to a maternal object. He will do anything to relieve the pain. This is when I talk about the traumatized boy within.

When a man is encouraged to look more closely into his pain, he will find that the uninitiated young boy inside feels terrified because he sees all support and understanding slipping away. It feels like physical withdrawal from drugs as he envisions a world devoid of warm, physical closeness. He feels he will fall apart if she is not around. This feeling is not the yearning for sexual closeness as much as the yearning for the soothing presence of physical, body closeness. This is very much a young boy's need for holding his mother's hand or lying close to her when he is frightened at night.

The uninitiated boy in the man will also feel terrified in a world where his physical needs are not being met. How will he feed himself? Who will keep his clothes clean? Who will get him to his friends? These fears seem irrational to an adult. But deep inside every desperate man these unspoken feelings are very real.

Engulfment

Many men first experience their intense feelings of dependence and abandonment after an initiatory separation has been forced on them. There is also a large group of men who have little idea of their latent abandonment feelings because they are still stuck in dependent relationships. These men feel engulfed by relationship and society's demands. These are good and sincere men trying to be good partners, fathers and citizens. They feel weighed down by others' expectations. They measure their manliness by others' definitions. They have not faced their Great Separation but are suffering the depression and discomfort of staying in the village too long. They often blame their spouse for their emotionally listless lives. They have not made their deep identity a priority.

For these men boundary setting means voluntarily running the risk of physical separation, often in the face of an uncomprehending spouse. Boundary setting always risks total separation. In this voluntary situation the risk becomes clear.

Men often talk of feeling selfish when thinking of setting boundaries, especially time boundaries. They feel that they don't deserve their own time, time to explore their inner life and prepare for initiation. As we will see in coming chapters, part of this feeling comes from the patriarchy, the father's world. Men are providers and protectors. They must spend their time making the world safe for their wives and families. This is a full time job, and makes them the disposable sex, disposable to society, disposable to themselves. Their mission provides no time for their own life. The patriarchy is not interested in a man's individual identity or personal search.

A man who is feeling engulfed will feel he is in a no-win situation, and he is right. He may rage or withdraw but he will still be stuck. He will blame the world but his dependency is inside him.

Declaration of Independence

Setting a boundary says, "I am ready to separate and can learn to emotionally take care of myself." Boundaries are psychological declarations of independence. A boundary is also a dividing line between the boy's world of the village and the man's world of the wilderness. By boundary setting in a relationship a man states he no longer needs a mother to watch over him. He also states he no longer is afraid of displeasing the mother and is ready to suffer the risk of separation.

A boundary needs two components to be healthy and initiatory. First the man must be able to willingly separate emotionally and even risk the end of a relationship. He must stop being a boy trying to keep a comforting mother object, and he must also stop basing his actions on pleasing a mother object who gives his life structure and direction. The test of a man's readiness for boundary setting is his ability to risk, and then face the consequences of his actions. As one of my clients put it, "I needed to be able to leave before I could set boundaries."

The second step in boundary setting is using the separation to move toward one's inner life. A boundary protects a man's initiatory path, his life path. The adolescent boy was separated during initiation in order to face his Ordeal. He was starting over and leaving what he no longer needed behind. Separation is always for a higher purpose. The litmus test of a healthy boundary is the insight a man finds in the midst of the pain.

John Gray touches on this idea in his book *Men are from Mars and Women are from Venus*. He talks about men needing their cave to retreat to, especially after a long day in the workplace. Men need time alone to unwind and make the transition to home and family. A man might sometimes read the paper or watch the news or putter in the basement. Women often see this behavior as a man walling himself off from the relationship. However, the cave is a healthy place, a boundaried place, a final frontier. If a woman will give a man this space, and he has healthy boundaries, the man will return to the woman, after a time, ready for relationship and intimacy.

Perhaps men need these spaces and intervals because of a hardwired initiatory pattern. This withdrawal may be an unconscious movement toward an initiatory space of aloneness and personal search. Many in the women's movement complain that men separate too easily. They don't necessarily buy the cave idea. They believe that the real problem for men is joining and relating. They are skeptical of talk of boundary setting. In some ways this is a restatement of the old complaint about men not being able to commit. Many in the women's movement feel there is an overemphasis on personal independence in society and in the men's movement. They are understandably wary of the rugged individualist, the man as cowboy, and the competitive society that evolves from this model. This is why they emphasize relatedness and the return to the feminine as the font of relatedness.

I do believe that men are taught to build walls instead of boundaries as a way of seeming independent and manly. This teaching is toxic to men as well as women. Wall building is a pseudo-independent construction with no real emotional separation and no real hope of joining in a healthy relationship later. The walls become another obstacle to a man's inner life and real relationship. However, returning to the mother is too dangerous for a man at this stage in his psychic life, too fraught with land mines and ambushes. Moving toward the world of men is a healthier, safer answer.

Women should have no fear of healthy boundaries. A separated man will also be a man who can relate from his inner life. An initiated woman will easily recognize healthy boundaries, and respect a man who sets them. However, women have the right to be critical of walls. For this is often the only kind of boundary they experience from men. Let me explain.

Walls

A wall is a pseudo-separation where a man withdraws more deeply into his defenses, usually numbness and addiction. Most men, as I have mentioned, are taught to be walled off. They learn to act and feel detached. This is the Boy Code. This is all in the patriarchal training manual, the code of the misguided warrior. Men are taught to be on a war footing emotionally when there is no war. Men must show no fears, much less abandonment fears, if they want to be considered manly. In the face of emotional pain men are taught to retreat behind walled bunkers.

This kind of separation neither separates a boy from a mother nor allows him to find a separate adulthood. In fact, the boy becomes trapped behind the walls of the village with the very mother he must separate from. Walls are purely protective. They insulate from pain. There is no higher purpose. There is no real separation. There is no growth. Walled off men never come out from their cave. They unconsciously choose safety over growth.

It is not a coincidence that the cowboy is the model of manhood in our society. The Marlboro man has sold more cigarettes by far than any other marketing icon. Cowboys are independent, have few loyalties or connections, and can move on at any time. The best cowboy never settles down. He seems separated. But for what purpose? The stereotype is that he goes around selflessly righting wrongs, as a modern knight errant. Closer to the truth is that he mostly smokes, wandering aimlessly through plains and drinking at saloons. These men are bunkered behind their walls unknowingly afraid to take the next steps of separation. Inside they feel safe. No person can hurt them. No woman can get to them. They often retreat into an addiction to relieve any pain they have. The dark mother complex has him in the grips of her greatest weapon, unconsciousness.

A man who builds walls is not open to any relationship that calls for the pain of honesty and compromise. Neither is he open to the pain of the Ordeal where he must face his aloneness to find his direction. Like all uninitiated men he is caught up in getting his own needs met and is obsessed only with how he can be loved and pleasured.

Boundary as Betrayal

Unfortunately, loved ones will often see a healthy boundary as a typical male wall. Uninitiated partners will not understand and will see the boundary setting as withdrawal or control, and as a betrayal. Separation for a man in our culture is invariably misunderstood. This misunderstanding is most painful when it involves an uninitiated partner.

Initiation in our modern culture usually means disappointing those who love us. Setting boundaries regularly brings a man face to face with being called selfish by loved ones. Sometimes boundary setting means looking at the fear and sadness in a loved one's eyes, a loved one who doesn't understand. Most of the time it involves facing one's guilt.

Men who set relationship boundaries find themselves having to disagree with their female partners about what constitutes love. There is an assumption in heterosexual society that women know much more about relationships than men do. Love and relationship are the domain of women. Women are assumed to be the authorities in the field. As Bernie Zilbergeld says, "Today's man is caught in a very peculiar position because the definition of love has become feminized."

Separation, like having caves, is not usually a female way of relating. So separation becomes fearful and foreboding for women as much as men. Some feminists don't help this situation by overemphasizing heterosexual relatedness as the panacea for all men. Unfortunately, we live in a modern, uninitiated society where women are just as much in the dark about a full heterosexual relationship as men are. Women are as much a victim of the patriarchy as men. And the Empress has as few clothes as the Emperor. Yet, in our society, women tend to write the agenda for relationship, and men rarely question the agenda items. Male boundary setting is rarely part of that agenda.

The healthy male mode of relating is not understood. I have experienced many responses by uninitiated partners to boundary setting. With one man an uninitiated partner responds that he only sets boundaries for her, instead of for his friends or family. Other partners react by calling him selfish or irresponsible. Another calls him cold.

A man will usually find himself criticized in one way or another for boundary setting. An uninitiated partner might also withdraw emotionally, including sexually, as a response to boundary setting. This is usually the greatest test of a man's abandonment fears.

Sex to an uninitiated man is often his only connection to anyone. At this point of conflict any man will be greatly tempted to withdraw the boundary. If he has gone this far he will be starting to come alive. Yet he will have many other feelings, too. He will be sensitive enough to feel badly about displeasing so many people, including his spouse and extended family. His guilt will tempt him to give up on his need to separate. His uncertainty, without Elders around, will cause him to waver. His sense of loyalty, as protector, will kick in. He may then go back.

Going back does not have to mean defeat. It is often part of the process. The important thing is that a man has tasted, just a little, the sense of manhood from the inside out. This cycle often happens several times before a man can make his boundaries firm enough to go the next steps of initiation.

The Warrior

One of the archetypes that I bring up in counseling when talking of boundaries is the warrior archetype. The warrior archetype in every man gives great guidance if a man can access him. For the warrior teaches a lot about boundaries and boundary setting. I have found that men who can get in touch with this archetypal energy gain the strength and wisdom they need to set boundaries. They can then also relate to their hardwired knowledge in a new way. The warrior is the archetype a man understands most easily.

Unfortunately, the idea of a healthy warrior has been just about lost. The modern West's idea of warrior is synonymous with destructive aggression and organized violence. A warrior wages war. In the best case, he uses violence for the higher moral purpose of his society. In the worst case, he uses violence for the less than noble political and personal ambitions of the mercenary. Whenever warrior energy is brought up in the context of the men's movement there is a negative reaction. For men are seen as primarily violent and the cause of most of the violence in our society. Women, especially, are afraid of warrior energy because they have often been victims of it in its shadow form.

Warriors have a bad name because of the moral ambiguity of war today, as well as the degeneration of the moral code of a warrior. Warrior energy also has a bad connotation because it is the manipulation of warrior energy by the leaders in our society that cause men to sacrifice themselves, and their own true feelings, for someone else's mission. However, the strength of the warrior, given the proper values and code, is necessary for every man to find within himself. Healthy warrior energy is an extremely valuable and effective energy. In the context of boundary setting it is the inner warrior who guards the boundaries. In every man it is warrior energy that sets the boundaries and cleaves to them in the face of any opposition. It is the warrior who guards the integrity of the initiatory journey.

An Eastern paradigm can give us insight into healthy warrior energy. The samurai of Japan had a code called bushido that laid out the philosophy and behavior of a warrior. The primary goal of the ideal samurai was to protect his lord and all that the lord symbolized. He would lay down his life instantly if his Lord commanded. He had little need or desire to focus attention on himself. He also had no desire to show his prowess by overcoming or intimidating someone not a threat to his lord. He was to protect his lord and the ethic his lord embodied with the least force necessary. It was actually a defeat for him if he had to use his sword. He should be able to understand dangerous situations far ahead of time and defuse the danger before violence was needed. A good samurai needed only to show his sword at the right time and opposition would dissolve.

A samurai was not interested in personal revenge nor personal honor outside his duty. He learned to sacrifice his ego to a higher cause, represented by the values of his lord and his own ethic of bushido. There was an ethic here whose purpose was to cure the natural egotism we all have. A samurai was only justified in disobeying his lord when his lord no longer followed a royal ethic.

Much of the literature of Japan centers around the *ronin*, the samurai who had no lord. Because of the social degeneration and chaos at the beginning of the 17th Century many samurai were downsized. Many of the best had to be let go because their lord lost his land or his life. Some of the greatest Japanese stories revolve around the moral choices that samurai made when they were tempted to use their impressive skills for baser purposes. Their greatest literature explored which samurai could keep to bushido and a higher calling and which samurai merely served their own ego.

A superb modern Japanese movie, *The Seven Samurai*, tells the story of this chaotic time in Japanese history when there were many ronin, as well as outlaws, wandering the countryside. This was a time when greed and opportunism, enabled by widespread violence, was rampant. The victims were always the poor farming peasant, unschooled in self defense or the martial arts, who toiled to make a subsistence living. Outlaws would steal any surplus, leaving the peasant just enough to survive and plant for the next year. Then the cycle would repeat.

This story tells how an extremely poor village sends out recruiters to try to find samurais hungry enough to work for a pittance of rice. One poor but extremely able samurai, who represents the highest goals of bushido, has compassion for the poor peasants and agrees to try to protect the village against a large gang of over 40 outlaws and ronin. He is prepared to die for the higher values of justice and compassion because of his quiet adherence to a life of bushido.

The odds are very much against him. In order to accomplish his task he goes out to recruit other samurai with similar ideals. He finds four other skilled samurai, a samurai impostor, and a young samurai wannabe. Their stories show different motivations for service, though none as pure as the leader. All in their own way show compassion for the peasants, without being maudlin. They strive only to protect the village. On the way they encounter a number of other samurai who are more interested in money and status and refuse the leader's offer.

The leader needs many more samurai but ends up with seven, counting himself. In the end the village is saved. (I encourage you to see how.) There is no outside reward. They were paid the agreed upon daily wage of rice. The leader moves on. The American movie, *The Magnificent Seven*, is based on this Japanese classic.

Today, there is emerging masculine consciousness of this healthy warrior energy as seen in this movie, as well as others such as *Kung Fu*, *The Karate Kid*, and a movie I will be talking much more about, *Star Wars*.

The Warrior Within

Just as with an ethical samurai, boundary setting using warrior energy is not aggressively destructive. It should be compassionate and primarily protective. It doesn't get offensive just to prove a point or win an argument. Neither does it get destructively angry as a way of hurting or revenge. It is not used to prove a man is right. It is used to help him find his right way.

Warrior energy is used to protect the value and the purpose of a man's life. It is first used in the initiatory process to separate from the world of the mother. It is the antidote to the passivity and unconsciousness brought on by the mother complex. Warrior energy is then used to protect the King, the emerging internal ethic and vision of the initiated man. Warrior energy protects and enables the right mission by protecting the initiatory process. This energy keeps a man focused on his personal search for identity and purpose, his personal mission, the true source of his manhood.

All healthy warriors must be obedient to a King. The King represents a man's soul identity and higher self. Men have to set boundaries and experience initiation before they can truly commit to a healthy relationship. Wives, lovers and friends are really looking for this type of initiated man. They are looking for the King in each man. They need not be afraid of a man with seasoned warrior energy. For the warrior protects the King.

A man will need boundary setting at each stage of his growth. I have talked of boundary setting from a mother object. Yet a man will also need to set boundaries in separating from the father. Mysteriously he will also need boundaries to ultimately separate from the Elder and all he represents. As such, warrior energy is needed most acutely at each new stage in a man's initiatory process. The warrior within helps to find and protect a sacred space. As a man separates from the village he moves closer to the sacred initiatory space where he will find all that he needs.

Chapter 5
Addictions: Life Behind The Wall

Much of the story of a man trying to separate from the mother object is about a man fighting addiction. Addictions are like an emotional umbilicus, connecting a man to a mother object and tricking the boy inside into believing he needs a mother for existence itself. The umbilicus is emotional and invisible; the dark Mother's spell of unconsciousness.

George Santayana once said that he didn't know who first discovered water, but he knew it wasn't a fish. We are an addictive society. It is hard for a man to recognize his addictions in the sea of addictiveness around him. Addictions keep a man artificially connected to a ready source of numbness at the very time he needs to face initiatory pain. Addiction is like pain insurance and policies are very cheap in our society.

Most men do not realize the myriad ways they are addicted or what the addiction is doing to them. The more obvious substance addictions, such as alcohol and drug abuse, are recognized when they cause serious harm to a man's reputation or career. Alcohol or drug abuse can also become obvious when it leads to domestic violence. A man who has multiple D.U.I.'s sticks out as someone with a problem. However, when serious addictions emerge publicly they are often seen as aberrations, the sins of some sick men.

Our models of manhood are often models of addiction. The training manual of manhood allows addiction as a reward for this false manhood, or an excuse for the pain of being a patriarch. On the other hand the man addicted to work, sex, rage, or money is seen more as macho than addicted. There is little social awareness that addicted men are still emotionally in their boy stage, or that they are a danger to the fabric of a healthy society.

That the emotionally regressed, addicted man is a cultural ideal is unrecognized. We are unaware of the disease much less the major symptoms. When watching old movies, especially old detective flicks, notice how strange it seems to see so many people lighting up at every opportunity. The ubiquitous haze of smoke gave an atmosphere of mystery and macho for men and sexual looseness from women. Nobody questioned the addiction or the danger of secondary smoke. Only today does the addiction seem obvious.

The Desperate Boy

Most often when a man comes into my office after suffering a sudden separation from a beloved mother object he will report that he got drunk. It is considered manly and forgivable in our society to get drunk and out of control because of love gone wrong. It proves the depth of the love not the depth of the dependence.

This kind of addictive behavior seems to be the universal reaction of a modern man in deep pain. I can always spot an addicted man when his first goal when entering my office is to get rid of the pain. I don't blame a man for wanting to eradicate the searing pain as quickly as possible. He has not been taught how to handle it any other way. Ignorance is his prison.

Most men will struggle their whole lives against regression to a passive, painless place which is the world of the young boy and the dark Mother. Think of a young boy around 6 years old. This is the boy inside that we need to deal with when understanding most addictions.

A boy this young has little experience in changing the world about him to get his needs met. For example, if a parent chooses not to feed him when he is hungry, he has few choices. He can cry, throw a tantrum, and make a nuisance of himself. He has no job, no access to money, no ability to barter, no leverage. He must wait until he gets the food he needs, usually from his mother. He depends on her to take away the hunger pangs. He depends on her to make him feel better. He is substantially powerless. This is the emotional place a man regresses to when he is addicted.

When a man first experiences the threat of separation his initial reaction will be anger, just like the little boy throwing a tantrum. If he becomes desperate, he will move from anger to rage. Unresolved anger is most often a man's gateway to addictions. Unresolved separation is most often the cause. The painful feeling of powerlessness is the catalyst. A raging man is a man gripped by impotence. A man's threatened separation from a mother object is usually his first conscious experience of powerlessness, and the cause of his deepest pain. The child's feeling of powerlessness within a man's strong body then leads to a dangerous situation.

Men have two unhealthy ways to deal with their inevitable anger at feeling abandoned and separated. A man can act out the rage, using addictive rage to try to bully a situation, stop a separation, and soothe himself with false bravado. Or he can medicate his rage with other addictions, hiding depressively behind his walls.

Rage

Anger is a natural emotion, even healthy. A man often needs anger to set healthy boundaries or to act against injustice. Rage, on the other hand, is learned and unhealthy. Rage is unconscious, uncontrolled anger. Most often a man will learn rage from his father or the patriarchal society. He will learn that rage can control those around him and lessen the feeling of powerlessness. He will also learn another patriarchal secret. Rage is actually soothing to the boy inside. It takes away the pain.

Most people would think a raging man was in great pain. Extreme, negative emotion leads one to believe that something is terribly wrong within the raging man. Yes, there is something wrong, but the enraged man is not feeling it. He is actually, at that moment, medicating his pain. Most men besides being addicted to a substance will be addicted to rage.

Trauma research has shown that the body releases opioid substances, called endorphins, into the system when the fight or flight response is triggered. Rage can trigger this response and release the narcotic-like chemicals that then wash the body. People can get addicted to this cycle of rage and release just as if they were taking a drug. The narcotic release is soothing and numbing. As John Lee says in his book, *The Anger Solution*, "Rage is a like a huge dose of morphine. It is a drug that is legal, plentiful, readily available and can be addictive!"

Most men in our society are taught to use rage for soothing and control. The soothing is physiological, the sense of control a way to handle feelings of impotence. Men then become addicted to the results.

The uninitiated man will always see his rage as justified. He will feel righteous in being angry. The dark Mother, the mother complex inside, will convince him he deserves to be angry, while keeping him unconscious of his own part in his problem. He will then have both the addiction to treat his pain and the means to rationalize his control. And he will have no motivation for a healthy separation.

Rage is the uncontrolled, mercenary samurai warrior who has no lord and no bushido. Anger is the healthy emotion of the good warrior, who uses anger to set boundaries and then experience the pain of initiation. Rage is the emotion of the dark, mercenary warrior who is afraid of initiation and would rather cause pain than experience it.

I have worked with many men who were rageaholics. This spectrum of anger addiction can go from the chronically irritable and depressed to the physically and emotionally abusive. Since this addiction is so widespread and common most men are surprised, sometimes shocked, to hear how their anger affects their loved ones.

Some men unconsciously use anger to medicate their depression. They can temporarily numb their fear with a hit of endorphins while treating feelings of impotence with another hit of adrenaline. They are desperate just to feel better. And this biochemical cocktail has often been pushed in the past by a dark patriarch. They are uncomfortable to be around yet are oblivious to how their irritability and sarcasm affects others. I call them lost ragers.

Other men have found that in addition to feeling better their rage can affect the behavior of others, especially loved ones. Rage can keep a spouse or children afraid enough to be respectful and compliant. Or rage can keep them from making any demands. Rage gives these men a momentary feeling of control and even adrenalized power. I call them controlling ragers.

Both these types of men act more from ignorance and desperation than malice. There can be rare physical altercations but more from impulsivity rather than planning. They often have a fleeting insight that anger is not working for them and they genuinely don't want to hurt those they love. They are hooked on anger but want to change. Their prognosis can be very positive when they seek counseling.

The far end of the spectrum involves men whose anger belies serious mental pathology. They will use any means, including serious physical violence, to control a mother object. These are dangerous men who rarely seek counseling. Some call them Pit Bulls.

Pit Bulls

These dangerous men use rage consistently to bully. They are on the most destructive side of the spectrum of rageful men. They learn rage as a way of keeping a mother object close and pliable. They rage or threaten rage as a means of control. These are abusive men who threaten physical violence and often use it when a loved one is not totally absorbed in them. They will systematically cut off their spouse from any meaningful relationship outside the connection to them. They must either feel physically close or be able to know their loved one is at home.

These men rarely come to counseling voluntarily. They are usually ordered to counseling by the court system. John Gottman, a research psychologist, has studied a sample of spouse batterers for decades. In the process he has monitored the physiological responses of these men as they got into controlled, nonviolent arguments with their spouses in their lab.

First of all he found that a sizable number of couples, identified as violent, were like men closer to the depressive side of the spectrum. The men were not consistently domineering and the women were not cowering under their domination. There were occasional outbursts that included pushing and shoving that didn't escalate into violence. These men were similar to those lost and controlling ragers. These couples were considered good candidates for counseling.

However, the rest of the group were composed of men whom Gottman felt were dangerous. He felt they should not be involved in couples counseling. In measuring their physiological responses he found that 80% of these men experienced the physiological arousal associated with anger: faster heart rate, increased perspiration, higher blood pressure. These were men accustomed to rage.

He labeled these men Pit Bulls because of their overattachment to their spouses. Gottman found that Pit Bulls "are strongly attached to their partners, albeit in overly dependent and controlling ways, and use violence to prevent abandonment." These men can feel shame about what they have done to their partners, after the fact. But they could become violent again if attempts at reconciliation were thwarted. These men consistently used violence, or the threat of violence, to keep their spouse close and controlled.

Some psychologists would say that these men, as well as other rageaholics, need more mothering to heal their deep wounds. They would insist that these men are not ready for separation or don't need separation at all.

Yet, most of these men are already attached to women who are understanding and nurturing. Most abusive men will choose dependent, nurturing women as spouses. These spouses will put up with most anything to keep the relationship going. They will give till it hurts. They will keep going back to be hurt. They unknowingly overmother like the dark mother. And their husbands stay emotional little boys.

Gottman says it is dangerous to the woman to be in counseling with many serious rageaholics and batterers. Trying for understanding will be counterproductive. The only hope for these men is for someone to empower their wives to stop mothering and to separate herself. Empowerment will give a woman the strength to stop acting like a mother object. The resulting separation will either force a man to deal with his emotional crisis, through fathering and Eldering, or force him to retreat to another mother object. Either way, at least the empowered woman will be safe. And the man will be given his best shot at healing and maturity.

I mention these men to show how dangerous this pattern of rage can become. Ragers consistently hurt, and sometimes kill, the very person they love. Men in any part of the rage spectrum cause pain rather than feeling pain.

The crisis of initiatory mother separation is the only way out for men stuck in their rage. A healthy and total separation leads to the world of the father and then the challenge of initiation. For the man who merely moves to another mother object, his path is often a deeper retreat behind walls. This is often the retreat to a substance, a mother object that will never get empowered and leave.

Deeper Retreat

Substance addictions are what most people think about when addiction is brought up. Addictive substances range from alcohol and hard drugs, such as heroin and cocaine, to soft drugs, such as marijuana and tranquilizing prescription drugs, to tobacco and caffeine. Some experts call these ingestive addictions, and include food under addictive substances.

Substance addictions are insidious because of the acceptability and prevalence in our society of mood altering chemicals. It's interesting that we accept mood altering substances for what they are. They temporarily alter our mood. The assumption is that we all require regular mood alteration.

Changing a feeling through addiction is like touching up an X-ray. The underlying problem gets worse as we put more and more effort into ignoring it. The underlying problem is the young, helpless, depressed boy inside who is looking for anything to make him feel better.

Addiction is the result of an aborted separation experience, leaving the young boy in a dark separated limbo. A man will be separated from a living, breathing mother object without any direction toward either comfort or initiation.

To the young boy inside, the separation trauma can be so severe he retreats, in utter desperation, to the only thing that he can count on for solace, a numbing substance. To the man who feels betrayed by a living mother object, the only reliable alternative feels like a comforting substance. The substance is controllable. The substance never leaves.

Most men retreat farther from life and into addiction because they have not been taught by society how to move on without dependence on a mother object. The natural place to find help in this transition is the father. However most of our fathers have themselves been fathered by a flawed patriarchy. When faced with the pain of separation the modern patriarchy turns to painkillers. With no reliable, mature father around a boy is thrown back on the patriarchy. As we shall see the dark patriarchy sees nothing wrong with addiction, as long as it keeps a man producing in the marketplace. And contrary to popular opinion, the majority of addicts are productive.

Signs of Substance Addiction

I can't be black and white when talking of substance addictions. There is not some concrete line which someone crosses into addiction. Often people question the number of drinks or pills per day that constitutes addiction. How many times or how many drinks or how many hours are often not helpful questions, because they muddy the real issue. If a man has two beers at night to relax yet works on his primary relationships and faces his life and identity issues then he is relaxing. If a man has two beers a night then goes to bed, depressed about work and with little communication with his wife or partner, there is strong indication of an addiction.

Throughout the ages people have ritually taken substances that alter consciousness. From the wine in the Mass and in bacchanals, to peyote for some native American rituals, to substances that shamans use in initiation rites, substances have been used in religious rituals. Substances have been used since prehistory for a sense of heightened awareness by artists as well as mystics. Certainly, for celebrations or conviviality, alcohol or other substances can give a sense of a special place and time. However, these uses of substances are meant to give a greater sense of connection, either in community or to a higher power. They can become a gateway to the inner life.

The addicted man is hiding. He is running from significant connections, even though he may seem jovial and friendly. He is trying to treat his depression with a liquid or a pill. He is either finding refuge in a euphoric feeling or he is unconscious. The paradox is that alcohol and many other drugs, such as opiates and barbiturates, are themselves depressants. After an initial euphoria they bring a man lower than when he started. So to continue the mothered feeling of euphoria a man needs to take more and take it more often. After a while he can no longer get the good feeling. Now he takes the substance to ward off the larger and larger depression of isolation, as well as withdrawal.

This whole cycle usually takes years, years of wasted time and accumulating depression. The end result is the body damage we talked about earlier, from the substance and from the depression. As in other forms of depression, addicted men also isolate themselves more and more from people and relationship. The addiction takes a man toward a feeling and away from significant people. So a man within the mother object addiction feels more and more alone and depressed. His only connections are his drinking buddies who share little except the same feeling. Or he connects with a mother disguised as a sex object while in the midst of addictive behavior. His only movement is withdrawal and retreat from any healthy emotional connection.

A man who is addicted will feel trapped in his life. He will feel caged, edgy, unable to enjoy the people around him, especially loved ones. He will continually yearn for the environment where he can use his substance of choice. Only then will he feel truly free, behind his walls.

The dark mother archetype, the mother who holds on long after she's needed, will always draw us toward unconsciousness and passivity. Those in the field of addictions call this unconsciousness the defense of denial. Connection to the dark mother object brings a blindness to one's own actions. The dark mother has a great interest in keeping us unaware and unmotivated. Most men who are addicted do not know they are.

I can tell an addicted man is making progress in counseling when he no longer dwells on his pain. There is progress when he no longer asks, "If I'm growing why don't I feel better?" Facing the pain, feeling it, is a sign of growth. This is a sign a man is preparing for Ordeal.

Just stopping taking a substance is not enough. Just stopping most often leads to being a dry drunk. Facing the pain of separation and learning the next steps is the only way out.

Men who wonder about their addictions to substances must ask themselves if they are using a substance to run from the pain and problems in their life. I am convinced that an addicted man needs an Elder to hold initiatory space for him and ask these kinds of questions. Holding space means the Elder teaches the steps of separation and helps a man stay in that questioning space until the next steps of initiation take hold. This Elder can be a counselor, minister, spiritual director, doctor. The Elder must be familiar with addictions and the peculiar steps of separation that substance recovery entails. Men need other men through every step of initiation. This step is no exception. I will talk much more about the Eldering process in future chapters.

I have found that the most powerful Elders for this recovery process are sponsors of 12-step programs. Finding these Elders involves going to 12-Step meetings such as Alcoholics Anonymous or Narcotics Anonymous and taking what is said seriously. Finding a sponsor and trusting him is crucial for separation and recovery.

The insidiousness and seductiveness of substance addictions is why many people consider alcoholism and other substance addictions a disease. It comes upon us unawares and keeps us unaware, aided by an addictive society. Yet we suffer unknowingly until much damage is done both to ourselves and to those around us.

I know few men who choose to hurt those they love. Yet addictive men do this regularly. A man must make a moral decision to stop an addiction, once he realizes he has a disease. The problem is bringing a man to the moral realm at all, where he is strong enough to both understand and make a choice. As we will see, it is up to fathers and Elders in society to bring a man to the moral realm, the realm of consciousness, the realm of the Ordeal.

Process Addictions

When talking of addictions most men think only of substance addictions, like alcohol or illegal drugs. These ingestive addictions are the obvious, and most reported, addictions. These are the addictions that catch the public eye.

There are also subtler addictions, called process addictions that are not as obvious. I discussed rage addiction earlier because rage is the cheapest, most accessible, and most prevalent process addiction. Sexual and work addictions are the other significant process addictions that are major detours on a man's journey toward manhood. Another, but less prevalent process addiction is compulsive gambling. For many men, a substance addiction, such as alcohol, will hide a long-standing process addiction, such as sexual addiction. The process addiction often precedes the substance addiction.

Process addictions have to do with behavioral processes, like emotional habits. They are behaviors that are done regularly to medicate pain, just as substances can. Our addictive society winks at process addictions, if they see them at all.

The process addictions are more subtle and destructive than substance addictions. After the danger of rage addiction, the sexual and work addictions are the worst process addictions. They are subtle because they don't seem to take away from relationships and responsibilities. No man has ever been jailed for working too much, and in our patriarchy there is no such thing as too much sex.

I will elaborate on work, as a process addiction, in the following chapters on the father. For now, I will mention that this process addiction is not only modeled but idealized in our society. While most sexual addiction is winked at, corporations seek and encourage the work addicted. This addiction can be hidden inside an aura of responsibility, productivity, even genius. And success often comes to the work addicted.

Not all hardworking, productive men are work addicts. The difference is whether a man has passed his Ordeal into a calling or is using work to resist the pain of Ordeal. A man stuck in the marketplace, the world of the father, is prone to depression from lack of meaningful work. Addiction often follows as productivity demands increase.

Work addiction has its origin in the father's marketplace. Sexual addiction begins near the mother's hut.

Sexual Addiction?

I maintain that addictive sex is the norm in our culture. Some experts on sexual addiction describe it as our "cultural sexual obsession" leading to a great divide between relationship and sexuality. There is a widespread cultural problem of objectifying women. This goes back to the projected mother object. Making a woman an object begins the process of using her for an addiction. Addictive sex, as a symptom of life behind the wall, ruins more relationships than any other reasons given in relationship how-to books.

The prevalence of certain attitudes about male sexuality contributes greatly to sexual addictions, and unsatisfactory sexual and personal relations. Most of these attitudes, like urban myths, are adolescent ideas that get culturally enshrined. The idea that men need sex to relax or to keep from being keyed up is prevalent. Jack Kennedy was reputed to have told a visiting prime minister that he needed sex every two days or he couldn't work well. Other men talk of needing release. Still others use their lack of sex to rationalize drinking. Too often sex is considered a survival need along the same lines as food and water. Without it, death follows, or might as well.

I am reminded of the famous adolescent ploy played out when I was young in make-out places across the country. An adolescent couple is deep into necking and petting when the boy pleads to go farther. When the girl is hesitant the boy talks about the irreparable physical harm he will suffer if they stop now. Ideas like exploding and never being able to have children are expressed. The boy pleads that getting off is the only cure. The responsibility is the young girl's. She alone can avoid a medical catastrophe.

Now "blue balls" is a painful condition. But I haven't heard of anyone dying from it.

Sex in our society has not gotten much past this primitive stage. In an addictive sexual encounter a man's sexual partner will often feel pressured and used. She or he will feel like a sex object, like a toy. And that will be an accurate assessment. Addictive sex involves using a partner to connect to a feeling, not to a person. In this case a man uses a person rather than a substance, or uses a person as a substance. This manipulation is the hidden agenda that creates the empty and violated feeling in the partner, and ultimately in the man himself.

Unfortunately, much of Judeo-Christian teaching endorses this addictive view of depersonalization, as long as marriage is involved. Evidently holy matrimony insures that there is a meaningful, personal relationship rather than an addictive one. The sacrament of marriage apparently covers a multitude of sins. Historically, the Christian marriage vows were taken to mean that the woman would have to please the man sexually, and on demand. The assumption was that men had this insatiable sex drive and women, with little sex drive of their own, owed the man sexual satisfaction. As St. Paul said, "Better to marry than to burn." Sex was considered a necessary evil blessed by marriage. The man's sexual drive would at least guarantee procreation. Throughout this religious history, sex was rarely considered an act of love.

Many of the marriage and relationship problems that couples have involve sexual problems. Much of the time the woman will complain that all the man wants is sex. And the man will not understand the point, of course he wants sex with his beloved.

Some of this problem can be attributed to gender differences. Women usually come at sexuality from a much more personal viewpoint than men. Most women need to feel close and intimate before they start feeling sexual. There needs to be a sense of significant and ongoing connection for most women to feel good sexually.

Most men, on the other hand, will say that they need sex first in order to feel the intimacy later. They experience closeness to their mate through the sexual act. Bernie Zilbergeld, in his book *The New Male Sexuality*, points out that "many men report that they do feel loving during and after sex, and some say they are more emotionally expressive after sex." He agrees that men often use sex as a healthy way of getting close and showing love.

These honest gender differences can be resolved with understanding and communication if there are no addictions involved. It is important for men to realize that women have a different style of movement toward sex than they do, and to respect that style. The uninitiated man's need to experience sexual intimacy first, on the way toward emotional intimacy, is not a sign in itself of sexual addiction. A man who is not sexually addicted will be able to hear his partner's personal needs and learn to become a good lover.

Sex as a way of sharing intimacy is a valid human characteristic. However, this way of achieving closeness can be a red flag. Sometimes the closeness the man seeks during sex is the archetypal closeness to the mother object and not to the woman lying beside him. This kind of closeness mimics a juvenile feeling of comfort and body relaxation. A man can unknowingly confuse this body feeling with personal closeness. When that feeling goes away, and loneliness creeps in, he will then want to have more sex, as an alcoholic wants more to drink, to achieve the feeling of comforting closeness again. In the process the man mistakes boyish satisfaction for adult emotional intimacy. The man mistakes comfort for love.

Terrence Real uses the term "sexual mother" to define this relationship. This closeness is boy to mother, not man to woman. It is really more physical than emotional. Meanwhile the spouse is not feeling closeness, but resentment. The boyish closeness does not constitute a whole relationship. Women start feeling like the object they really are. They feel more like a mother, comforting a child, rather than a woman loving a man.

I've talked to a number of women who "give in" because their man "needs it." Patrick Carnes described one woman who felt like she was "something to drain her husband's body so he could sleep." This addictive sexuality is the regressive sexuality of the young boy. Women instinctively feel this.

I have counseled men who have sex every night like clockwork, and their wives accept this. I have counseled other men who would have sex every night if they could. I have counseled men who obsess about sex regularly every day. They are proud of their desire. They imagine every man wants the same. They punctuate their desire by the obvious, "I'm a man aren't I?" Sexual desire makes them feel manly.

I am always concerned when I hear a man say he would have sex every night if he could. Society might think him manly for having such a strong libido. I wonder how much he uses sex, or sexual fantasy, as a refuge from his problems and pain. I wonder how much sexual obsession keeps him from exploring other parts of his relationship and his life. Again, there is nothing wrong with sexual pleasure. But what place does it have, like other addictions, in keeping a man a boy?

Sexual obsession is always a sign that a man has lost direction. He tries to fill his emptiness with seemingly harmless behavior that few people recognize as addiction. Ironically, when a wife or lover does hear of a man's possible sexual addiction they immediately recognize the truth there. They immediately realize why they have felt so used. The presence of an addiction does not show there is no love in a relationship. It shows that a man has much work to do in finding healthier ways to fill his emptiness.

Sexual obsession is a sign, not of manliness, but of powerlessness. It is vital that men understand the hidden sexual addictions that we all have been taught to have. The norm for sexual conduct in our society is addictive sex. Few men are taught differently. When I mention to a man that there is sexual addictiveness in his life he will recoil under those strong words. I don't say this to blame or shame him. I tell him so he can understand what is going on around him and inside him. A man needs to know the parameters of his mission and who the enemy really is.

Some estimates show that 5-10% of men have clinical sexual addictions, those resulting in severe consequences to a man's life such as loss of job, public shame, legal action, imprisonment. It is the rest of us who have to find how sexual addiction affects our lives and relationships, without the warning of public consequences. This addiction is insidious.

Pornography

One of the surest signs of sexual addictiveness is a man's use of pornography. Pornography is the smoke that exposes the fire of sexual addiction. Pornography elicits a wink and a smile from man to man. Yet most men are embarrassed to reveal this habit to women they love. And most men have been ashamed to admit this habit to me as their therapist, not knowing that I assume that the majority of the men I see have a high probability of being addicted to pornography.

Pornography is often the gateway to sexual addiction. Men swim in an ocean of soft and hard pornography and media sexual innuendo. One of the main reasons pornographic viewing is so deeply buried in men's emotional needs is because pornography is often a boy's first experience of adult sexuality. This imprinting linking sexual excitement with a flat page or screen fantasy is very powerful emotionally, so powerful this imprinting is close to feeling hardwired.

Pornography is not harmless. Women partners' reactions to discovering pornography in their man's life is a clue to how destructive this compulsion is. Most women who discover pornography in their partners' lives react intensely and painfully. Women often rage to cover the intense pain they feel. Their reaction is the same as discovering an affair.

Men are often in surprise and shock at this reaction. Yet a woman's instincts are usually accurate. A man is not having an affair with a flesh and blood woman, but he is having an affair with a mother object. This object has many bodies and looks. The dark mother can be a shape shifter. She keeps a man passive, having only to open a magazine or press a few keys to call up a web page. She keeps a man unconscious, repressing his shame while comforting his boyish needs.

Women often intuitively know that there is something wrong for this is proof that a man has separated love and sexuality. Sometimes she is the one loved. Sometimes she is the object. She feels awful to rarely be both loved and sexually exciting. All sexual addiction separates healthy, mature love and sexual comfort. Pornography is the minor leagues for major league sexual and relationship problems.

Sexual Trauma

All men have been sexually abused by our sexually obsessed culture that objectifies women. However, up to one in four men have been personally sexually abused. And 90% of these men have been abused by someone familiar to them. Unfortunately, sexual abuse of men seems to be minimized or ignored. Yet physical sexual abuse can widen the gap even more between men and a healthy sexual response. Not everyone who is sexually abused will suffer damage to their sexuality. But physical sexual abuse on top of cultural sexual abuse has the potential for sexual trauma.

This cultural denial of male sexual abuse may result from the assumption that men are basically promiscuous anyway, so an early sexually exploitative experience is not seen as harmful. Maybe men are seen as oppressors so often that they hardly can be seen as being oppressed. Sexual abuse of women, as a widespread social reality, was courageously uncovered by the feminist movement. Maybe that is why women are seen as the only people being abused.

Men need to know that their compulsive sexual behavior of the sort that is blatantly dehumanizing is often the result of having been severely sexually dehumanized themselves. This is not to excuse the behavior but to explain it. It is also meant to show a man a way out. The mission is to start dealing with the pain of abuse, after the destructive behavior is controlled.

Men who have been abused sexually have been traumatized. When a trusted person, male or female, is also an abuser the betrayal and manipulation severs the natural connection between sex and love, just as pornography does. The betrayal often freezes a man emotionally at an early developmental stage and an earlier time in his history. In other words, the boy is stuck.

Sexual trauma keeps a man stuck in the village in a more profound way than any other experience. His rare comfort will be sexual pleasure. He is not able to grow enough to understand the far more satisfying experience of a loving sexual and emotional relationship. He will find himself habitually performing behaviors, ritually, that mirror the abuse that was done to him. His life will alternate between seemingly endless depression and short bursts of sexual highs. The high will inevitably be followed by guilt and the familiar depression. The traumatized man will then become obsessed with getting the next high, to the exclusion of the rest of his life. This is how sexual trauma works.

Men who have been sexually abused by another man sometimes feel bisexual. They feel the need to have impersonal sexual relations with another man, often an older man. They feel a need, a deep ritual need, to relive an emotional connection on a sexual level. I have found that these men are not looking for sexual comfort as much as the male archetypal recognition from a father figure. These men have a gaping father wound. When this wound is sexualized the guilt and confusion is paralyzing. This homosexual behavior has the genesis in trauma and not in healthy homosexual behavior. These men are not primarily or naturally homosexual. This traumatized stuckness can be addressed with special emphasis on working on the father wound discussed in the following chapters.

Men who have been abused by a female can have a much harder time separating from the dark mother. Women who abuse identify with the dark mother's need for control and keeping a male child a boy. Sexualizing the mother bond in a direct way intensifies the already omnipresent cultural abuse. This is a trauma that can be healed in the conscious separation from the dark mother.

Acting In

Sometimes a man will not act out his sexual trauma by performing sexual acts. He will act in. Possibly because of a stronger sense of social right and wrong received from a father figure, a man may be able to keep inside the sexual drive for comfort. He will be able to contain destructive sexual behavior. But there is a price. He will often find he has little sexual desire. He cannot make love with a loved one without feeling conflict and pain. So he unconsciously numbs, numbing his penis as well as his emotions in any loving situation.

Sometimes this man will be forced into sexual fantasy for comfort. Fantasy and masturbation, usually brought on by pornography, will be his only satisfying ritual. The results will be the same. Guilt and depression will follow. Some of the man's guilt will be around his regret at not feeling sexual excitement about the woman or man he loves. Other times this man will totally shut down sexually. He will revert to a substance, and retreat deeper behind his walls. Often the substance, especially alcohol, became addictive because he was using it originally to fight his sexual depression.

More and more men, both traumatized and not, are actually suffering from a lack of desire sexually, especially with their partners. These disorders of desire don't mean a man has erectile difficulties. They point toward a lack of sexual excitement or motivation. The paradox in these men's lives is that the desire lessens as their commitment to relationship increases. For many of these men, the problem is that they are unconsciously burying the addictive sexual conflict between emotional intimacy and sexual excitement.

Left with the choice of emotional intimacy they become shut down because they are not able to endure the sense of engulfment and power-lessness that intimacy brings them. The sense of engulfment could be the result of sexual trauma. It could also be the result of poor boundary setting in the total relationship and the feeling of engulfment by the mother complex. In either case, the feeling of engulfment must be dealt with before sexual healing can take place.

I must mention that there is another reason that a man may have lessened sexual desire, even impotency. When a man has walked farther down the path of initiation and thus sexual healing he may have times of erection difficulties and less of a need for genital sexual fulfillment. This temporary condition has more to do with sexual initiation and the way out of sexual addiction. This situation is dealt with in the chapters on Ordeal.

A Way Out

When I talk to men about their sexual addictions, especially in their monogamous relationships, they gape in disbelief. Things like fetishism and longstanding promiscuous sex are their standard for sexual addiction. Anything less seems normal. It is hard for men to accept that we have all been sexually abused, some very personally, by a sexually obsessed culture. We have all been programmed to disconnect sex and love. We have all been acculturated to love objects, not persons.

Part of the reason that men resist any thought that their sexuality is addictive is fear. They believe that my clinical answer is abstention, celibacy, cold turkey. It is not. Sex is a good thing. When making love is really making love the experience is one of the most edifying a person can have. Men who have experienced sexual love with a loved one cannot believe the wonderful difference.

The deep healing of any addiction requires voluntary movement toward initiation. I have rarely met any man, no matter how deeply wounded sexually, who has not healed after redirecting his warrior energy toward initiation. As in all addictions the healing is in moving toward a meaningful life path that replaces the aimless wandering of an addicted life. The initiation process is as much a transition into love as a transition into manhood. Initiation makes a man a loving person who can literally make love. I must act as Elder in my work with men to witness to this healing and transformative way out. I must witness to hope. I must also honestly warn of a process that is neither quick nor painless. I must warn of the Ordeal where pain and healing are like brother and sister.

The initial steps of initiation always involve disconnecting from impersonal attachments of all kinds. The initial steps have to do with a man summoning enough warrior energy to draw a line in the sand. Setting this boundary means not going back to the impersonal sexual expression that detours from the path of initiation. Separation from the dark mother means never permanently regressing behind that line.

Moving On

Once the warrior awakens to creating boundaries and becomes fearless in moving toward the painful initiatory path he has exhibited one of the most courageous actions a man can take. He has gone inward on the path to manhood. Boundary setting starts the separation from any addiction. But the crucial step is the move toward voluntary separation and initiation.

Seeking other men for understanding and connection to healthy masculine energy can help overcome the need to stay hidden behind the wall, close to the hut. Often in seeking a way out a man can take his doubts and shame to another man whose life journey he respects. This is about taking steps from behind the wall. Men need men to mirror their own healthy masculine yearnings. This is also about starting to learn initiatory humility in asking and receiving honest feedback and support. The man he confides in could be a good friend as long as he is a friend who is good. This man can also be a colleague, a minister, a counselor, a man who sponsors other addicted men, any man who seems to be walking a path of honesty and integrity.

This big step for the man with the awakened warrior is the movement toward connection to father energy. Father energy gives a man strength to finish his separation from the mother complex and move into the world of the father. Reaching out to another man is a start in finding father energy. Father energy can be carried by any older man who has traveled his inner road. Father energy is needed by a man of any age who has a father wound.

The uninitiated boy is stuck in the world of the mother, by the mother's comforting hut. The most likely reason for his stuckness is the lack of masculine, fathering energy. The father brings a boy the courage and the support to move into his world, helping him face the inevitable pain. As we will see it is the father who gives the boy the strength and wisdom to finally separate from his regressive comforts. It is the father figure and his message who lead a man out of the world of addictions.

A man needs powerful relationships with important people to grow.

This is the opposite of the popular myth that a man can go it alone. At this point he needs strong fathering and then wise Eldering, a strong masculine presence. Addictions keep a man unrelated and unmotivated. When things get painful, as they inevitably will on the journey to manhood, an addicted man will move toward an addictive object and away from the men who can help him.

For most men, the father and what he represents is the answer to overstaying in the mother's world. His is the relationship that holds the key. He is the way out from behind walls. He is the way out of the mother's hut. We are an addictive society because there are not enough good fathers and Elders to guide and lead men into their manhood. We, men, are regularly orphaned by absent fathers. Yet the young boy inside needs a father to grow, even into his young adulthood. The archetype of initiation cannot be denied without destructive consequences. The following chapters will describe the next initiatory steps and how we can find answers in the world of the father.

Chapter 6
The Age of the Father

A boy is hardwired to become a man. He is hardwired to be initiated. Yet his hardwiring is dependent on the actions of other men. His hardwiring is dependent on a network of older men. Other men must consciously turn on the hardware. If a boy is kept from men who will guide him to manhood, his destiny is blocked.

It is a misunderstanding that most men languish in the world of the mother because of comfort. This is not the real story. Most men are stuck in the world of the mother because other men have not taken them away. The most important happening for the young boy in his quest for manhood is the emergence of one man, a good father. This man becomes a bridge to other men who hold a key to his destiny. The father brings the energy of separation, the mirror of masculinity, and the motivation to search for the life mission. The father starts a man on his road to manhood.

The connection to a mother object of any kind means overstaying in the world of the feminine. A man who stays too long sees the world through the eyes of a woman. He often finds himself living out the dreams and wishes of a woman. Sometimes he stays with a woman whose dreams he despises. In either case, he finds himself spending most of his energy obsessed with keeping her happy. He lives the dark side of the saying, "If mama ain't happy, ain't nobody happy." He assumes that if he pleases a mother object, he will somehow be happy too.

Indigenous people instinctively knew this feminine obsession to be wrong for the boy and destructive to the community. Both men and women did not let it continue. Mothers, poignantly but purposefully, handed their boys over to fathers and Elders. They knew it was time. Fathers, then Elders, knew their role and willingly took over responsibility for the boy's growth.

Modern men do not benefit from this wisdom. Most modern men are stuck in the world of the feminine. In modern times the mother has been blamed for this overstaying situation. Men, even today, are thought to be victims of devouring, controlling mothers, helpless to get away. Early psychology blamed everything from masturbation, to addictions, to homosexuality on the smothering mother. Blaming women has historically been the civilized way for men to succumb to the mother complex, while trying to save face. It is easy to blame the woman, not the complex.

The fact is that modern young men are stuck in the world of the feminine because older men leave them there. The dark mother merely colludes in the process. The dark mother merely seduces an already lost boy. In any case it is not the flesh and blood mother, or mother/wife, who is the culprit here. She is most often the scapegoat.

Separation and initiation always involves an older man. An indigenous boy never left the village by himself. He didn't know where to go or what to do. He was stuck until an older man came and took him away. In modern times young men still need older men to show them the way. The father is the first older man the boy connects with. His presence and wisdom is crucial to a boy's growth.

Assistant Mothers

In the recent past fathers were, at most, considered assistant mothers. Margaret Mead, a noted anthropologist, once quipped that fathers were a "biological necessity but a social accident." Since early 1800's, fathers were felt to be doing their parental duty if they provided a financial base for the family and stepped in when discipline was too much for the mother. Otherwise parenting was left to the mother, including the teaching of morality and social graces. Modern American fathers were taught that they were not needed in childrearing. So fathers unknowingly deserted their sons, stranding them in the mother's world with no way out.

Much of the literature of the contemporary men's movement centers on the lack of good fathering. Robert Bly was the first to point out the woundedness that many men feel from lack of fathering. He talks of the changing role of fathers since the Industrial Revolution. With the coming of technology and the moving of the workplace to the factory, the father became an absent member of the family. Factories replaced fields. Sons saw their father off early in the morning, greeting an exhausted man late in the evening. A son knew little of what his father did all day, where previously, in agricultural societies, fathers taught their sons what they did by working side by side with them. Fathers were no longer in the loop of initiating their sons. As Anthony Rotundo says, "mothers were now expected to mold the characters of their sons, a task that in previous generations had always belonged to fathers." Sons were abandoned to be initiated by their mothers.

Today, the lack of a healthy father presence is the most significant cause of a boy's loss of masculine direction. We are all products of stunted or skewed initiations because our fathers didn't know better. We are all often at a loss about how to father our own sons. We are all terribly at risk for seduction by the dark mother. We are all at a loss for what it means to be a man from the inside out. This is what Bly talks about when he emphasizes every man's father wound.

Masculine Energy

But what is the role of the father in a boy's initiation? How have we been wounded by his absence? Where does he lead us? Where is he today?

The father for indigenous people is the son's first significant experience with masculine energy. When the father is present with positive masculine energy he starts the process of separating the boy from passively receiving from the mother and moving the boy toward an active state of motivation for his search for masculinity. By doing this he performs a mini-initiation for the boy, awakening a hunger for emotional risk and exploratory pain.

As we shall see, a significant part of masculine energy is the energy of separation and individuation, which inevitably involves pain. Masculine energy involves facing the pain of separation from the tragic world of addiction and regressive relationships. The father is the first, necessary bearer of this separating energy, while giving the boy a vision of wholeness beyond the pain. He gives meaning to boundary setting and is a model of a mature, boundaried man.

In most indigenous tribes the father took over the guidance and discipline of the child after a point, usually at age 7 or 8, and started to introduce him to the man's world. He gave him the message that now he would have to experience pain and discomfort on his way to getting his needs and the tribe's needs met. This pain was not seen as the enemy, as in the mother's world, but as a necessary part of manhood.

The initial pain was separation from the mother and the world of immediate and easy gratification. The father started to teach delayed gratification for a purpose more important than comfort. The father taught the boy how to face the world outside the hut. He introduced the boy to his world, the world of the marketplace, the world of the hunt, and the world of the survival of the tribe. The survival skills that the father would teach, as well as the modeling of manhood, would be necessary for the boy to survive his coming initiatory Ordeal. The father would guide the boy in starting to see the world through a man's eyes.

The Initiated Father

It seems that the crucial time today's father needs to assert his positive masculine energy is still when the boy turns 7 or 8. About this time the boy is starting to confront the world outside the hearth and hut, symbolized by venturing to a modern school. The boy learns that there is a world outside the hut that he is destined for. He learns that this new world has different rules from the world he came from.

The father represents the strange, outside world to his son. If the father has been initiated he will very consciously take the boy away from the feminine hut, the kitchen and family room, and tell the mother he is taking over the next step in the boy's growth. He will then introduce his son to the world of the marketplace, the world of strangers outside of family, to the social world outside the home. In this way the father is a crucial transitional figure on the boy's road to initiation. He starts teaching a boy how a man acts with strangers. He starts to teach a boy the rules of the world of men.

The father, not the mother, should start setting the rules and the discipline at this age. An initiated mother will understand this and welcome it. She will not get in the way of the father's influence or try to protect the boy from the father's strength. She will start to go through her own grieving process at this point in letting go of her son. This will be part of her initiation.

The father teaches a boy how to interact in the larger society. The initiated father will see this world as an exciting, adventuresome place. He teaches a boy that strangers are potential friends. In this he builds on the message of the good mother, who has given the boy a sense of hope and trust. He also gives a boy the beginning of a comfort level around other men. In this way a father teaches a boy he can reach out to other men and follow his hardwired instincts. An initiated father will not see other men as competitors and dangerous strangers but as sources of support and wisdom. He will see other men as potential fellow journeyers, as brothers in initiation, healthy patriarchs, or Elders who can give wisdom and direction. He will impart to his son the goodness of the community of men.

The initiated father starts to teach a boy the wisdom of the Elder. The world of the father shows a boy that anything of value needs to be struggled for. And the father starts to show that value resides within. The father does not shield a son from pain, especially emotional pain. Instead he acknowledges the pain and encourages the boy to learn from it. In this he prepares the boy for his eventual Ordeal.

The initiated father teaches a son how a man relates to a woman without turning her into a mother. In this way a father gives important lessons about committed, adult relationships. An initiated father will not treat his wife as a mother object. He will model healthy boundaries. He will not be terrified of her anger or dependent on her approval. Thus, he will give a son the example of how to treat a woman with respect, as a companion and true partner. He will also give a son the wisdom to choose a woman who can be a true partner.

In all that he teaches, a father lends his son his own strength and wisdom until the son is strong enough to find his own inner wisdom. As Lewis Yablonsky, author of *Fathers and Sons*, points out, "A son who has a close relationship with his father is thus constantly examining his own behavior from his father's point of view." An unfathered boy will soon be overwhelmed by the choices and responsibilities of his new world away from home. He can then turn into an overwhelmed man who does not have the strength or enthusiasm for an adult life. An initiated father lends the strength for the boy to discern good decisions and the strength for the boy to weather his mistakes. This experience gives a boy confidence that he will eventually succeed in a man's world.

The father is the first and most important model of manhood that a son encounters. A son will carry the imprint of his father in his soul, for better or worse, for the rest of his life. The ideal is for a son to want to live his life with the passion and dedication of his initiated father. The ideal is to see his life as filled with potential for opportunity and meaning, in community with other men and women who share that optimism and hope. The initiated father opens a son up to the camaraderie of brothers, the power of healthy patriarchs, the wisdom of Elders, and the companionship of a committed life partner.

The Modern Age of the Father

The modern man ideally needs a father between the ages of 7-14, as did primitive boys. However, modern men seem to have the boy's need for emotional fathering for a much longer time. I see most men's need for fathering extending past age 14 to around age 36. We all probably need good fathering at least until our mid-30's. Because we are an Elderless society, a society without formal initiation, a man's initiation now is left to chance. If this were an initiated, mature culture boys would have the opportunity to mature much faster. However, in a modern or uninitiated culture, it seems to take a man at least until his mid-30's to find a sufficient amount of healthy fathering energy to move into psychospiritual initiation.

This extra stage roughly corresponds to psychologist Daniel Levinson's developmental stage of neo-adulthood. Levinson studied a cohort of men from their days at Harvard in the 1940's throughout their life cycles. He used his study to find if men go through developmental stages their whole life. While older psychological theories seemed to show development stopping at young adulthood, Levinson was one of the first modern psychologists to show that men develop throughout their lives. Levinson showed that adulthood was not a monolithic end state culminating in death. Instead he showed that men could keep growing past their 20's.

Levinson feels there is a normal structure to most men's lives throughout their lifespan. He claims in his book that men are not considered full adults in our society until around 35. Until then he is a novice adult. After that he is ready to become a full-fledged adult. A man has a great need for a mentor during his novice phase, according to Levinson, in order to make the transition to full adulthood. A mentor can make up for a lot of missed fathering, as I will talk about later.

Carl Jung also talks of a man being able to start the equivalent of the initiatory process only after 35. His idea of maturity and initiation he called individuation. He felt that a man was not ready for his journey of individuation until much later than adolescence. He felt a man was not ready until the second half, or afternoon, of his life.

J.R.R. Tolkien wrote a series of books on a fantasy world complete with long histories of many cultures, multiple languages, and mystical geographies. He wrote a myth. Like any myth his story contains many psychological truths. The hero of his story is a relatively young hobbit, a boy trying to become a man. The hobbit culture has different stages of hobbit social development. There is a hobbit term called the tweens, a time between hobbit childhood and adulthood that extended from 18 to 36. Hobbits weren't considered adults until 36, after their tweens. Tolkien also seemed to sense modern man's dilemma of psychological growth in giving hobbits an extended adolescence. Or maybe he sensed modern man's desire for more time to prepare for adulthood.

Contradicting our social norms, the 20's is still the age of the father. The father figure is still needed during the age of the tweens. For many men their own father is exhausted by this time. However, some fathers come into their own when a son reaches this age, especially if they have just completed their own initiation. For others there is the hope of a second father whom I will talk about in a forthcoming chapter.

The Father Wound

If the father is absent, or bears negative masculine energy, two things may happen. The boy may be frightened to advance, retreating back to the mother. Then he tries to live out his mother's dreams and obsessively tries to please the woman he loves. Or the boy unites with the negative, competitive father of the dark patriarchy, a process called identifying with the aggressor. Then he lives out his father's dreams or the dreams of the patriarchal society he is a part of. In neither case does he find his own manhood.

The 20's is the age where the father wound first appears for men. I have counseled many men in their 20's who are stuck in their tweens because of their father wound. They feel this great social responsibility to be an adult, yet see little in the model of their father that appeals to them. So they wander in this limbo of overwhelming expectation and little motivation. They fall prey to the passivity of the dark mother. Adulthood to them is more like a disease than an adventure. They cannot identify with their father's life yet they are hardwired to follow a father. So they stay a teen in a man's body, ashamed and scared and in need of a father figure who can give them a different vision of male adulthood.

There are other men in their 20's who identify with a remote, successful, uninitiated father. They want to follow their father's lead. They have learned to identify with a flawed vision of manhood. They usually don't feel their father wound until later in their life. I do not see these men in their 20's. They are too busy living out their father's dream. Their father wound appears at mid-life, when they begin to catch glimpses of the dead-end road they are on.

The Traditional Father

If a father is not initiated he may not see the need in his son for masculine energy. Or he may use his son to try to get the masculine energy he never got. An uninitiated father is usually either absent from his son's life, or he is competitive with his son for a sense of lost manhood. He will, by a variety of unconscious ways, leave a boy stuck in the mother's world with no power or insight to get out.

Absent fathers are playing out their assigned roles in a traditional way, using the traditional training manual. We talked of the traditional role of father as family protector and provider. Traditional marriages are survival focused and men are responsible for the economic survival of their family. There is no need for the father in child raising, except in matters of extreme discipline. That traditional father mission concentrates on the financial well-being of the family, and depends on the father being a remote model of responsibility, industry, and ambition. In many ways the traditional family is seen as an economic unit whose goal is to raise sons to head their own economic units.

As we will see in a coming chapter the father's worth has become equated to his net worth, leading to work addiction as the norm. As in Victorian times the worth of the whole family, especially sons, is also attached to the father's net worth. Men substitute the quest for money for the quest of the inner life. Work success has become the father's test of manhood, his initiatory Ordeal. For the modern father the most important role of guiding his son through the perils of his mother separation and inner initiation was lost. The traditional father was unaware it was ever there. As Anthony Rotundo says, "By the early nineteenth century, when the work of middle class men began to pull fathers away from home, fathers yielded their traditional roles of shaping the character of their sons."

I have talked to many men who couldn't understand why their wife left them, or why their children left with their wife. They believed they were following the guidelines of fatherhood. Invariably they would talk of how well they provided financially for their family. The most repeated comment would go, "I gave them everything they asked for." They felt they had done everything by the book. And they had.

I have also talked to many men who have felt love and pity for their father. These men knew their fathers would do whatever they could for them. They loved their fathers for that. They also realized that their fathers did not have what they needed to keep from feeling overwhelmed in their quest for respectability for their families and themselves.

Creating a Father

An uninitiated, traditional father will ignore his son because he is in pursuit of patriarchal masculinity. He unknowingly abandons his son, withholding the needed masculine energy. He does not know better.

Because of the boy's hardwired need for the masculine, most unfathered boys will go elsewhere, randomly picking up bits and pieces of masculine stuff from the environment. He will imagine what being manly is. He will create a montage of masculinity as his model, like a poster hung on the wall in his bedroom. In the words of Frank Pittman, "Without a 'father in residence', we may go through life striving toward an ideal of exaggerated, even toxic, masculinity."

The uninitiated son of an absent father will imagine what a good father is and long to have this imagined father as an answer to the emptiness he feels inside. He will also long for this masculine figure to bring him along the way to manhood. He finds that the bits and pieces of masculine energy he picks up from older men is not enough to fill his void or guide him on his way. He will ceaselessly look for other answers.

Many times this answer translates into a young man's desire to become a good father himself. Some men try to get a good father by being a good father. They unconsciously try to create the family they never had. They eventually become both father and son. Thus, they try to achieve manhood through their own family and their own fathering.

These men, though following a traditional path, have added a new twist to the modern father's role. This baby boom twist is often a wonderful benefit to their children, especially their sons. These modern fathers are changing the traditional Victorian role by putting a lot of effort into child raising and a lot of love into their children. They are getting close to their children. They seem to be drawing on some deeper archetypal father energy in getting closer to their children. They are also drawing on the best parts of their own fathers' lives. More importantly, they are learning from their own pain of growing up.

This new form of involved fatherhood is a crucial cultural addition. Many modern fathers need both support and praise for this fathering work. Though there is a ways to go, these fathers are giving significantly more masculine energy to their sons. They are also giving their daughters a good foundation of self-esteem and self-confidence. They are good fathers.

In the process these men are also unconsciously providing some healthy fathering energy for the boy inside themselves. This is a form of second fathering that is more and more prevalent in today's world. It can bring a man farther along his path than the traditional father can. These men have a closer tie to childhood as well as to their own sons. They give their boy inside some exposure to the fathering they didn't have.

Unfortunately these fathers give much more to their sons than they are able to give to their boy inside. Their own father emptiness is still not filled. This emptiness most often comes out in the lack of a healthy, passionate relationship with a wife, who still is more of a mother. It also comes out in the confusion these fathers feel when their own sons become adolescents and need help in career choice and life direction. These fathers still suffer from the absence of connection to initiated men.

The Competitive Father

The men's movement talks of the traditional absent father, away at work or reading the paper. This father has little to say to his son and is a mystery to his family. However there is a whole other class of father that is more involved with his son, but in a dark, negative way. This father competes with his son. As we will see, the patriarchy is based on this competitive father using his son for his own needs. Many men are also personally affected by their own competitive father in ways that block their journey to manhood.

There is a Greek myth that relates to father competition which Freud used to make a point. Freud talked of the Oedipal struggle for a young boy. This psychological struggle was based on the myth of Oedipus, who eventually and unknowingly killed his father and married his mother. Freud stated that a son would naturally come in competition with his father for his mother's attention. If a son did not give up this need to have his mother to himself he would run up against an angry, powerful father. Since a boy was much smaller and more vulnerable than his father, the wise and healthy son, according to Freud, would give up his mother need and align with his father. He would then identify with his father's dreams and desires. In this way a son would avoid being destroyed by the competitive father.

In Freud's view this alliance with father, through fear, was a good thing, since it bolstered the patriarchal culture of obedience to the fathers. As we will see, identifying with the aggressive, competitive father, without separation, is not necessarily a good thing.

Many men have a difficult time at the birth of their first child. The attention, nurturing and concern that they had gotten from a mother object suddenly leaves as the mother turns her attention to the infant. The husband turned father can find himself feeling abandoned and jealous. Unless the father is initiated he will see a son as a competitor. Resentment builds toward the infant, a resentment which can go on throughout that child's life. The son of a competitive father can feel that resentment in the form of competitive criticism and demeaning behavior. Demeaning behavior can turn into emotional and physical abuse. The father can feel that he can find manhood by vanquishing his son. In this way he thinks he can win back the mother object.

This abuse cycle is probably the most wounding a son can experience. However, there is a way out of this cycle for the son and the competitive father. It is Freud's answer. It is the dark patriarchy's answer. But the price is great. In the competition the son can let the father win. Any success the son does get he offers up to his father. Unconsciously, the son honors his father by honoring his father's dreams. The son lives his life for his father. In this way the father is not threatened and the son feels safe. The son identifies with the competitive father and seeks manhood through that model. In this way the son also feels close to his father. In effect the competitive father uses the son to live his own dream and to make himself look like a man. The father can get a sense of pseudo-manhood by feeling responsible for his son's success. In turn the son will identify with his father and his father's dreams as the only way he knows to get the fathering he needs and a feeling of manhood.

Most sons of competitive fathers will be extremely focused and motivated. They will be driven. Their focus will be on money, status, athletics, or whatever constitutes the father's dreams. They will be unconsciously living the father's script. They will not have taken time to consider their own dreams.

If a boy does not succeed in living his father's dreams, the father may put him down unmercifully, punishing him. This son is then driven back to the mother object, usually in the form of an addiction. He is the man who gives up. For he has only one ideal, and that is unreachable. He has only one road to manhood, a road he cannot negotiate.

However, if the son succeeds in his father's dreams both can reach their goal. The father feels successful, and the son feels secure in a readymade identity. Loyalty to a father is not a bad thing, but after a certain point there is a high price. The price the son pays is the relinquishing of his own vision and the path to his own identity. He lives someone else's identity. He is the one who, at mid-life, most profoundly feels the failure of success. He is the one who gets stuck in his father's world, never able to separate and find his own manhood through his own Ordeal. For the competitive father never lets go.

The Sins of the Father

If a father is not initiated, he provides his son with a faulty model of adulthood. All our fathers have unknowingly colluded in creating our faulty training manuals. This fault is the origin of the father wound. We are all heirs of this wound, passed on from father to son for many generations. The wound acts like an original sin that is born in our souls as the body emerges from conception.

I have worked with many men who have struggled with the wounds from their grandfathers and great-grandfathers. Often they live what seems their personal tragedy, when it is really the family tragedy of many generations. Sons wrestle with the demons of their ancestors without realizing the root of their struggle. Most of us have been wounded by fathers who, in turn, have been wounded by their fathers. Most of our fathers were well-meaning but naive though some were desperate and competitive.

In fact the vast majority of fathers have done whatever they could to be the best their sons and daughters needed. Most fathers have knocked themselves out for their families. They have used their masculine energy in the only way they knew how. This is the sadness and sense of tragedy that most men have to face on their initiatory journey. There are few bad guys or enemies here. Yet the wound exists. And facing the pain of the father wound is a crucial step on the journey toward manhood. Love and truth can exist side by side. Awareness of our own father wound can help each of us understand our father's father wound. Seeing one's father as also a brother in pain and ignorance can lead to compassion. When a man can see his father as also a brother he is well on his way to healing his father wound.

Identifying with the Dark Patriarchy

In most cases the father wound led us in desperation to the initiation promised by the dark patriarchy. The closest we would come to a feeling of manhood was in identifying with the values and lifestyle of the dark patriarch. The dark patriarch was probably all that our fathers and grandfathers knew of fathering energy. And the dark patriarch is the embodiment of the competitive father.

We all have an urgent, archetypal need for father energy. The road to manhood goes through a father. In the absence of our own father's initiated energy we have learned to absorb mostly pieces of ersatz masculinity from places beyond our family. Our hardwired need eventually forces most men to identify with the masculine energy emanating from the father culture around us. In a sense we have all been forced to identify with this competitive father in the form of the patriarchy. We look to the patriarchy to initiate us. If we don't identify with the patriarchy we risk not being considered men by family, friends, society. When we do identify we become competitive, or a failure.

In this culture there is little idea of the need for fathering other than patriarchal fathering. And there is no thought of a step beyond the patriarchy, no thought of the necessary father separation. So men get stuck in the village with divided loyalties, loyal to a mother object at home and to a patriarchy in the marketplace. Neither of these loyalties gives him the direction he needs. Neither parent figure points to a space beyond the village, the sacred space of true initiation. The next chapter talks of how we are all forced into pseudo-initiation by a patriarchal society in the absence of a healthy, initiated father culture.

Chapter 7
The Vader Voice

The Father's World

The father represents a view of the world outside the family and the mother's hut. To indigenous peoples the father's world wer as the marketplace of the village. Boys in indigenous villages knew that the world of the father was like a half-way house and school on the way to initiation. The father shared necessary masculine energy and taught skills necessary for initiation. He also showed the son that he no longer needed the nurturing of the mother to survive.

In modern times the father's world is first the world of the school and then today's social and business world. The modern father's world brings us to a fuller definition of the patriarchy.

The word patriarchy comes from the Greek words meaning rule by fathers. In my belief and proposed definition a patriarchy is a culture permeated with a world view and values of older, not Elder, men in power. Theoretically a patriarchy is as humanly healthy or unhealthy as the psychospiritual evolution of the men engendering its cultural values. However, I will often merely use the naked word patriarchy to name this cultural organization because I know of no patriarchy in Western civilization that is not dark.

In my view a dark or negative patriarchy consists of fathers who are uninitiated. Another definition of patriarchy would include a society with no knowledge of the role of Elders in initiation.

Patriarchies are always steeply hierarchical. In a patriarchal hierarchy the higher a man ascends the assumption is that he is wiser no matter how he got there. Father knows best. In this world children, women, and young men never reach that level of wisdom.

In a patriarchy, the father's world holds the highest values and goals of the culture. In my view of a modern patriarchy there is no awareness of a world outside of the marketplace and the village. Uninitiated men have not experienced the other side of Ordeal. Elder values are nonexistent. The father's rules are the last word in manhood.

In our modern patriarchy, the highest values reside in the world of business, and power is used to protect commerce. Manhood success is measured by material success. From a patriarchal viewpoint the marketplace is where manhood is found. This is the place a man is initiated. From the view of a patriarchal society, the marketplace is the only reality a man should aspire to. Profit is the true bottom line and financial success is the ultimate criteria of manhood. There is no next step. There is no realization that a man must separate from the father, as well as the mother, in order to become a man. In a patriarchal society there is no room for Elders and the inner journey into a deeper reality.

Here, the father wound goes even deeper than the wounds from our own fathers. The patriarchy tells us that identifying with this marketplace father is the end of the line, the goal of our manhood. Much of modern society's yardstick for male maturity is based on Freud's Oedipal struggle. Our cultural assumption is that the end of male development results in the son's identifying with the father, causing a boy to also identify with the patriarchy, the greater father.

In our cultural scenario, the boy learns to be the good son of a father culture that values the hard work and productivity of a marketplace reality. By the fruits of this productivity, a son moves toward manhood. He becomes a good provider to his family and a good, contributing citizen of his community. In this psychological scenario, the more a man identifies with the rules and mores of the father culture the more mature he is. The more productive he is the more of a man he is.

The patriarchy is the real author of our flawed training manual. The patriarchy wounded our fathers who unknowingly wounded us. The patriarchy now creates the deeper father wound in all of us, because it takes advantage of our archetypal need for fathering. If the patriarchy fathered us, and then let us go to Elders, it would be a blessing. But our patriarchy stops at the village boundaries, refusing to acknowledge the reality of the wilderness, withholding the path to a deeper manhood.

Patriarchal Reality

Most men see themselves as realists. They don't want to be seen as naive, idealistic, or crazy. For them there is only the one reality, the reality of material success and social well-being. The assumptions of their life go unchallenged. For someone to say that there is another reality outside the village, is threatening. Going along with the program means staying within the agreed upon reality of the patriarchal culture, within our modern consensus reality.

A consensus reality is a reality that everyone in society unknowingly agrees to. It is a world view or paradigm that goes unquestioned. Questioners are considered heretics or lunatics. An example of consensus reality from another time in history can give perspective on the patriarchal paradigm we now live in.

During Galileo's time in the early 17th Century, the earth was considered the center of the universe. That reality had all kinds of implications for the reality of everything else. Because the earth was at the center of the universe, mankind was the center and reason for all life. God was up in heaven, above the moon, where unchanging truth resided. The pope, known as Papa as he is today, knew truth better than anyone else because he was intermediary between God and the people. Society was structured on a hierarchical order with God at the top, patriarchal authorities in the middle, and the rest of us looking up to find the truth. The father archetype was paramount because the father was the stepping stone to God.

In Galileo's time, the Bible was true in every word. And it talked about the sun revolving around the earth. As Martin Luther said of Copernicus, "This fool wishes to reverse the entire science of astronomy; but sacred scripture tells us that Joshua commanded the sun to stand still, and not the earth."

The people who said that this geocentric universe was wrong were labeled as crazy or evil. These people pointed to another reality that was foreign and uncomfortable to consider. This reality was also a threat to the patriarchal church which controlled the life of the Western world at that time, and to the patriarchal governments who received their authority from the church. A new astronomy threatened the very foundations of their patriarchal culture. It created the possibility of a different consensus reality, a new mythos that actually held the seeds of our modern, political democratic ideals.

Copernicus and Galileo were correct of course. They had the truth. They were also at odds with the current consensus reality. And so were punished for believing in another paradigm. They were seen as disloyal to Church and God and the current father's world. They were seen as sinners.

Today, our consensus reality is still represented by the father. However, the father is no longer the pope, but the free market father, the commercial father of mercantilism and the democratic marketplace. In Galileo's time people were taught not to believe their own eyes. The Church would tell them what they were seeing. They were expected to see the world through the Church's eyes. In our culture, the patriarchal consensus reality tells us what is true. We are taught to see the world through the patriarch's eyes. As Sam Keen points out, "In the secular theology of economic man Work has replaced God as the source from whom all blessings flow."

Modern men are unknowingly affected by a view of manhood that is essentially a view of uninitiated men. Thus, society itself acts as a dark father. This dark father keeps us stuck in the marketplace to bolster its own view of reality and its own gain.

Take a corporation that is extremely competitive and hard-driving. It is probable that the culture of this corporation assumes that an employee gives most of his life to his work. He works long hours, is on call, and does whatever it takes to get the job done. A man's highest values are expected to coincide with the corporation's highest values. Though phrases like family values are mouthed as most important, the corporate family still demands the primary allegiance.

The patriarchal consensus reality in these corporations is that profit, winning, status, money are the highest values. Other cultural considerations are secondary. William Pfaff, a syndicated columnist, writing in *Notre Dame Magazine*, states: "A change in belief about the responsibilities of corporate management also has taken place. Maximized return on investment capital … is the sole appropriate criterion for corporate decisions. The notion that 'social return' may be as important as fiscal return in assessing corporate conduct is ruled out." In many corporate cultures one is literally expected to give one's life for these values. In return for unquestioned loyalty, the father corporation promises care of the good son for life.

Sam Keen calls this new culture a "corpoarchy." The corpoarchy now defines much of our modern consensus reality. The corpoarchy has in many ways replaced the matriarchy and patriarchy in providing every man's social parenting. Anyone who tries to live their life by other values, such as family or a wider spirituality, will be seen as weak. To the corpoarchy, this person will be a traitor, or at the least, naive or incompetent.

As we will see, the values that indigenous people lived by were not discovered in the marketplace. Marketplace values were derived from values found in the initiatory wilderness, the other side of the soul and spirit. The marketplace itself had no mystery, no answers to their deepest questions. It wasn't made for that. It was a tool, a vehicle only. Fathers deferred to Elders in the realm of values.

In an Elderless society, fathers, in the guise of patriarchy, fill the vacuum left by the absence of Elders. In many ways, the problem is not the excesses of fathers as it is the dearth of Elders. Elders have not shown us a new reality and haven't taught us how to find our own voices.

The Father Inside

The father, both in indigenous times and today, symbolizes the values of the well-ordered and efficient marketplace. In itself, the values and goals of the marketplace are good and necessary. The father's role in giving a boy the ego strength to negotiate this world of material survival and creative productivity is crucial. Also, the father's masculine energy is vital in leading the boy away from the kind of narcissistic, playboy mentality of the dark mother. The problem is that the marketplace is not where a man found his maturity. Our modern problem is that most men are stuck in the father's world, overstaying in a world of incomplete manhood.

Most men stay stuck in the patriarchal world because men hunger for a father's presence and a father's voice. Because sons hunger for masculine energy, a subtle thing happens inside every man. Sons unknowingly incorporate their personal father, as well as their patriarchal father, inside their psyches. These fathers, once inside, survive in the shadows of their mind, speaking to them of life and manhood. This is the origin of the father voice in every man. The father voice is absorbed into every man because we are hardwired to absorb it. Our father's words, influenced by the patriarchy's words, then become like a software program inside our minds, a program that we didn't know we had, running ceaselessly.

All of us have normal talk in our heads most of the time. Unfortunately we rarely think about who is talking or the origin of the voice. Men who start the inner journey become aware of a male voice inside early in their journey. These men then start to wonder where those words come from. However, most men just assume this masculine voice is their own, containing their own thoughts and values. Uninitiated men assume all their thoughts are their own. Not being familiar with the inner life they are naive about their own inner workings. They rarely question that these voices and these words may come from somewhere else.

Unfortunately, some inner voices speak the words of others. What uninitiated men don't realize is that, starting as children, we all record the repeated dialogues from the most important people in our lives. Our brains are like tape recorders, picking up and storing important conversations, especially from fathers and other older men. These other older men could be teachers, coaches, priests, or media heroes we see on TV. These stored conversations, these tapes, are often the sources of the words playing in all men's heads. If these tapes contain the words of initiated men we possess wisdom that will bring us a long way toward manhood. If these tapes are of uninitiated men, carrying the patriarchal voices, these voices bring us very flawed wisdom and a great amount of shame.

This patriarchal voice lives in the deepest parts of our own psyches. This is both the voice of society telling a boy how to be a man as well as the voice of his own father's expectations. Frank Pittman calls this voice the "male chorus." The chorus speaks for the masculine consensus reality. In our society it can be a good voice up to a certain point in a man's development. However, this voice invariably turns negative if a man strives to find his own initiatory path, outside the marketplace and outside the consensus reality of our time. Like the engulfing mother the competitive father tries to keep the boy in his domain after the boy is ready to move on. The patriarchal voice warns a man in stern and shameful ways if he strays outside patriarchal reality.

In my work I often deal with dreams as part of therapy. Invariably in the first part of a man's therapy his dreams will contain a dark, shadowy male figure who is trying to hurt him with a knife, gun, stick or other phallic object. Sometimes the dark male presence tries to destroy him with an explosive. This male figure is most often the patriarchal archetype of the dark father that the man carries inside of him. Bombs and guns most often represent the angry words of the father aimed at the boy, explosions that destroy a boy's self-esteem and confidence. Knives, spears, and other long thin objects often represent the tongue of the father, using words meant to harm. These dreams are one proof of the dark patriarchal voice, and that presence that resides deep in every man.

The Vader Voice

The patriarchal voice resides in our unconscious. Unless the personal voice of a healthy, initiated father is strong, the patriarchal voice of our culture becomes our de facto father. The voice of a personal, uninitiated father merely strengthens and adds credibility to the voices of the patriarchy. Most of us have powerful patriarchal voices inside because our fathers trying to help us unreflectively passed them along to us. For most men this patriarchal voice says things like "be in control, work to take care of the family, don't let the company down, don't let them see you sweat, winning is the only thing, real men don't make mistakes." The patriarchal voice carries the commandments of the masculine mystique that Frank Pittman and Warren Farrell talk about. As Pittman points out, "when we see men overdoing their masculinity, we can assume that they haven't been raised by men, that they have taken cultural stereotypes literally, and that they are scared they aren't being manly enough."

One of the strongest messages of the patriarchal voice is its incessant command to "be productive." This message plays in most men's minds, including mine, with the relentless monotony of a misbegotten mantra. It seems to speak everywhere, not just at work, but at home or anywhere else where there is any free time. It speaks while trying to relax or be with friends. It starts to speak the moment one awakens and it reminds us if we sleep too late. This mantra creates a great deal of agitation if it is not followed. For in the patriarchy the proof of manhood and the source of self-esteem is in productivity, only in productivity.

After the patriarchal voice gives its commandments it often adds the call words "asshole," or "dumbshit," or "sorry fucker." The voice acts like a tough sadistic drill sergeant with a new recruit. This is why I call it the Vader voice. Like Darth Vader, the voice is there for its own dark purposes, the purposes of another Empire. Like Vader it tolerates no disloyalty or failure. There is more to say about Vader later.

The irony for 99.9% of men is we are all ultimately failures in the patriarchy. Few of us ever reach the top. There are few CEOs of corporations or generals in the Army or Hall of Famers. There are even fewer presidents of the United States. I have talked to many successful executives who have thought of themselves as failures because they never made it close enough to the top. Yet the top is the only place the patriarchy really recognizes manhood. In the patriarchy there are thousands of losers to one winner. The winner is a man. The rest of us are still boys.

The Vader voice keeps reminding us of our failures, to shame us into continuing. This voice is so toxic because the losers never realize they are in a no-win situation. The truth is the patriarchy only prepares a man to be a winner. It prepares a man to soar, feeding his flying fantasies all along the way. Yet the system is set up so that most men crash, feeling like failed sons. Most men don't realize that the gaming tables are rigged until it is too late. The system is set up to shame, and to keep men boys serving someone else's needs.

Fortunately it is never too late. But the answer is very unpatriarchal and paradoxical. As we will see, a man can only become a mature man by facing and integrating loss and separation. Loss is actually the doorway to manhood. Initiation involves learning to form an alliance with loss, in the depths of one's own person. But the patriarchy cannot recognize loss as a good, and despises separation seeing it only as disloyalty. Real manhood is outside its consensus reality. The Vader voice doesn't speak of loss as an opportunity. Loss is only a tragedy and a sign of failure. The image of the winner is the image of manhood.

The Dark Father Outside

The patriarchy is the embodiment of the competitive father. If a man also has a competitive father the Vader voice is doubly damaging. Many competitive fathers call their sons losers by word or action, magnifying the power of the patriarchal voice. As Kindlon and Thompson point out, "a father's ultimate psychological weapon is criticism, because most sons remain acutely sensitive to a father's put-downs well into adulthood." However, the corporate patriarchal voice is the Vader voice most men encounter daily. The boss and boss's boss all the way up the ladder are taught to demean in order to control, to sap confidence to insure against separation. The corpoarchy is jealous of its sons because it needs its sons desperately.

I have encountered many burnt out businessmen who work long hours exhausting themselves for bosses who never get enough. Their confidence is shot. Their self-esteem is in shambles. All they want is some sign of approval. The only approval they get is the chance to keep their job in the hopes of getting the father blessing they yearn for. The corpoarchy knows of this archetypal need for a father's blessing and uses it well.

A successful businessman has a boss who is patronizing and demeaning much of the time. Less frequently the boss praises the man, telling him he is indispensable. Though the man knows that he needs to leave the position because of this uneven treatment he stays on for years. He doesn't realize that he has transferred his desperate father need to his boss. He doesn't realize that he lives for a father's approval, even if it is erratic and often followed by criticism. He doesn't realize that his competitive boss is acting like a competitive father. Many of his coworkers do not understand this man's passivity, nor does his wife. They don't realize, as he doesn't, that his father voice, now the voice of his boss, tells him he deserves such treatment as the price for a father's guidance. To everyone else he is a winner. However, his patriarchal voice, magnified by the dark voice of his boss, doesn't allow this self-concept. He continues to feel like a loser who couldn't make it without his boss. In some ways he unconsciously stays a loser so he can still have a father.

A man comes into counseling because of work stress. He is burnt out on a job he doesn't like. He is good at his job and is well respected. He makes a very good living for his family. Though he has the skills to move to other work he doesn't take that risk. He is depressed and starting to drink too much. His father worked for the same company for 40 years. His father didn't especially like the work but the pay was good and he supported his family. The son's patriarchal voice told him to stay in one job for the good of the family. The Vader voice said that risk was wrong if it was only for personal meaning. His own traditional father supported this cultural message by telling him that all jobs were for pay and not for selfish enjoyment. The patriarchal voice, and his own father's, sapped his hardwired motivation to find the answer to his burnout. Maybe his father gave his son this advice for his own good. Or maybe his father couldn't bear seeing his son making a success of his own thwarted dreams of freedom.

Facing the Voice

If the patriarchal voice is not identified and dealt with, a man will be emasculated by it. He will mistake this voice for the initiating father who will introduce him to manhood. He will then be unconsciously acting from values and attitudes that he doesn't realize are affecting him so profoundly. He will be working from the illusion that he is his own man but he will be like a computer with an undetected virus inside.

The first thing a man must do when wrestling with father separation and his own personal journey is recognize that all the voices in his head are not his own. To a man who considers himself self-sufficient this idea is ludicrous and threatening. Yet a man must start to realize that the consensus reality has shaped him, involuntarily, in ways that rob him of his freedom. He must realize his choices are contaminated and his freedom compromised. To realize this takes humility.

Secondly, a man must realize that the patriarchal voice has no interest in him becoming a mature man. The voice only has an interest in a man being a good son. Like Freud's theory, the patriarchy sees a man's maturity as residing in the patriarchy, no farther. Manhood, according to the patriarchy, resides in the marketplace, not the wilderness. And the son's job is to serve the marketplace.

Thirdly, a man must realize there are other voices, outside the patriarchy, that can give him wisdom about his masculinity. These voices are found outside the village. A man must realize that he must take risks and go to unknown territory to find these voices. These are the voices of Elders and initiated brothers. In risking he must also face the pain of suffering the loss of both the mother's comfort and the guidance of a father's voice. The greatest pain is often the sense of aloneness in moving toward the wilderness of his own soul.

As in the primitive initiation rites a man must separate from the father's world of the marketplace on his road to manhood. The separation moves a man from a state of unconscious obedience to a conscious place of choice. The Ordeal brings a man to the first truly free choices in his life. He must leave the marketplace as a son to return to the marketplace as a man.

One of the most important parts of the work I do is to help men recognize the patriarchal voice inside. This is easier said than done. For most men the patriarchal voice and its unspoken marketplace assumptions have become an overriding source of direction in life. The voice is their compass and counselor. It is also their prime motivator. The voice is a refuge when all else is confusing or threatening. Even when the voice is demeaning, when it is the Vader voice, it is more comforting than the lonely confusion of separation.

I have worked with a number of men who started to question their patriarchal voice and found themselves overwhelmed. One very earnest man came into a session horrified. Without the patriarchal voice he could find no other voice inside to motivate him or give him direction. Without the voice he felt he would fall apart. The shock of how much of his life was ruled by this negative, unconscious voice was frightening to him. The greater shock was the terrifying challenge of separation.

Star Wars

Luckily there are also positive new lessons to be found in our culture, and positive voices to listen to, that speak to the steps that heal the father wound and deal with the Vader voice. One of the great myths of our times, and one that we have all grown up with, is the Star Wars myth. This myth speaks to men struggling with the father wound and the patriarchal voice. I will follow this myth throughout the rest of this book, for it offers many clues to modern men's dilemmas.

Myths and fairy tales carry the psychological and spiritual truths of a culture. Joseph Campbell, our greatest mythologist, studied myth and fairy tale all of his life. He saw them as containing lessons for all of us in living a more human life. He felt that "in myth the problems and solutions shown are directly valid for all mankind."

George Lucas knew Campbell and respected him. He actually used many of Joseph Campbell's insights in writing the trilogy. In doing so he has built a modern myth based on ancient truths.

As Michael Meade points out, myths talk about another reality so they often start out "once upon a time" or "in a time different from our time" or "in a place unlike any other place." Myths talk about the other side, the world inside, the inner reality. They talk about psychological truths rather than the truths of the senses. They talk of the world of the spirit rather than the world of matter. Brother David Steindl-Rast says that myths are not real, they are realer than real. The Star Wars myth starts "a long time ago in a galaxy far, far away." Now we know we are talking about psychological and spiritual truth. Now we know we're talking about a reality outside our consensus reality. We are talking about the other side.

In the Star Wars myth, the initial protagonist is Luke Skywalker, a great name for a hero who aspires to go beyond the village. He does not know his father. He is being raised by well-meaning relatives who are both uninitiated. His aunt and uncle continually try to convince him to stay in their compound, where it is safe from the wars raging in the galaxy. Well-meaning, uninitiated relatives will always be in the grip of the unconscious feminine which protects from risk and pain and keeps a man close to the hut.

Luke, however, is in the grip of the initiation archetype. He longs for the challenge of finding his identity by following his initiated father's path, the path of the warrior. His father once modeled positive masculine energy. He was not destructive with his power nor grasping for status and success. A Jedi Warrior had a code of protecting the weak and the altruistic community of the Jedi culture. He was a warrior similar to a samurai. His father's masculine energy and absorbed voice was already taking Luke away from the safety of the hearth, represented by the compound, and the wider village, represented by the family business.

In the Star Wars myth Darth Vader turns out to be Luke's father. The word vader means father in Dutch and is a play on vater in German. The obvious play on words renders Darth Vader the Dark Father. Here is the father wound on a cosmic level. Luke's father has not only betrayed him, he has betrayed the civilization that Luke grew up in and the Jedi code of ethics that Luke yearns to follow. The father wound always feels like a betrayal. It always hurts at the core of our manhood.

Darth Vader tries to use his son's power to consolidate his own negative ambitions. He is the competitive father who has no interest in his son's individuality. The betrayal leaves Luke dazed and confused. Darth Vader does feel love for his son which ultimately saves them both. However at the time he has succumbed to the temptation to power in the galactic marketplace. Vader has turned his back on the Force, representing the other side, the place of true spirituality and his own true identity. He in turn is controlled by the Dark Emperor, the archetype of the dark patriarchy.

Darth Vader tries to turn Luke from his path and have Luke serve Darth's own power needs. Darth offers as a reward the power of this side, power in the galactic village. Darth threatens Luke with death if he will not turn. In other words, Darth will take away his support and motivation. He will cause Luke to fall apart, to be a nonentity in the life of the village.

Darth also goes after Luke with a phallic sword and ultimately wounds him by cutting off his right hand, the hand of power and patriarchal productivity. Darth knows if Luke does find his own identity Luke could take away his power and the power of the Empire. Darth knows the threat of the son who is initiated.

Luke faces a terrible choice. He can be loyal to his father and join the Empire. He can be loyal to his mother and go back to the compound. Or he can risk death or humiliation by finding his own path as a Jedi warrior. One's own path of individuation will most often be seen as a betrayal by the wider society. It will be seen as a great breach of loyalty. The son will necessarily experience a conflict of loyalties. For most men the hardest accusation to endure is the one of being disloyal. Yet a boy has to be disloyal if he is to mature and find his own identity. Good old boys make lousy men.

To be a man a boy must ultimately separate from the father and the patriarchy. If he has good, initiated fathering his father will encourage the separation and prepare him for the emergence of the Elder. If his father is absent and he relies on the patriarchy for his fathering, the Vader voice will discourage any separation. If he also has a competitive father, separation will be labeled betrayal. A man will then be stuck.

Luke is in great need of an Elder who will lead him out of his loyalty dilemma. He will need to distinguish a true Elder from the dark father who promises a pseudo-initiation. If he is lucky he will find a second father who can start the healing of the father wound and prepare him for the coming of the Elder. Or he will have to face the Ordeal, surprised and in crisis.

Many unprepared men are stuck in the world of the father, without an Elder, a crisis ready to happen. This is, I believe, the genesis of the midlife crisis. For many men the stuckness is in the world of work, and the patriarchal voice talks only of work as initiation. The next chapter talks of how men get stuck in the pseudo-initiation of marketplace work as a way of trying to find manhood while staying loyal to a father. This chapter deals with work as addiction.

Chapter 8
Thank God It's Monday

"I've been very busy lately," was the response of the Governor when asked the name of his recently born granddaughter. He didn't know her name.

If productivity is the highest value of the patriarchy, then busyness, related to business, is a very high virtue. I talked about addictions in a previous chapter. These were addictions related to the young 3-6 year old boy inside. They included the substance addictions and two process addictions, rage and sexual addictions. These addictions are great obstacles to mother separation, seducing men on a false path toward maturity.

There are other process addictions that a man can develop blocking the initiatory path. One is particularly subtle and insidious because it is respectable. This process addiction mimics some healthy qualities of the mature man, such as service and dedication. However, this addiction merely reflects the highest goals of the marketplace culture, promising manhood without the wilderness Ordeal. Like other process addictions, this set of habits and behaviors has a spectrum from mild preoccupation with work and career to overwhelming obsession.

Work addiction concerns the boy inside and his relation to his father. This boy, around age 7 or 8, needs his father to guide his next steps. This addiction concerns the man stuck in the marketplace, trying to contact father energy and find his manhood. It concerns the patriarchal voice that talks to a man of productivity, advancement, the journey of business, and being a good son.

Work as Initiation

Workaholism is the story of a man trying to deal with his father wound. Work addiction is also the culture struggling with a collective father wound. This wound can be anaesthetized by a near total dedication to the patriarchal pseudo-initiation of manhood through marketplace success. Sometimes a man takes up his father's dreams, the scripted plan for his son's life, and follows a similarly addicted father. At other times, in the absence of his own father's script, he takes up directly the patriarchal script of his Elderless society.

The patriarchal script speaks of success in the marketplace as the primary test of manhood. In the patriarchal society, the journey of manhood stops at the marketplace. The false Ordeal of manhood then takes place in the marketplace, not the wilderness. In this patriarchy there is no other side, no wilderness beyond the village boundaries. Yet the initiatory yearning persists. Entrepreneurial men often talk proudly of the "jungle out there," unconsciously trying to make the marketplace a real wilderness. They talk of survival of the fittest, as if they were actually in a death Ordeal.

Thus, by default, the patriarchal voice replaces the good father. The dark father takes the place of the Elder. The Vader voice of this marketplace elder pushes a man to be productive and profitable as proof of a successful Ordeal. This process takes advantage of a man's hardwired needs for fathering and Eldering. The payoff of the addiction is the false sense of manhood the man achieves.

Unfortunately, this false sense of manhood does not fill a man. It can never make a man feel good from the inside out. As Jan Halpern, a psychologist and executive coach, says, "What all the effort comes down to is this: Work is used as the narcotic to run from low self-esteem. It is the temporary fix that makes the workaholic feel good." And Jan should know. She interviewed 4,000 executives as part of the work in writing her book, *Quiet Desperation, The Truth about Successful Men.*

The work addiction usually reaches crisis proportions at middle age when a man has achieved success without the real peace he has been looking for. It is then he starts to feel the reality of his pseudo-initiation. As an Elder has said, he has gotten to the top of the ladder of success only to find that the ladder is on the wrong wall.

Cal

Cal has been married for 26 years. He and his wife, Carla, have raised four children. Cal is rightfully proud that he has put four children through college even though he has never been to college himself. He has finally reached a level of success that includes a Mercedes parked in the garage of a showcase house. Cal talks often of how he has "had to work 12 hours a day, 6 days a week just to stay ahead." He will also talk of how he didn't enjoy all that work and would have rather "won the lottery a long time ago." His own business involves a lot of standing and physical work, and his limp and slow gait show the results.

Cal's parents divorced when he was 12. He ended up living with his widowed aunt for his 4 years of high school because he couldn't get along with an alcoholic mother. His father moved out of the area after the divorce and had little to do with Cal.

Cal started working in high school and "has been working ever since." Though he sometimes talked of the joys of retirement, he always figured he'd have a short "sprint" of a life and never imagined a life without his work. He measured his worth and his manhood on how much, materially, he could give his wife and family. He would often remind Carla of their hard won survival in the "reality of that unforgiving world out there." He saw himself as a very good father and husband, though he was sorry for how little time he gave his children. He was a good man, using his patriarchal script in the only way he knew how, by providing and protecting. By marketplace standards he could be considered a "man's man."

Carla had other ideas. She had expected that once the children were raised they could enjoy life as a couple. Cal would cut back on his work so they would have more time for each other. She didn't want all the fruits of a more affluent lifestyle. She grew up with little and needed little. She wanted more time with her husband and a relationship of warmth and mutual respect. She wanted to share their inner lives as well as their outer ones.

Cal, who was known as a bear with a heart of gold, told Carla she was "crazy" to think he could cut back. She had to "start looking at reality." When Carla asked for more time than money Cal took this as a criticism of his manhood. He was being a man, and it wasn't enough. He saw her as living a good life without the worries he had. To him, she was either naive or ungrateful. He was really more hurt than angry at the slap to his manhood. However he exhibited the only defense most men have learned, a show of righteous anger.

In fact his anger had gotten out of control in the last few years. This was why Carla had insisted on marriage counseling. This good man had started throwing things in the direction of his wife while yelling profanities at her. He would then minimize his short bouts of anger, often blaming Carla for her unreasonable demands.

Cal didn't know how to handle any criticism of his manhood, especially by the damsel whom he thought he saved. He hadn't been taught by a father how to handle his pain or an intimate relationship. He couldn't understand what sharing his inner life meant. He was becoming proof that uninitiated, though good, men can be dangerous men.

Cal was stuck. He was being a man to his family in the only way he knew how. In his mind he had survived the Ordeal of years of hard work. He had suffered his initiatory wounds. He had followed the voice of his patriarchal Elders. He had found the values of his materialistic culture and made them his own. He was a Man and deserved a Man's respect.

I felt truly sorry for Cal, as I feel sorry for so many men who have been betrayed by a pseudo-initiation and a dark father. His wife did provide an alternative for Cal to stop his dead end journey before it was too late but he couldn't understand that alternative. Since he was unaware if his inner life he had no place to go, except to work.

Cal could only minimize his wife's complaints, including charges of abuse, and go on working as a way of satisfying his craving for initiation. Unconsciously, by working he was also satisfying his archetypal craving for the fathering and Eldering he never had. No matter how many men complain that they work only for others, they are really working to fill a deep, gnawing craving in themselves. Wives do not understand this need, though they instinctively, like Carla, see the addiction as self-serving. They don't see the misguided activity as a search for manhood. They also fail to see how much their criticism tears at an already open wound.

The Religion of Business

Many men who are work addicted are seen as pillars of the community. And they often are. They are the ones who volunteer for the high profile boards and governing bodies. They are the ones elected to local posts of responsibility. They are often quite skilled in their work and try to broaden their impact. Often, these are men genuinely interested in the community as they see it.

These men then become the marketplace Elders for other men. Marketplace work is their deepest value, and productivity is their mantra. Business becomes their religion. They are usually the ones who talk about the need to protect the marketplace as hallowed ground. Since men have a hardwired need for the sacred place of initiation, the marketplace replaces the wilderness as their sanctuary.

These men then support any politician who places the marketplace first. They speak of the market system as inevitably producing social good. Any work that produces income becomes a sacred calling, so they support all activities that get people back to work. Sin is not participating in the market. So they are righteously indignant if anybody is able-bodied and not productive. Their religion says that what is good for business is good for mankind.

And there is a truth to what these men are saying. Material survival, and the leisure time that comes from a surplus in the marketplace, does come from market efficiency. Involuntary poverty is not a good thing. Not being able to work and support a family is a tragedy. The problem is that this truth stops short of where human values lie. Leisure does not bring manhood or meaning in itself. Neither does uninitiated work. Material security is a jumping off place, not a destination.

In 1947 Simon de Beauvoir, a French woman and pioneer feminist, talked of men in this country. It is an interesting observation across time, gender and geography: "In the United States one is always concerned to find out what an individual does, and not what he is; one takes for granted that he is nothing but what he has done or may do; his purely inner reality is regarded with indifference, if, indeed, any note is taken of it."

Men treat work as religion because the stakes are so high. Just as the alcoholic will try to find the spirit through drink, the workaholic tries to find his sacred destiny through work. The irony is that a mature man does often live out his destiny through his work. But it is not primarily income producing work. It is a sacred work that can be found only beyond the marketplace.

Cal didn't understand his wife's needs for companionship and relationship. It wasn't that he didn't love his wife or care about her happiness. He just didn't get it. One of the symptoms of a workaholic is his obsession with the marketplace as a way of feeling good about himself and feeling like he has a place. Start talking to him about any topic and the conversation will quickly get around to his job or his field. Other than that he is often silent. The alcoholic needs his alcohol to feel confidence. The workaholic needs his work to feel like he is fulfilling all his manly roles: father, husband, productive citizen, civic leader, and philanthropist. Work as pseudo-initiation gives a man an identity. It is also the place he feels most comfortable and most respected as a man.

Work and Father

Psychologically, many work obsessed men have received some positive fathering energy. Their wound is not as deep as the neglectful father. Their father had in some way started the separation from the mother and shown them the lesson of pain for a higher purpose. Many fathers of workaholics have given their sons a sense of guidance and competence. These fathers are not ruthless insider traders and capitalist pigs, the robber barons of the modern age. These are more often good men who gave all they had, passing on the only manhood they knew. Their sons are also men who have a real sense of marketplace justice and fair play, given them by their fathers. Good men.

Many workaholics are the product of a hardworking father and an emotionally distant often depressed mother, both in different ways wounded offspring of the patriarchy. These men do not understand the need for an intimate relationship because they did not have a mother who was able to bond emotionally with her husband and her son. I talked in an earlier chapter about the reasons this might be true, including a mother who was depressed or seriously ill early in the child's life. These men need the maternal object of wife only in the home, raising the children, providing the secure homestead. They are unable to understand the need for an emotional partner. They are most comfortable and secure at work. They live their whole active life behind the wall, unaware of their inner life.

Cal's mother was a depressive who actually left the family when Cal was a teenager. She was overwhelmed by her own life and understandably had little emotional energy left for her children. When a maternal object, his wife, asked for love, Cal didn't know what that meant in any relational way. Love meant meeting his wife's needs, her marketplace needs. Love, in return, meant being needed and respected for his protection. For men like Cal respect is much more important than love.

Cal had not taken the next step because he didn't know there were next steps. He already knew the lesson of pain for a higher purpose. He didn't realize that the pain he needed to face was in the wilderness within, rather than in the external marketplace. He also didn't realize that his higher purpose involved a much more complex journey. And he didn't realize that there was a life that had a sense of deep satisfaction and meaning different from the ultimately empty feeling gotten from a large bank account and multiple plaques on the wall. Finally he didn't realize he had a wife who loved him but for different reasons than he thought.

Cal had been betrayed by a patriarchy that promised a satisfaction it could not deliver. One of the signal betrayals of the workaholic is that he gives his lifeblood for a work he is not called to. That is his greatest sadness. Many a man may be very skilled at his chosen profession, yet not find the work that gives him deep satisfaction and sense of purpose. He may never realize he has followed a father's dream rather than his own. He has taken any job instead of his sacred work. He has stayed a son in the patriarchy.

Many men stay a son because of their love for their father and all their forefathers before them. We are all hardwired to look to fathers for our manhood. Most of us have been the recipients of an unselfish father love. We have been recipients of the care of a man who has gone out of his way for us even though he didn't know the right way.

As one man said of his workaholic father, "Ultimately I realized that I was unconsciously keeping Dad's pattern going in me as a way of honoring him. As crazy as it sounds, that was my way of loving him." Many good sons of good fathers do the same.

The Good News, the Bad News

The good news is that workaholics in many ways are much closer to their manhood than those with other addictions. They have absorbed much that masculine energy has to offer, often from their fathers. They have developed many skills that would allow them to survive in the wilderness.

They have shown they can endure pain. They have also showed courage and focus. They often have an abundance of warrior energy. They only lack an Elder to explain their next step and expel them from the marketplace.

The bad news is that most workaholics need the sudden, unwilling separation from the father, and the patriarchy, to get their initiatory energy again. A job tragedy is, paradoxically, their main hope. Men will often experience this tragedy as a betrayal, only later realizing it was necessary. Hopefully they later see the crisis as an opportunity, setting the stage for initiation.

Many men experience the tragedy, or betrayal, in modern times as a job loss. Downsizing is a common betrayal today. When the patriarchal father has no more use for the son he lets him go. As I have said, the corpoarchy is ultimately narcissistic. Let the sons beware, even the most skilled ones. The dark father has his own needs to meet. He is ultimately competitive.

Job tragedy could also be from illness or injury. In this case the separation can be more sudden and complete. The depression is also more profound. This is very insidious because the betrayal can most often only be attributed to a deity or higher power. A man will then treat his God as the demonic father. His anger will keep him from seeing the injury as an initiatory wound and a major step in his Ordeal. If a man succumbs to the tragedy and his own anger he will lose the opportunity of his lifetime. His loss of faith will be the real tragedy.

The most subtle tragedy is, paradoxically, the man who has been successful. The marketplace has many rewards suited to a man's uninitiated desires, suited to his addictions. These rewards are like a drug, numbing him to his own deeper desires and his own inner pain. Often they numb him to his interior boredom, boredom from doing work he is not innately interested in. One of the biggest false rewards of the successful man is a woman who gives him the respect and pleasures that the pseudo-man needs. Often, in mid-life, when he starts to feel his boredom and emptiness he will blame wife or friends. He will miss the tragedy inside while he looks for another challenge outside. If he is able to see his boredom as the pain of an internal wound he has a chance.

In our modern culture retirement seems to be the ultimate reward for patriarchal productivity. The reward is the free time to enjoy life without the responsibility of a job. However, real enjoyment, minus addictive comfort, is not in his playbook. Instead of joy a successful man has to face inner and outer emptiness. At first there is brief euphoria. Later, not having found meaning in his inner life, he flounders in an ocean of meaningless time. What meaning he found in life revolved around work. Most often he will finally pay the price for ignoring his inner life by a needless crisis of health. Statistics show that for many men health declines steadily the first years after retirement. For others the boredom catches up triggering chronic depression.

If a successful man can understand his depression just before and after his retirement as initiatory he has a chance of finding the enjoyment retirement promises. Free time becomes a wonderful opportunity for using hidden talents for a higher purpose. It is never too late to go through initiation. In this case the initiation propels a man through two stages, boy to man and man to healthy patriarch, on his way to becoming a wise and happy Elder. More about these transitions later, especially the initiation to enlightened patriarch.

The tragedy of workaholism is that the man looks initiated. He even starts to believe it himself. Yet he has not gone through the pain of finding the underlying values that direct his talents and lifestyle. The man is still a boy and a son. He has lost the opportunity to feel a man from the inside out. The uninitiated man, because of his deficit, uses his responsible work to dodge healthy relationships with wife, children, friends. Like the alcoholic he uses his addiction to numb the pain of the work of relationship. He has no idea how to relate to anyone outside of a work context. This man has many acquaintances but few friends, especially other male friends. His marriages often become financial partnerships rather than love relationships. Jan Halpern writes that of all the executives she interviewed only 10 percent claimed to have married for love. Divorce then becomes a poor financial decision. Many successful workaholics can't bear the thought of divorce simply because they can't bear the thought of losing half their estate.

Workaholics have no idea how they would act if they wanted to have a healthier relationship. So work becomes a refuge from uncomfortable family and social situations. Work also becomes an obstacle to connecting with other men who could motivate them to another level of initiation. Many men cannot realize their tragedy and live out their lives not knowing what could have been. Many more are starting to realize their tragedy and looking for answers.

Cal was pressured by his wife to come to counseling. He did start talking about slowing down and "retiring at 55" as the first rumblings of another movement. He was starting to realize he didn't know how to enjoy himself. He saw Carla as the one who enjoyed life for both of them. He was willing to start questioning his need for work and the disappointment his life had given him.

Work vs. Job

I believe that most men who near maturity must leave behind the patriarchal workplace, where they are treated as perpetual adolescents. A man separating from the dark father needs to consider three alternatives in the marketplace.

One alternative. He needs to work for himself, start his own business. Many men, especially middle managers, have been spurred on by job betrayal to find more life-giving work, often as an independent businessman. Sometimes downsizing has triggered their initiatory Ordeal. At other times burnout finally brings a man down. As an example, a recent AARP poll shows that 46% of baby boomers would choose another job if they had the chance. As we will see, job loss or burnout has brought them to their work calling. As Mark Gerzon points out, "Those who are self-employed or who can run their own shop outlive those who are trapped between superior and subordinate."

Many men are ready in terms of talent, skill, and experience to be healthy patriarchs, that is men who have the latent power and wisdom to lead a community and even a culture in a different direction based on Elder values and respect for personal call. Younger men are looking for their blessing and mentoring. These are men on the brink of finding a meaningful call and living a life of fulfilling service during midlife. Job loss or burnout triggers the initiatory archetype. However they must be humble enough to go through initiatory Ordeal as older men. As I will describe later this healthy patriarchal stage can be reached through the inner work of initiation. These men can psychospiritually get a two for one initiation: boy to man and man to healthy patriarch. But it takes a great deal of humility and perseverance. Fortunately these men often have the strength of character to accomplish this very thing. They are the ones who can risk the move to meaningful work.

A second alternative. He can work in a business or corporation but be given the freedom to freelance, to create and innovate as he sees fit. He must be given the freedom to follow his own vision even though the overall vision of the institution is not what he can wholly agree with. This involves a man setting strong, healthy boundaries with his company and risking separation if the company does not respond. A man who has gone through Ordeal, and separated from both the good and dark father, is able to take those risks because he knows there is significant life beyond the corporation.

A third alternative is to find a job with significant responsibility in a corporation, profit or nonprofit, that closely mirrors one's own values and goals, even though the pay and status is less. Again the need for initiatory humility. So many men are highly talented and greatly unappreciated. If a man has faced Ordeal and separated from the patriarchy he is no longer hung up on status or financial success. He is value driven. He can often find real meaning in taking a lower status yet highly fulfilling job because he is finding the satisfaction of the inner life. He is also serving his community in a most effective way.

These alternatives are dependent on a man finishing the initiatory process. They depend on a man being able to see the difference between a work and a job. As we will see, the initiation process is the key to a man finding a work that has intrinsic value to him, as well as needed value to his community. Values and character are then the guarantee that a man does not use his work and power for his own narcissistic ends. Initiation guarantees that a man will not collude with a dark patriarchy or identify with his negative father voice. Like Luke, he will not join the dark father for supposedly good ends.

Chapter 9
A Second Father

Sometimes the possibility for good fathering seems hopeless. The unconscious generational betrayal in our society continues to this moment. Blind fathers lead blind sons. Where are the older men who can see? Is there only one roll of the dice in the father game? Is there only one game? I believe not.

In a sense, a man never stops looking for a good father. He is looking for someone to reflect his maleness in a positive way. He is looking for a champion, a guide, a wise coach, a manager in his corner, a scout who can tell him what's around the next bend. We all need someone to walk with us before we walk alone. We are not hardwired to be mature. We are hardwired to look for men to prepare us for manhood.

A Second Chance

As I have mentioned, I believe the age of the father in modern society extends until a man is in his mid-30's. These are the 'tweens', between childhood and adulthood that go from adolescence through the age 30 crisis. This is the time of the strongest father hunger. Men try to fill that hunger in different ways. Most men fill the hunger by identifying with the patriarchy and its values as the only substitute for the missing father.

David Ray, a poet and English professor, wrote a memoir in 2003 called *The Endless Search*. He talked of the fatherless boy who "is ever seeking his lost father or the replacement who might stroll into his world." He continued, "Back in the 40's I began my own list of potential fathers—and by father I mean not bearer of seed but bestower of human kindness and companionship, a man with some flicker of interest in a boy's future. My father had seldom shown me that special attention before he got a ride west, leaving my mother, my sister, and me without a clue for many moons." He concludes that "By the time one reaches senior citizenship, the list is staggeringly long." David ultimately couldn't find a father any better than bartenders "who offered a home as good as I'd ever had, and booze to numb the pain."

In the traditional family fathers are usually exhausted by the time sons become teenagers. The patriarchal father role takes a great deal out of a man without giving much back. The patriarchy uses and abuses most men, including our own fathers. For this reason Warren Farrell calls men "the disposable sex." In the role of protector by provider, men give their all in the marketplace for their family. They often have nothing left for their sons, even when they start to realize they neglected their sons to begin with. In addition, fathers, who love their sons dearly, are at a loss as to how to help their sons in other than traditional ways.

Yet, how does a man, today, get the fathering he needs to go the next steps. How does a son find the energy and motivation to leave the world of the dark mother, where he is obsessed with either addiction or finding the right woman? Must he be on an endless, disappointing search?

There are alternatives to this dark situation. Men of any age have a second chance. There are ways to absorb the positive fathering energy we need from men who have something to give. There are men out there who can give what we need. They can become, for a while, our second fathers. They can take us farther down our path, where we can find the masculine energy we need to strengthen us for the coming Ordeal. For the Ordeal comes, bidden or unbidden. Second fathers know the Ordeal. They have the power to prepare us.

Mentor

The key to understanding good fathering is the motivation of the father. A good, initiated father will be focused on the growth of the young son. As opposed to the competitive father, the good father will need nothing from the son to make him a man. As we will see in the characteristics of a mature men, a good father is interested in the welfare of the next generation rather than his own welfare. He has found his manhood. He is not looking helplessly for an unreachable traditional manhood, to the detriment of his son. Neither is he trying to find his manhood by vanquishing his son.

Finding a mentor is one way to get the right fathering. Mentoring is a process of an older man taking a younger man in his protection and interest, and teaching him the ropes. It is a term that is usually used in the business world, especially for young executives. It is also a term that is being used increasingly in the volunteer movement when talking of older men helping poor urban youth. General Colin Powell has come out strongly to lead American efforts in helping fatherless young men get the fathering they need through mentors. Mentoring is found whenever an older man takes an interest in a younger man without dark, narcissistic motives. As Sam Osherson says, "For many young men, mentors truly become the better fathers they yearn for."

Daniel Levinson says that one of the main tasks of the novice adult, age 17-33, is to find a mentor to guide him. The mentor fosters the young man by believing in him, helping to discover the newly emerging talent in his newly discovered world. According to Levinson, the mentor is usually several years older, a person of greater experience and seniority in the world the young man is entering. Most often the mentoring relationship develops in a work setting, but is not confined to the work arena. The relationship is often intense. Levinson calls it a "love relationship."

Even if a man has had good enough fathering, the mentor can act as a transitional figure from the world of parents to the world of adults as peers. In this way he prepares a man for the coming of the Elder and the claiming of his full adulthood. The mentor is a mixture of parent and peer. In a way he starts the separation from father. In another way he completes the work of father.

Most mentoring needs to come from men who have already accomplished their goals. Mentors need to participate in the grandfather, senex or wise old man, archetype. Traditionally grandfathers have retired from the world of the marketplace. They are at another stage of life, closer to the detachment that good fathering needs. They are closer to the other side.

Archetypally, sons and grandfathers have a natural connection because both are closer to the other side, the wilderness place where spirit and death also reside. The son has newly emerged from the land of death, through birth, and the grandfather is preparing to go back, through death. This closeness to spirit and death really symbolizes detachment from the everyday marketplace world, and the temptations of the competitive father.

In a sense we are all looking for a "grand" father. A mentor can fill that role. But first we have to be humble. There is an old Zen story about a proud man coming to a monk for guidance. The monk invited him in for tea. As the monk poured the tea into his guest's teacup the tea overflowed the cup and still the monk continued to pour. Finally the proud man asked why he continued to pour. The monk stated that the proud man was like a full teacup. The monk could not fill him with his wisdom before the man emptied himself of his own righteous opinions.

If a man will be open to a mentor he must look for a man who has the qualities he wants to learn. Usually these are marketplace skills or talents that serve a higher purpose. The primary link between a mentor and a mentee is the love of the skills the student is trying to learn. The love of these skills will be what draws the two together in the first place. However, a good mentor teaches his skills as a way of preparing a man to find his own unique direction. It is usually a mentor or a good father who will notice and point out the peculiar talents a man has. A good mentor will point a man in the direction of his gifts and not necessarily toward where he will achieve success in the world.

I am reminded of the movie, *The Karate Kid*. Mr. Miyagi is drawn out of compassion to the young boy who is fatherless and devoid of marketplace skills. He has no motive other than the call of generativity. The boy is drawn to Mr. Miyagi because he wants to learn his considerable skills at martial arts. Later, he continues to be drawn by his mentor's sense of peace and quiet confidence. In the process of learning these skills the boy learns to develop confidence in his talents and in himself. The boy learns he is capable of focusing on a worthy goal that involves his gifts. He learns that he can respect himself. He does not learn his life direction yet, that will come from his Ordeal. But he has found the confidence and learning base to face his initiation.

A mentor is usually not a boss, for bosses too easily become competitive fathers in our patriarchal society. Most bosses are forced to use their subordinates for their own gain, for the security of their own job, because of the corporate culture they live in. They have a hard time being interested in the well-being of their "sons." They also have a hard time finding pleasure in the skills of someone who may surpass them. Sam Osherson talks of the process of cannibalism, where one generation "may cannibalize another by stealing its energy, its ideas, and often, literally, what it produces." In seeking a mentor a man must not be naive about cannibals, substitutes for competitive fathers.

Another disinterested man in a corporation can be a mentor. An older man in the same field can be a mentor. Older men who have successful marriages can be a mentor for purposes of learning about healthy relationships.

There is an old Zen expression, "When the student is ready the teacher will come." The problem is that we are taught to be competitive with other men so we are not open to mentoring. We are not open when a mentor appears. We are taught to be better than other men, not to admit our weakness and ask for help. The modern training manual assumes pride not humility. This manual assumes control not submission. The dark patriarchy admits few mistakes, for mistakes are a sign of weakness. We are not taught to be ready for a good teacher. We are taught to be suspicious of an older man wishing us good. We feel unnaturally uncomfortable asking for help. I say unnatural because it was the most natural thing in the world for thousands of years for a man to look for a mentor.

Probably the most available mentors for the wider role of second father are those in the helping professions such as counselors, social workers, psychologists, pastoral counselors and spiritual directors. Today, there is also a new field composed of business coaches and consultants that try to move beyond just nuts and bolts to fostering growth of personality and character. There are also executive volunteer organizations, composed of retired successful businessmen, who have something to give without needing status in return. These mentors can help a man to find his gifts, negotiate the web of corporate or institutional relationships of the workplace, and prepare a man for the pain and wonder of his Ordeal.

Older men who are genuinely interested in the welfare of younger men are out there. Invariably they have gone through their own Ordeal and have found their deeper values. They have separated from the patriarchy and are no longer motivated to use younger men. They have a lot to give even though they might not realize it. Younger men need to find the humility to look for them. Society needs to create ways of making a mentor relationship a normal part of a man's growth.

Pseudo-initiation

One of the most important functions of a good father and mentor is to protect and educate young men on the pseudo-initiations that occur during this novice adult period. Most men in their 20's are so hungry for fathers and the bridge to manhood that they jump into the pseudo-rituals of manhood that our society has to offer.

Marriage is one such ritual. I have counseled so many men who have married in their early and mid-20's because that was expected. This ritual allowed them to seemingly become a new man, even though they felt no change inside. The hunger for manhood was strong. Unfortunately marriage is not a rite of initiation. It does not produce men. As we will see marriage in mature cultures was the right of a man only after initiation. A good modern father bears this message.

Sam Keen relates a story that illustrates this point, as well as the power of a mentor. Sam had just gone through a divorce after a long marriage. Another relationship with a young woman was also falling apart. He was, at that point, also starting another love affair "to heal the wounds of a failed romance." He was going through the Great Separation with all the pain and confusion that entailed. He was obviously being pulled back to another WOMAN, albeit a young one. He was desperately in need of good fathering to bring him his next steps.

He was eventually brought low and forced to the humility needed for openness to a mentor. As he wrote, "My life was coming apart at the seams." His mentor was Howard Thurman, a college professor who was "a friend for 25 years, a grandson of a slave, mystic, philosopher." Howard gave him advice at that time that Sam felt was the best advice he ever got. Howard talked of two questions a man must ask himself. The first is "Where am I going?" The second is "Who will go with me?" Howard then emphasized "If you ever get these questions in the wrong order you are in trouble." Howard was a true second father.

Another pseudo-initiation that a good father and mentor needs to warn about is the early temptation of a high paying job. When I was in my 20's the goal was 30 by 30: a salary of $30,000 by age 30. By the late 80's it was to have a salary that doubled your age. I've lost track of what this pseudo-initiation axiom has become today. The money itself is not really the problem here. Money is amoral. The problem is that this superficial standard of manhood is the opposite of what initiation is all about.

One goal of initiation is to find work that has inherent meaning and satisfaction. The pseudo-initiation of a manhood standard of salary minimizes any sense of meaning or identity. This high-priced act of pseudo-manhood will never give a man the feeling of manhood from the inside out. A good father will recognize gifts and talk of the skills needed to survive in the marketplace. However, he will already understand the false standards of success in the dark patriarchy. He may have succumbed to them at one time himself and learned better. He will emphasize the need for matching training to talent. He will disprove the illusion that the paycheck will prove his worth. Knowing the marketplace, the good father will also know that for most men who have been initiated the money will follow in abundance if they choose from their initiatory calling.

It is easy to pick out men who are looking for manhood in their net worth. In one way or another they will mention either how much they make or how much they spend. These men are trying their best with the fathering they have gotten. They are being fathered by the patriarchy and their own patriarchal voice. They are victims of pseudo-initiation and need the support of men who know another way.

Second Fathers

The rise of men's groups in this country is a major sign of the father hunger that grips so many men in this country. I believe that men's groups that are formally or informally part of the men's movement are one of most important ways that we can get the healthy father energy we need. For a men's group, as a whole, can give a man much of what a birth father has missed.

Men's groups can be professionally led, structured by a men's organization like the Mankind Project, or leaderless yet coherent meetings formed by a number of men committed to each other. Some have gone for as much as twenty to thirty years with some men coming and others leaving.

Most men feel an immediate resistance when considering joining a men's group. This feeling is a testament to our modern father culture that separates men through the dark philosophy of social Darwinism whose message is compete or die. Men are taught to immediately armor themselves in a warrior mode when meeting another man. Then the hierarchical dance begins with each man measuring where he stands in the pecking order, as in whose pecker is bigger. This is not a situation that leads to trust or vulnerability or hope of any support.

However, 95% of the men's groups I have heard of are living out a totally different men's culture. Within them is a sense of brotherhood. In groups like this men become like loyal, caring brothers, even in loving confrontation. The group as a whole seems to create a father space, generating the healthy masculine energy men are looking for. Most men feel this connection soon after joining a group.

In my experience a man who enters a group first experiences healthy father energy by feeling a validation of his masculine way of experiencing the world. Men who have not escaped the dark mother world often believe any criticism of their masculine way of feeling. Since emotions in this world are considered the domain of women, men continually feel their emotions are somehow invalid. They are deemed either shallow, uncaring, aggressive, disconnected or a number of other negative judgments. If men are not supported and recognized for their natural masculine feelings they are left only feminine feelings, or they feel guilt for their own healthy masculine ones. No wonder men tend to numb out at this choice. When I have seen men being recognized and supported in their feelings I invariably see a profound sense of relaxation and gratitude come over a man, that is after the shock wears off! Father wounds start to heal at this point. The boy inside starts to smile.

Another way that men get fathered in a men's group is by championing each other. This goes beyond support. As men get to know each other they pick up on the strengths and talents of each other. In reflecting these talents back, especially marketplace skills, the group invariably works on bolstering a man's confidence based on their own experience. I have seen so many men take risks in following their talents and dreams as a result of their brothers acting like a championing father.

Of course there is also healthy confrontation. Men in the group have to be ready to confront each other when they feel someone is taking a detour off their path. This is especially true when a man regresses back to former unhealthy behaviors or attitudes. Confrontation, though, does not have to be aggressive or demoralizing as in the patriarchy. Like a good father's admonition it can be firm but caring.

The greatest risk a man will take in his life is in facing his Ordeals, the times of intense inner transformation. In helping a man face his painful separations and his biggest fears a men's group also performs its greatest service.

Our Invisible Sons

Have you ever given yourself a pep talk trying to give yourself the confidence and the motivation to do a good job? Have you ever wondered who is talking to who? Doesn't it feel like a coach talking to a player, or a boss talking to his team, or a championing father talking to his son? This may be the closest you have felt to connecting with the boy inside. And the closest you have come to being a second father. Think about it.

We all have an invisible boy inside. He is the personal archetype of the *puer aeternas,* the eternal boy inside. He could be any age. He is often unfathered. He is like a relative we know very well who has been orphaned. He has been with us since we were his age. He is with us today. And he needs our help.

This invisible boy is in great need of fathering to make up for any fathering he has missed. He is still looking for a father. He is actually that part of us that we feel when we have a father yearning. He shows up often in our lives, trying to get our attention, our father energy. Yet most of us feel shame when he comes, for he is only a boy and he feels and acts like a boy. And he makes us feel so small.

So we orphan him again and again. We are ashamed of him because he brings back feelings of boyish fear, or childish anger, or hopeless infatuation. He is the boy who finds it so hard to leave his mother for fear of not being taken care of. He is the one who feels small and powerless in the face of a critical father. He is the one who gets into a rage when his plans don't work out and he feels humiliated. He is the one who makes a wife into a mother, a boss into a father, the world his center stage.

This inner boy is in continual need of a second father. But first he needs to be acknowledged. He needs to become visible. Then he needs to be taken seriously and loved. When this happens he will be ready for the healing that second fathering can bring.

He shows up most often when we are weak and regressed. Regression is a psychological term that refers to anyone unconsciously sliding back into old behaviors and attitudes that we have had growing up. They are often states of mind that are inappropriate for a present situation because they are seen or experienced from a child's perspective. The resultant behavior is at best ineffective, at worst seriously destructive.

As John Lee says in his wonderful book *Growing Yourself Back Up*, "when we regress, we go from clear thinking adults to talking, acting, and sometimes even looking like children who are not getting their way." He goes on to say, "We feel powerless and out of control." This sense of being small and weak is the most powerful sign that the inner boy has shown up and he is scared.

Sometimes this boy is carrying a trauma that is so painful he is terrified a lot of the time. Sometimes he is suffering the feeling of invisibility and powerlessness of being ignored much of his life. Sometimes he is so angry at his treatment he lashes out violently, with a boy's rage and a man's body.

Regression is both a tragedy and an opportunity. The tragedy is that a boy shows up who has been hurt and unseen for many years. He is lost and in pain. The opportunity is that the boy shows up to be fathered and healed. I have been talking about the boy inside who has a hard time leaving the mother's hut. I have talked about the boy inside who follows the patriarchy because of his father hunger. I have talked of the father wound. The opportunity in regression is finding the part of ourselves that most needs healing. The opportunity is finding the orphan.

Refathering

I mention regression because there is another major way a man can get the good fathering he needs. Regression is the way that most men come to meet the boy inside. And there is a new way a man more consciously gives the boy inside the fathering he needs. This way has been championed effectively by John Bradshaw. It is called inner child work. Much of this is outlined in Bradshaw's book, *Homecoming*.

This work involves dealing directly with the boy inside. It is possible to be a good father to ourselves. This is a process that Bradshaw calls reparenting, and I like to call refathering. We can consciously get good fathering by being a good father. This work takes as much effort as parenting a biological child. The boy inside needs as much attention and education as any child. The work involves taking a step that seems crazy.

Remember when I talked of the voices inside our head and the self-talk that goes on so normally. Well, the boy inside has a voice, too, that has been speaking for a long time. This voice tells us his needs and desires, as well as his fears and insecurities. Most of us do not hear or recognize the voice because we weren't taught there was a voice, or a boy. Yet the boy is there and he is us. And the boy is suffering from a father wound. He actually carries the pain of our father wound.

When I start working with a man in counseling I immediately start working on understanding and setting boundaries. If a man can start setting boundaries I know he is prepared to start his initiatory journey. He has enough strength to start separating from the mother object. I know he is then ready for second fathering. My next step invariably is to help the man get in touch with the boy inside. This boy needs to be fathered through several stages before the man is ready for Ordeal. Reparenting is a crucial way to get that fathering.

I encourage men to contact their boy inside by starting a dialogue. In this dialogue there are two speakers. One speaker is the man as adult and concerned father. The other speaker is the boy. The dialogue should be written at first. Like a play script, one line will be the father, the other will be the son. I ask the man to start by asking the boy a question. This question could be: "How do you feel?" or "What do you need to feel better?" Then I ask the man to imagine what the boy wants to say, what he wants, what he feels, what he needs and write down those imagined words. Then the man, as father, answers this boy's needs or feelings as he would his own son.

This dialogue always feels very artificial at first. The boy's voice, as it is written, feels made up rather than natural. However, the dialogue becomes very real quite soon because the boy inside does come out. I didn't create him for purposes of this book. He's there. He's real. He's hardwired inside. He's an archetype, the puer aeternas, the boy inside we have been talking about all along. He carries our life experience as a child and bears our childhood wounds. He's the part of ourselves that will always be a child. He's the part that takes over, at times, in inappropriate situations. He's the part that gets addicted, dependent, rageful because of his hurt. He needed an understanding father back then. And he still needs us today.

John Bradshaw encourages letter writing to open the dialogue. He instructs the man or woman to write a letter to the wounded child who is the age they are working on. The letter should tell the child all the things a child needs to hear but often doesn't.

John Lee calls this awareness of the boy inside, especially when he takes over our feelings, conscious regression. It's tough to be aware that we can act immature and childlike at times. It's tough to let ourselves realize that we have had a temper tantrum or a moment of dumb remarks or a sense of boyish powerlessness. We're supposed to always feel like a man. It's tough to realize we often feel like a young boy, especially under stress. Yet conscious regression can be a gateway to healing and empowering that boy. Regression is normal. Conscious regression turns potential crisis into opportunity.

The Youngest Boy

Different issues come up when starting a dialogue with the boy inside and learning to understand him. These issues help identify what child we are dealing with. There are three ages that I have found most prevalent. One is the boy who is under 6 years old. The other is the 6-12 year old. The third is the adolescent of 13-16. The ages are approximate and can vary from man to man. The issues are more universal.

First, the youngest boy. A man who has just been forcefully separated from a mother object is in emotional crisis. He is dealing with the under 6 year old boy. The boy who is under 6 is in need of the type of fathering that keeps in mind that the boy still has some mothering needs. This boy is usually frightened and in need of reassurance that he will be taken care of physically. He needs to know he will have enough to eat, will be kept warm, will be protected from aggressive adults, will not be left alone. This is the boy who holds our abandonment fears and is terrified at the thought of not being close to mother. Abandonment is this boy's issue. Desperate loneliness is his strongest feeling when he is not romantically connected to a woman.

The youngest boy inside will naturally look for this reassurance from an outside woman as mother object. His greatest fear is being alone. He doesn't realize that a good father can nurture and protect him, too, in the situation he is in. He doesn't realize that he has gotten the mothering he needs, and that his happiness now lies elsewhere. The good father starts the process of the boy connecting with other good men, while transitioning the connection from an increasingly regressive mother object.

Most men going through the Great Separation find they have great, terrifying abandonment fears. Their fears seem so irrational and unmanly. And they are. The man is really experiencing regression to the youngest boy in all his fears and desperation, his intense abandonment feelings take control over all others. Others wonder how a man could get to such a level of dependency on a woman. They can't see the terrified boy inside. They don't realize that this boy/man never had help in the natural process of separation. They don't realize that part of this man was never able to move on from mother.

For most men, this crisis is the first time they have felt this child so clearly. Once they are introduced, the bond can be emotional and effective. Once the reality of this boy is experienced, a man finds compassion for himself he didn't know he had. This is not the "feeling sorry" for himself that most men despise. This is not self-pity. This is the beginning of a true sense of love for self, embodied in the love for this defenseless child. This compassion is also the foundation for future self-esteem.

Greg was a very compassionate man until it came to himself. Then he could be self-critical and feel totally useless, a victim of the Vader voice. Greg grew up with a depressed overburdened mother and an abusive, competitive father. He was going through a divorce when he came for counseling and was feeling intensely lonely. He knew that divorce was the best thing, but he couldn't control the desire to go back to a bad relationship. Like many men, his loneliness was overwhelming his better judgment, a sure sign of the youngest child.

Greg was very surprised when I told him he was probably feeling the same loneliness he felt when he was very young and couldn't get his mother's attention or nurturing. He was more surprised when I told him that the young boy was still inside at the present moment and was feeling the double hurt of past and present abandonment. He listened carefully when I explained that the child needed his attention, or that child's feelings would probably force him to go back to his wife for her attention.

After much hesitation he was willing to try to contact that young boy in his own compassionate way. Greg started a dialogue with the youngest child. This child will usually not speak very much at first. Remember, the young boy has been there one's whole life, first possibly ignored or mistreated by others, then later ignored by us. In Greg's case a depressed mother had little to give, while his father was running a business that left no time for children.

Greg's child, whom he called Little Greg, didn't speak much at first, except to say he was afraid of many of the men Greg was around at work. That was all he could get out of him. I explained to Greg that this was not unusual with the son of a competitive father. He also told Greg he was very frightened of his wife's anger. Later it became clear he was frightened because he feared anger was a prelude to being ignored and left alone. Little Greg was starting to talk and he now had a name.

As the adult, Big Greg, the second father, started reassuring the young boy inside. He also started hearing random words inside his head like "ice cream cone," "milk shake," "cookie," especially when passing an ice cream stand or bakery. Realizing that this may be Little Greg, he took these words as requests. Greg would stop, if at all possible, at the time he heard the words, and he would order the requests. It was clear what he was to buy. It was also clear that he felt quite satisfied and safe while eating the nurturing food.

Food would seem a small thing, but it symbolized Greg's openness to take care of even the most basic of needs. Greg learned slowly that he could take care of himself and didn't need a mother object to nurture and protect. He would listen for Little Greg's fear, especially in the face of his wife's anger, and tell him he was protected and safe. Though he might fear his wife's abandonment, he told Little Greg that he should never worry about being alone and unprotected again. Big Greg would never leave him again.

Greg started to feel a warmth toward himself and his struggles. He could feel a protectiveness toward the youngest boy inside. He could give himself a break, knowing he was balancing old hurts and healing old wounds. He could learn to be alone and feel curiosity about the world about him, not desperation about living abandoned and lonely. Greg, the man, learned to see the world with less fear and more hope by moving into the world of the second father.

The Middle Boy

The boy inside between 6 and 12 has other issues. While the big issue for the youngest boy is abandonment, the middle boy has issues of recognition and confidence. His need for fathering concentrates on being recognized for his talents and his competence. This is the boy starting out in school and then the work world.

A good father is usually the first to recognize a child's gifts, regardless of their connection to the world of work. He also introduces a boy to the joys of following a talent or interest to its fulfillment. Boys at this age are naturally curious and resourceful. They ask many questions about how the world works. They love to experiment and risk. A good father tells a boy what he can do well, as opposed to the patriarchal voice which usually talks about his shortcomings. The good father encourages risk and experimentation, as opposed to the Vader voice that talks of safety and eternal obedience. The good father upholds a boy's talents or interest even though they might not coincide with his own. In many ways he tells the boy that happiness does not come from following someone else's agenda.

The good father is firm yet supportive. He gives the message that manhood comes with a price tag of risk and pain. Yet this father also models the peace that manhood can bring. The good father provides a template for manhood that the boy needs until he is old enough to find his own manhood. This father lends his ego strength until the boy has enough of his own.

This middle boy inside is the hardest to contact. He is usually shy and has little confidence. He tends to hide. He does not want to take risks. He is afraid of making mistakes. He is usually work addicted, but not in a job that holds his interest or uses his talents well. He will take risks within his work addicted role, but he won't risk going on his own to find his real talents and identity. He often has regressive security and relationship needs from the wounded youngest boy. He is usually filled with shame.

A man who is reparenting this boy inside needs to be like a mentor. He needs to start looking at himself, as he would look at a juvenile boy, in terms of his emerging gifts and talents, not in terms of his marketability. Most importantly he needs to shield the boy inside from the Vader voice. The second father must encourage and see the goodness in each endeavor, not reinforce the negative male chorus inside. Just as the patriarchal voice starts to berate, the second father voice needs to uphold. Just as the Vader voice seeks to unman by criticizing any unpatriarchal role, a good father needs to bestow manhood by recognizing innate talent and vision wherever it leads.

As a counselor I must often interrupt a man when he gets down on himself, or starts to call himself a failure. I must point out to him how he is taking his Vader voice seriously. He is forgetting that this voice comes from somewhere else. He is believing a voice that is really not his own. I must continually remind him to stop and discern which voices are talking. Then I must use the voice of a second father in showing his strengths, gifts, and accomplishments. I especially need to remind him to be gentle, but realistic, with this middle boy. I remind him that this boy, who is hurting, has had too much criticism in his life already. No boy deserves that.

Most men are not in the job that best uses their gifts and talents. Many men are in jobs that don't use their best talents at all. This middle boy of 6-12 holds the key to a man's natural gifts. His interests and enthusiasms start at this time. This is the time when authentic dreams start. If a man wants to find his real calling, he starts with the middle boy.

This is also the time the father wound starts. This is the time that talents go unrecognized and interests go unsupported. This is the time the boy starts to be placed in the patriarchal mold through institutions such as school and church where alternatives are limited and expectations become a burden. This is the boy who desperately needs a second father.

Dialogue

Once a man experiences the boy and believes in his presence a dialogue can begin. As I've said, this dialogue can be on paper or in one's head. Once this dialogue becomes more natural, the talking can go on at any time and in any situation. The most effective dialogue is around a present situation. Any intense, negative feeling will often come from a wounded boy inside, especially those that seem too strong for a given situation. Dealing directly with that boy and his needs will often calm the negative fears and release positive adult energy.

An example: a man might have negative, irrational feelings about his boss. Though his boss may be critical or too demanding the feelings are overwhelming and spill over into life outside of work. The strong, negative feelings probably come from a wounded child inside. A man might start a dialogue by asking what the boy inside, of any age, thinks of the boss. The boy may say that the boss doesn't like him. The boy may actually be afraid of him. The boy may say that the boss always puts him down. It may come out that the boss reminds him of his own critical father.

Now the man knows that he is dealing with the middle boy and the issues are around recognition and risk. A conscious man will realize that the boy is experiencing a transference reaction from the father to the boss. Because of transference the boy will then react to the boss as he reacted to his father, which explains an anxiety that takes up his whole world. The boy will feel unprotected and anxious, with no place to turn. Where can an 8 year old boy turn? It is the boy who feels he has no choice but to stay with the only father he knows. As a result the man's work will suffer because of a crippling anxiety, and a hopeless depression. He will really be reexperiencing feelings of the boy that have been inside for a long time.

If a man realizes this fear and where it comes from he can reassure his boy inside that he will be protected. The man, as second father, can remind the boy that he will be taken care of, even if the boss fires him. He will remind the young boy that the boss isn't his father, that he now has a father that won't leave. He will reassure the boy that the man can be fired, not the boy. And the man is perfectly able to find another job. He has choices. He will reassure the boy that he does have talents, even if his boss won't recognize them.

Over time this kind of dialogue will usually calm feelings down and allow the man to work with much less anxiety and fear. Then a man will be able to more clearly look at his alternatives, and possibly be ready to risk. An uninitiated man would say that this advice to the boy is facile and not realistic in the world today. A man just can't be so detached from his job, especially if he has a family to provide for. Here is the Vader voice again. Here is the voice the man must choose to ignore. Here is the voice the boy inside must be protected from. Surely, a mature caution must be present in any decision. But, most men are more influenced by the boyish fear of the middle boy. And the Vader voice will always take advantage of that fear.

The Second Father—Obi Wan

In the Star Wars myth, Luke is stuck in his family's small village. Luke feels he "will never get out of here." His uncle Owen is a well-meaning but uninitiated man. He has taken the place of Luke's father. He is generous. Although it is unclear, at first, how much his uncle is keeping him around the farm to protect Luke, or how much he is using Luke for his own vision.

In any case, he is not a second father.

Uncle Owen does not understand Luke or his talents. Neither does he champion Luke's dreams. He unwittingly keeps Luke from his identity by trying to mold Luke into following safer dreams and values. In fact, it is Luke's aunt who tells Owen to "let him go." She recognizes that Luke is not a farmer because "he has too much of his father in him."

Uncle Owen refuses to recognize Ben Kenobe's name, calling him "a crazy old man." It becomes clearer as the story unfolds that Owen is trying to protect Luke from the fate of his father. Owen has decided that he must protect his family by shielding himself and Luke from risk and danger. He purposefully lives far from the center of the community. He teaches Luke how to hide. He shows Luke that risk is not worth the rewards. He gives the message that to follow one's inner calling is too dangerous. He shows Luke that initiation is foolish. Uncle Owen is a good man caught in the no-win patriarchy. His message is to fit in and don't make waves.

Luke is rescued by Obi Wan Kenobe, a Jedi master. Obi Wan lives alone, on the same plain, in a humble hut. He is an old warrior and wise man. He is past his prime, yet he is ready to use his warrior talents for the good, especially when asked by the Princess. It is clear that Obi Wan recognizes Luke as having the soul and talents of a Jedi warrior. Obi Wan understands Luke. He loves the same things Luke does. This understanding is symbolized by giving Luke his father's laser sword.

Obi Wan starts teaching Luke to be a Jedi warrior. He immediately enlists Luke in a very dangerous mission, not protecting Luke from pain or risk. When Luke balks at the mission, Obi Wan points out Luke's patriarchal voice by simply saying "that is your uncle talking." Obi Wan says that Luke must do what he feels is right.

Luke then experiences the Great Separation. His uncle and aunt are killed. Fortunately, unlike many of us, Luke has a second father right there to get him through that trauma and guide him to his next steps. Luke says he wants to become a Jedi and learn the ways of the Force. This is contrary to the patriarchal society which considers the Force an ancient, defunct religion. This is also contrary to the patriarchal Empire which acknowledges no force above its own.

Luke is moving toward the other side. Obi Wan is there to support him on the journey to that transition, while protecting him from the patriarchal voice. Obi Wan starts to teach Luke what fathers need to teach, all about warrior energy. Fathers need to teach the focus and discipline of energy. They teach how to contain energy instead of dissipating it. Fathers teach skills of reaching goals through enduring inner pain, rather than running from it into addiction. Fathers teach boundary setting, the special skill of the warrior. Fathers teach of the larger world and how to negotiate it.

As Luke starts out, he learns immediately about the world of uninitiated men. He finds himself in the most unusual bar in the history of movies. He has not learned boundaries. He is trusting and naive. He almost gets himself killed. Obi Wan does not protect him from the bar by having him wait outside. He does protect Luke from getting killed. All fathers need to lend their sons their strength, until the son finds his own. This is why fathers need to continue to make some decisions for their sons while respecting the son's emerging skill at making his own.

Obi Wan soon starts teaching Luke the skills of the Jedi warrior. He gives Luke a remote to practice with. He counsels Luke to feel the Force flowing through him. He tells Luke to "act on instinct" instead of trusting his eyes. He encourages Luke to "stretch out with your feelings." He gently starts introducing Luke to the inner life, the source of his strength and identity. He encourages Luke by telling him he can do it.

This initiated second father is not only teaching skills, he is pointing to another reality, the other side. Luke will contact this reality through his feelings and instincts. He shows Luke, though Luke does not really understand yet, that there is another reality both within Luke and in the world. Second fathers prepare men for this reality, a reality the patriarchy does not recognize or understand.

Ultimately Obi Wan recognizes Luke's unique identity. He does not force Luke to see the world with his vision or to follow him endlessly. Obi Wan does not keep Luke a perpetual son. He does not use Luke for his own purposes. Instead he says to Luke, "Your destiny lies in a different direction than mine."

Obi Wan lets himself be destroyed, a profound lesson of manhood we will take up later. Immediately, he becomes a good voice in Luke's head. He becomes a good father voice to counteract the patriarchal voice. He stays with Luke, reminding him of the virtues of a good warrior. This is one of the greatest gifts a second father gives, his voice that endures in the psyche of the son.

When Luke is about to attack the Death Star he hears Obi Wan's words "Use the Force." Luke then turns off his targeting computer. He refuses the rational, the logical, the technological, the patriarchal answer. Instead he goes inside toward a part of himself his second father assures him is there.

The Adolescent

In the course of dialoguing, a man will eventually come into contact with the adolescent. The adolescent will be 13-16 years old. He will still need some fathering during a crisis. However he will be drawn to experimenting with a place far from the father, at the very edges of the village. He will be starting to separate from father. The wise father, as Obi Wan did, will encourage this.

The adolescent, like Luke, will start wondering more and more about the wilderness and the promise that it holds. And he will start looking for brothers and friends as a preparation for his initiation. The next two chapters talk of this adolescent and what his concerns are. As the younger boys inside start to heal, the adolescent's needs become stronger. We are coming to the far side of the father's world in adolescence. The adolescent is at the village boundaries wondering about the wilderness out there.

Chapter 10
Midlife Brothers

A t some point in a man's life he realizes that he is at a crossroads. He may not know exactly what all the stakes are, but he knows he must make some crucial decisions that will greatly affect the rest of his life. This is a time in most men's lives toward the end of the age of the father.

This time, after the mid-30's, is often referred to as midlife. Most men have been to this crossroads often in their earlier life but never recognized it as such. Maybe they didn't recognize its urgency because there was some instinctual knowledge that there was still time left in the age of the father. Maybe there was nobody there to explain their situation. This crossroads is really a place near the boundary of the village. One road leads back towards the village. The other road leads to the wilderness.

A man's outside age continues along a biological continuum from year to year. However, a man's inside age can fluctuate depending on the wounds and deficits of the boy inside, and the outside stressful circumstances the man is experiencing. Under stress, a wounded boy/man, wandering at the crossroads, will run back to the village. He will either run toward the mother and her comfort or the father and his directions. In other words the man will regress to the boy under 12.

There is also an adolescent boy inside a man. This is the boy who can act more like the man we all recognize in the street or in the executive suite. He loves the games of adulthood. He loves the risks and challenges. Yet inside he is still struggling with leaving boyhood behind. He also struggles with what it really feels like being a man from the inside out.

The crossroads is the place of adolescence, at the outskirts of the village. Adolescents like to be at the edge, hanging around the village boundaries, yet keeping a respectable distance from the wilderness. Part of him yearns for the freedom and adventure of the wilderness, as well as the experience of the mystery of manhood. This is his adolescent inside. However, the younger boy inside is often afraid to think of unconsoled aloneness, without rules to follow and a role to play.

In helping a man to make the next steps toward manhood, he must be introduced to the adolescent within and to the place where the adolescent hangs out. A confused, unguided, angry or depressed adolescent inside can be a significant obstacle to a man's growth, keeping him in the village long after he needs to leave. This is the adolescent Robert Bly talks about in his book *The Sibling Society*. Bly talks of how most men are stuck in adolescence, are stuck at the crossroads. He talks of adolescents that never grow up, because they have no Elders to prepare them for the wilderness. He talks of a culture of regressed adolescents disguised as men.

The adolescent is the older boy inside. Men need to consciously contact the adolescent within if they hope to find their manhood. This is the boy of 12-16 years. He has many crucial tasks to perform before he is ready for initiation. Preparation involves finding initiatory brothers, separating from father, finishing the separation from mother, and preparing for the sudden presence of the Elder.

Midlife

Most men are not ready to take up adolescent issues until long after they are young teenagers. In this culture there is precious little good fathering and Eldering energy to bring a man past adolescence to initiation. This dearth of initiated men causes most men to top out in a perpetual, unhealthy adolescence. Men are ill-prepared for what will become painful midlife issues because they have not had a healthy adolescence.

For many men, an insidious dissatisfaction of life creeps up in their late 30's and 40's. This is the time of the stereotypical midlife crisis. Daniel Levinson talks of the time between 35 and 40 as the normal midlife transition from novice adulthood to full adulthood. Levinson feels this normal transition need not be a crisis even though there are big changes going on. I agree that this time need not be one of crisis if healthy adolescence, Levinson's stage of novice adulthood, has been dealt with. However we are a culture where we are led to skip a whole stage of growth, the stage of healthy adolescence.

Men are unprepared for the adolescent transition because men are stuck in the father's world. Where the healthy adolescent is prepared to move on to the wilderness, a patriarchal man is taught that the marketplace is the end goal.

For most men who have gotten to the crossroads, the crisis is not from mother separation, though there are usually these residual issues to be dealt with. The crisis is from the growing awareness of betrayal by the patriarchy. This is the time a man starts to realize that his ladder of success is on the wrong wall. The satisfaction he was promised is not there. He realizes he does not feel like a man even though he looks like a man in the mirror. He may not realize his dissatisfaction as betrayal. But he realizes a mounting and insidious discomfort with his life.

He also realizes that he is unprepared to answer the questions that are starting to plague him. Questions such as what work do I really enjoy doing that can also support my family? Is this the work I want to do the rest of my active life? Have I wasted my talents and energy? Is this the woman I want to spend the rest of my life with? Is this the kind of father I want to be to my children? Is this the reputation I want in the community?

Men often tell me, in a defeated tone, that they are horribly late in dealing with their issues, because they are in their 30's or 40's. They feel ashamed. They feel depressed. It is hard to convince them that they are really not too late. They are at the crossroads, again, with time to take the right turn this time. Now they have to deal consciously with that uninvited but thankfully persistent adolescent.

Adolescent Unbidden

When we experience this increasingly frustrated adolescent inside at midlife he has become angry and aggressive. He has been ignored for a long time by most men who have followed the rules of the patriarchy. He will not be denied. If a man will not deal with him consciously this adolescent will take over unconsciously. An unconscious man in his 30's or 40's or even 50's will encounter this unruly adolescent in the form of adolescent behavior. To a traditional, patriarchal man his adolescent behavior comes as a great surprise, to others it is a shock. Often the unbidden adolescent has just gotten a man into trouble through some uncharacteristic, irresponsible behavior. This could be anything from reckless and aggressive driving, to having an affair, to hanging out in bars, to spending into big debt. Sometimes the adolescent shows up, unbidden, in the stereotype of the midlife crazy who breaks his neck with gold jewelry, buys a red convertible, dates women half his age, and acts half his age. Other times he arrives quietly, staying hidden, but creating havoc.

Midlife Adolescent

There is a strong connection between modern midlife and unfinished adolescent issues. As a man's outside age moves past his mid-30's he is ending the age of the father. The adolescent issues of separation and individuation surface again forcefully. For a man to take up these issues effectively he has to realize the signs of the healthy adolescent.

First he must realize that his restlessness about following in someone else's footsteps is a natural sign of his own growth. The restlessness is the yearning of the adolescent to go on his own. He must realize that even the restlessness of the unbidden adolescent is really the unguided adolescent looking for initiation. The initiatory archetype is at work here. A man at this stage yearns for the unknown as a place of discovery, more than a place of danger. The yearning to create one's own path, away from the crowd and the village, has the marks more of unrealized dreams than unrealistic fantasy.

A man at this time will often fantasize about leaving his job and his home, sometimes even leaving his family, to start over in a small town where he is unknown and unexpected. They think about starting over like they did in their 20's, except now they're in their 40's. Sometimes men think wistfully of their college or high school years and the different decisions they could have made. All these thoughts signal the adolescent inside, who is still in his teens, wanting to finish his tasks and his dreams.

Unfinished dreams is the stuff of the unbidden adolescent. It is also the place where all healthy adolescents need to start. If a man reacts to his freedom fantasies without shame or hopelessness, he can start to contact his inner adolescent, just as he contacted his younger boy. He will realize that he doesn't have to leave home or family to start over, for the journey is really an inward one. He will start to take seriously his adolescent dreams and hopes. He will start to take seriously his adolescent within.

The adolescent within needs to be taken seriously. His restlessness about having to obey needs to be honored. His discomfort with living someone else's dreams must be recognized. His boredom with the traditional rewards of society must be accepted.

His need to separate from the patriarchy must not be ignored. This is the time when a man often has a falling out with his mentor or other second father. To a man who doesn't understand, this is a tragedy. A man who understands realizes this is inevitable. The adolescent must separate from the father. Sometimes the separation is as hard as the connection was good. As Daniel Levinson writes, "Most often, however, an intense mentor relationship ends with strong conflict and bad feeling." However, as he writes, "After the separation, the younger man may adopt many of the qualities of the mentor. His personality is enriched as he makes the mentor a more intrinsic part of himself." The adolescent needs to go on alone, yet, like Luke and Obi Wan, the mentor's voice still encourages.

Alf came to me because he was having chest pains that were found to have no medical basis. Though he was relieved to find that his chest pains were not serious medically, he decided to take them seriously anyway. He was starting to realize that the stress of his job might be worse than he thought. Though he was quite successful in his career he also realized that he no longer looked forward to going to work every day. He also felt that the orders he was being given, as financial officer in a small corporation, were not in line with his own ethical code.

Alf had been laid off two years before because of downsizing. At that time he had been desperate to get another job, because of the impact on his career and his dreams of financial success. Alf had gone to school with boys from very well-to-do families, even though his own family lived modestly. A good part of his motivation to be successful was to finally fit in with this crowd, who never quite accepted him in high school. When he was more candid, he admitted that he wanted to be more successful than most of them just to show them up.

Alf was a humble, ethical man and a good father. He didn't realize how much his competitive, unguided, stuck adolescent was running his life. He had taken his present job primarily because of the money and opportunity. The job looked fine on his resume. Because of his reservations, he didn't necessarily plan to stay more than a couple of years.

Alf's boss was a hustler. He seemed to feel fine about bending the truth because he knew he would pull things out in the end. Alf was not so sure of his boss's judgment, and he was sure he didn't believe in warping the truth as much as this man did.

Alf was also questioning how much he enjoyed his work for its own sake. He started to question how much his job was just a vehicle for his career and status needs. He did enjoy a challenge. He enjoyed studying the big picture and devising financial plans that were creative and effective. He enjoyed creating teams of people from different backgrounds and managing them. He did not necessarily enjoy the day-to-day number crunching, nor did he enjoy taking orders from someone whose judgment he suspected.

Alf was miserable. He was so miserable that he impulsively quit his job, after arranging for a decent severance package. Alf figured his boss wanted him out of there anyway because of Alf's problems in supporting the boss's judgments. His boss was a competitive, narcissistic patriarch who needed yes men to prop his ego.

In counseling with Alf I encouraged him to stop impulsively looking for another job. I tried to help him, as second father, by letting him borrow my judgment that he was not in a desperate situation and that his talents would be recognized in a number of career areas. I gave him the benefit of my experience in telling him there were other facts about his life that he was unaware of, and that he might need these in making future decisions. I told him that much of what he was going through was not abnormal psychologically, though it was not necessarily what the patriarchal society considered normal.

I first tried to get him in touch with the adolescent inside. I tried to show him how his adolescent was following a career track only because he still felt less than his peers. We talked about how useless and meaningless this dark competition was. I encouraged him to look at his numerous accomplishments and start to appreciate the gifts and talents of that neglected adolescent.

I talked about his father. I showed him how his father was a good, ethical man who happened to be depressed. This man had no time to father Alf as he struggled with his own career as an insurance salesman. Alf's father never fit into the corporate world, nor was he a success. He had a hard time helping Alf find his talents. He had little stamina to give Alf the strength he needed to make choices about corporate life.

I talked to Alf about fathers and second fathers, and how those in his life were unable to give him the self-esteem he needed. I suggested that he didn't have to attain material success in order to feel like a man. I then talked of the steps the adolescent within had to go through to feel like a man on the inside. I encouraged Alf to go within to find his answers.

I challenged him, as an Elder, to find the other dreams of his adolescent, the ones he never lived out. Healthy adolescent dreams, the dreams we all had at 16, are often the keys to our true direction. He would need these dreams as a starting point for his coming Ordeal.

When I talked of the patriarchal separation and the need for Ordeal, Alf understood. He recognized my emerging Elder voice. He was starting to become ready for the confusion and chaos of the coming months. He promised he would not neglect his adolescent and abort his Ordeal.

Besides individual counseling I talked to Alf about joining a men's group. I was doing some of the work of second fathering and Eldering. However, Alf also needed brothers. Brothers would be crucial in his coming Ordeal. Brothers would help prepare him for initiation.

Healthy Adolescence

Adolescence is the time of significant relationships outside the family. The adolescent has a need to separate from family, mother and father. He needs to experiment with being a separate person, though he still needs a good father as a safety net. This experimental time is the time of transitional separation from father. He separates partially, developing significant relationships with peers, especially male peers.

Friendship is the new relationship that this time brings. Friendship allows a man to significantly separate from family yet get the support needed for the initiatory journey. Friendship with other men gives a man significant masculine energy, without a regressive pull toward the patriarchy. Friendship with a woman allows for support, without the regressive pull toward the mother object. In this chapter I will talk about the necessary bonding in friendship that men need with other men.

Adolescence is the time when a boy experiments with the edge of the village, where all the other adolescent boys are also hanging out. In some African societies, even today, the adolescent boys have their own daytime huts, still in the village, but away from family for most of the day. They return at night to the family hut, not ready for total separation, yet much more attached to their brothers than their family. I repeat. All men have a hardwired urge to bond with other men. The urge is there because the need is there.

All men have a deep need for brothers. The natural tendency for young adolescents is to explore friendship and teamwork with other boys, in preparation for many adult pursuits that benefit the community. For example, in primitive societies men had to learn to work together in intricate patterns of behavior and nonverbal communication in order to be successful as hunters and provide for the community. Cooperation was vital for survival. Teamwork was born way back then.

Today the overpowering urge men and boys have for sports has a lot to do with this hardwired need to team up. The hand and head signals in football, baseball and basketball mimic the silent hunting signals of our distant fathers. The high of winning as a team often brings the deepest satisfaction that many men feel. The bonds of the team often override the bonds of blood. Men often talk of team as family.

This same sense of bonded togetherness for a purpose comes out in war. Sometimes the closest many men have ever felt to another person comes in war, facing death, with each man covering his brother's ass. The warrior yearns to fight with other warriors. Though men don't miss the violence and destruction of war, they often miss terribly their brothers in war. The sense of a warrior's loyalty to each other is really the strongest motivation men have to endure the violence of war. The military has always taken advantage of this loyalty to make men fight in the first place. Forget about why we are fighting or what we are fighting for, just don't let your brother down. Men are hardwired to care about their brothers.

Competition

It is a cruel paradox that the dark patriarchy uses healthy male aggressiveness and turns it into the competitiveness of keeping men apart. Where men are kept apart as brothers there will usually be some kind of violence, disguised as unhealthy competition. Adolescence has always been the time of the brother, except in our modern society.

Friendship to a person who is taught from an early age to be independent and competitive, is confusing. Men are told of teamwork in corporate America, and team players are supposed to be rewarded. But my experience suggests that the teamwork really rewards the topmost, dark fathers while the team players are often betrayed. Men band together at the corporate level to get an edge on their coworkers rather than to help each other.

Men in our society see groups of other men as instant competition rather than as avenues of initiatory cooperation and support. The negative father voice, intent on sabotaging growth, tells men how many ways other men will beat them out if they are not careful. As I have said, the patriarchy is designed so that there are many losers and very few winners. The system is designed for a man to be a great competitor or a loser, pitting men against men for the patriarch's gain.

In our culture manhood is defined in terms of a dark competition. The playing field is the work world. Other men are obstacles to manhood, not brothers or friends. There isn't much room for a lot of men in this world. Competition supposedly weeds the men from the boys. In this environment it is easy to see how men do violence to other men. Men are taught to believe they are in it alone. Men are taught that ultimately no other man will help. Men are taught to be selfish, and not think past their own needs and the needs of their family.

Stuart Miller writes in his book *Men and Friendship* that most of modern life demands that we be ready to compete "thereby ever-honing us to belittle, to criticize, to search for flaws." In earlier times competition did not mean what it does today. Even in Greek antiquity the idea of competition was to bring out the best in each opponent. Michael Meade points out that the word competition actually comes from the Latin words which mean to petition together. In the Greek case, each man's petition was for the gods to bring out the best in each other. Competition was a kind of mini-initiation in which brothers helped each other find their best selves.

Michael Gurian in his book *The Good Son* shows that competition can be a kind of nurturance between men, especially between a father and a son. He calls this masculine way "aggressive nurturance." It can be a way of teaching in a language a growing boy understands. As long as competition has the value of calling out natural talents as its highest goal, it can enrich both a man and his community. In this way it becomes an important preparation for initiation, both as a way of receiving fathering and a way of bonding with brothers.

Male friendship is one of the most potent forms of triggering the initiatory archetype and gaining a sense of strength to do the initiatory work. Patriarchal competition is unnatural. Competitive violence is not what men are made for. Men are made to bond for gaining strength and courage. The dark patriarchy, however, is afraid of initiation. The dark patriarchy only wants talents that serve its cause, strengthening the bond of father to son, not brother to brother.

Finding Brothers

It sounds strange but men have intimacy needs for other men. This is not sexual intimacy, but a sense of closeness and trust. If men do not feel close to other men they will look to have all their intimacy needs met by women. This is not how we are hardwired. For men, it is not essential to have a friend who has a bosom in order to have a buddy.

Stuart Miller talks of the difficulty of finding deep male friendships. When he mentioned writing a book on male friendship to colleagues he was astonished to hear their warnings that he should not write a book on homosexuality. They were worried for his career. Stuart is not gay and did not intend to write a book on homosexuality. The idea of deep male friendships was too foreign for his colleagues to understand in ways other than homosexuality.

Most men I meet in counseling will automatically think of a woman when they want to share their deepest feelings. One struggling man felt stuck because he felt most men "extremely boring." To him, his newfound women friends were quite interesting. This man was succumbing to regressive maternal forces, as do most men, by obsessing sexually and emotionally about one interesting "friend." This detour took energy away from his own internal journey and a marriage that could be saved. When he did start connecting with other men, sharing his internal journey, he stopped obsessing.

Stuart Miller talks of the danger of even a good relationship with a wife or significant other. He says that "the problem then arises that, as rich as his relationship with his wife may be, he eventually suffers from claustrophobia, from a sense of being suffocated in the arms of the Great Mother, an archetype he gradually projects on his spouse as his relationships with men become less vital."

Men's groups, formal or informal, are a form of friendship extremely helpful to men's development. As well as providing second fathering they provide brothers. This is why I recommended a men's group to Alf. Men's groups are the analogue of ancestral tribal bonds. In men's groups the bonding of members is a crucial step for the healthy adolescent within. It is the key to healing the adolescent as well as preparing for healthy maturity. Men seem to quickly develop a different sense of themselves in a conscious men's group. The archetypal need to bond gets stimulated early. The adolescent immediately seems to feel a lift and a desire to go the next steps, and face the initiatory pain. Young men have always started the initiation with their brothers. Brothers lend courage for those first steps into the wilderness. Brothers understand those first steps.

In my experience men feel a support that lifts up their sense of a male, valuable self. Brothers give different feedback than fathers and mothers. They tell us of different parts of ourselves. Brothers have less of a stake in our life direction. They don't succumb to the manipulative temptation of the mother's dreams or the father's ego. They are as open as we are to questioning the patriarchal rules or the matriarchal pleasures. They yearn as we do for satisfaction and the inside sense of manhood. They provide a safe place for us to experiment with other ways of relating and being.

The Mature Adolescent

In the adolescent subculture, no longer is the adolescent just taking from parental figures. Now he is asked to give also. At first it is very hard for the adolescent to realize that others have legitimate but sometimes contradictory needs. He will make a lot of mistakes in this learning process. Brothers help us learn the give and take of the next steps. We can make mistakes with brothers and not feel judged or guilty. These mistakes can teach an adolescent the beginning of relationships of equality and mutuality.

Brothers can provide a second family to help us leave the first. We are not hardwired to go the whole initiatory journey alone. Most of the journey is with men as fathers, brothers and Elders. Only the last part is alone. We need the strength of other men to face that Ordeal of aloneness.

Once a man is able to grow past early adolescent issues he is ready for late adolescence and the time of initiation. He will have the yearnings of midlife, yearnings for a greater sense of self and more meaningful direction. The regressive adolescent fantasies of sex and success will feel less and less satisfying and attractive. His need to fit in to the adult world of the patriarchy will seem more and more irrelevant. He will become more uncomfortable with the empty values of pseudo-adult responsibility and rewards. His fear of other men will dissipate. He will realize the satisfaction of good friendships and his ability to give of his emerging self. He will start to learn the blessing of having brothers.

Han Solo

In the Star Wars myth Han Solo is the prototype of the unguided adolescent. He is in it for the money, partly because he is in deep debt to the loan shark, Jabba. The assumption is that he gambled, somehow, and lost Jabba's money. He is single and answers to nobody but himself. He is unmoved by the larger struggle of good and evil in the galaxy. He is obsessed with the marketplace.

Han is in the presence of a mentor, Obi Wan, yet Han sees no strength in him, nor any use for the "old religion" of the Force. His initiatory urge only comes out in his need to take reckless chances in smuggling or evading bounty hunters. His big adolescent toy is the Millennium Falcon. He is proud of it and what it can do, just like any adolescent is proud of his "wheels." He boasts about it constantly, as if it makes him manly.

Han continually displays the persona of a man including calling Luke "boy" throughout their first encounters. His reaction to stress and danger is always the dark warrior's reaction, anger and focused violence. He doesn't learn from Obi Wan that there are other ways of the mature warrior. He is immediately attracted to Princess Leia, but acts with bravado toward her. He hides behind his male persona and ends up acting more adolescent. As a maturing young woman, she is unimpressed.

Finally, the only thing that keeps him in the story, and close to the initiatory process, is his sense of brotherhood with Luke. He has his money. Leia is ignoring him. He won't go on the suicide mission of destroying the Death Star, a true initiatory experience. Yet he returns to save Luke from Darth Vader's destruction. Han somehow does not fall prey to a dark competitiveness with Luke. He must sense from deep inside that brotherhood has some answers for him. Maybe he is tired of the loneliness behind the persona. He saves Luke from the destructiveness of the dark father, as good brothers do. In doing so, he finds a new family. Luckily, the second father is Obi Wan Kenobe. Luckily, that brother is Luke Skywalker. This bonding to a brother, who has a second father's values, becomes a key to a whole new life.

Questions

In working with the adolescent inside a man has to continue his refathering and guidance just as he did for the younger boy inside. In speaking with the adolescent he will often find a dissatisfaction with his life direction. As he feels more he will feel his adolescent. He will find an anger at patriarchal fathers and any authority that seems heavy handed or manipulative. He will often find a sense of hopelessness. Most of the time these feelings are a sign of a growing readiness for initiation. These feelings are really the start of initiatory depression, the first step in the coming Ordeal. A man who refathers his adolescent inside listens to these feelings and the inevitable questions these feelings bring up. If a man takes his adolescent seriously he turns a crisis into an opportunity. Good fathers, unlike patriarchs, encourage questioning even of the fathers themselves. A man who ignores his adolescent dissatisfaction and questions remains stuck in depression and in an unhealthy adolescence.

This crisis of doubt is also where friends as brothers come in to help. A good friend will take a man's questions seriously and add many of his own! Questions will start to become common, dissatisfaction normal. But for this to happen a man must risk sharing his internal life. He must risk sharing his doubts and deliberations with another who may be walking the same path. He must risk misunderstanding, even ridicule. He must risk leaving the protection of the patriarchy.

Friends who are ready to become initiatory brothers will not shame or minimize this risky sharing. With initiatory brothers common questions will emerge. This banding as brothers can happen at any time. A man does not have to be in a men's group for these connections. This kind of connection, in a men's group or anywhere in the world of men, will cause initiatory energy to rise.

This energy of connection will also inevitably draw Elder energy. As we will see, Elder energy draws a man deeper into his questions and confusion.

The Elder takes the adolescent very seriously, continually testing whether he is ready for Ordeal and its answers. One significant test is whether the adolescent can stay with the discomfort of the questions. This is when fathers hand a boy over to Elders. This is when brothers are crucial to the midlife dilemma. Brothers can keep a man from running scared back to the village. As in a good team or a good platoon, brothers can keep each other going, even in the face of extreme fear.

Chapter 11
The Elder W

This short chapter is about the role of the Elder, at this point the Elder within, in the life of the initiate, and in the life of a man. His role is so crucial that it is archetypal. As I said about archetypes, they are universal human experiences that we carry in our psyches. Because the Elder experience is archetypal, the Elder is sleeping within every man, waiting to be awakened. Men who are ready, most of you who have read this far, will recognize him starting to emerge and speak.

The Elder

The Elder is the archetype of the *senex*, or the wise old man. He represents a wisdom and awareness beyond our personal history, beyond the boy's experience. He represents a viewpoint of life beyond the marketplace. He represents a new form of consciousness that holds the key to the boy's manhood.

The Elder represents a totally new view of life, a view that is often in opposition to a man's conventional, familiar beliefs. He represents a wisdom beyond personal experience. The indigenous peoples viewed this wisdom as coming from their ancestors, as well as their gods. The Ordeal was the time to be introduced to these ancestors and to face their terrifying gods.

We can view this archetypal wisdom as slowly being learned over generations and millennia. Jung called this archetype the "2 million year-old man" inside. He saw this wise man archetype residing in the collective unconscious of every man's psyche. The indigenous people viewed this ancient wisdom as residing in their ancestors, who were accessible to them through Ordeal and prayer. They also saw this wisdom in the Elders who were watching over them.

In an Elder society, the Elder appears when the adolescent is nearing readiness. He suddenly becomes prominent in the lives of the boys growing toward initiation. Older boys notice the Elders looking at them from a nce trying to tell if they are ready. They test themselves in preparation or their coming Ordeal. Boys expect the Elder to come and change their lives profoundly. They wonder if they will succeed or even if they will survive. They are often of two minds, wanting their manhood yet fearing their test.

In indigenous times the Elder provided a clear path to their manhood. His presence was a daily reminder of their next steps. Boys took some comfort in knowing that they would not be sent to Ordeal before the Elders' wisdom recognized their readiness. They also had a deep sense that the Elders wanted them to succeed, and would guide them through the process. They knew that the Elders would push them beyond their known limits and the limits of the village. They knew that the Elders understood mysteries beyond the village that held the secret to their manhood.

In an Elderless society, there are many older men but few Elders. When there are no Elders there is no witness that there is an essential reality beyond the village boundaries. There is only the illusion that somehow manhood takes place in the marketplace, by young men mimicking older men. There is the illusion that initiation only involves the persona. There are no Elders to point to a whole different time and place of transformation. So there are no clear pathways to maturation. Authentic initiatory longings for a special, unique sense of self are crushed, or go unrecognized.

Real adolescent dreams become unrealistic fantasies without the Elder's translation and guidance. When the Ordeal time gets close in an Elderless, modern society, a man is caught totally unawares by his feelings of alienation, aloneness, dissatisfaction. As I have said, this time usually comes when a man is in his late 30's or 40's. If unheeded the alienation reappears in his 50's or 60's. This Janus time of midlife comes totally unexpected.

An unaware man in the grip of unsettling questions doesn't realize that he is experiencing the awakening of the Elder within. Besides experiencing the yearnings of the adolescent for something more, he is experiencing the answers of the Elder. The Elder sees the world from a totally different perspective, different from the father or mother. The Elder knows of possibilities that are beyond the consensus view of manhood. He knows that a boy is made for a more profound and meaningful life than the unEldered marketplace holds.

Questioning one's life direction and one's priorities is a sure sign the adolescent is ready for something more. Questioning the direction and priorities of society around him, and his place in these priorities, is a sure sign the Elder is starting to emerge in a man.

Perhaps a man is starting to question his job. Is my job something that betters society? Does my work reflect who I am now? Do I have more to give than this job allows? Are my talents really being utilized? Do I make a difference in the bigger picture' ᵗ⁻ my life more than just about me? Those are the questions of the Elder.

Sometimes the question: g has more to do with relationships. What persons in my life can I really count on to support my deeper self? Is my marriage a witness for other couples to emulate? Am I a friend who is honest and caring enough to confront destructive behavior in those I care about? Should I go out of my way to share my wisdom with those younger than me? There is the Elder.

A man may question his faith. What are my bottom line values? Do I live them out and walk my talk? Do my life goals include the good of others? What does it really mean to act morally? Is there such a thing as a spiritual call? There is the Elder.

The Elder archetype bears the wisdom that our crisis of alienation and separation is necessary. He bears the paradoxical message that this painful crisis is an opportunity. This internal sense of a different rightness can be viewed as intuition. This intuition can be seen as the voice of the ancient Elder within. The Elder within gives us the sense that we must go past what we are taught is real. He coaxes us to find reality for ourselves, even if it is dangerous. The Elder causes us to question other's views of what is good, even if the vast majority agree. The Elder always questions the consensus reality of the marketplace and the village, as he lives in the emerging man.

Yoda

In the Star Wars myth, the Elder is primarily represented by Yoda. In Greek myths Elders are like the sky gods expecting obedience without questioning, demanding subservience from on high. The patriarchy is primarily based on Greek myth. In Celtic and Germanic myths there are trolls and elves and dwarves, spirits of the earth and intuition. These Elders bring an earthy, nature wisdom. This wisdom comes from unlikely, overlooked places on the ground, where wisdom has been stored since aboriginal times.

Yoda represents the Germanic myth. He is 900 years old, a true senex and bearer of much ancient wisdom, pre-technical but very strong. Yoda represents prehistoric, pre-Christian wisdom. Especially to modern, Western eyes, Yoda's wisdom is packaged in the unlikeliest, countercultural way. Yoda lives on the other side, and incorporates its wisdom. He knows the Force. He has been taught by the Force. Few in the technological, patriarchal galaxy even know of him, much less reverence his wisdom.

When Luke is just about ready, he is led by his second father to Yoda. Actually, the galactic situation causes Luke to be thrust into his Ordeal prematurely. Yet he has an Elder, though a very frustrated one, and that makes the difference. Again there is that Zen saying that holds a truth about Elders: "When the student is ready the teacher will come." Often readiness is just a sincere desire to do whatever it takes to become a better person, and the humble action to seek someone with more wisdom.

On first meeting, Luke is at least irritated with Yoda, if not downright scornful of him. Luke says, "I'm looking for a great warrior." He expects a traditional, cultural warrior, a veteran of many wars. Instead he finds a cross between a dwarf and a troll who acts like a little child. Offhandedly the dwarf comments that "war is not what makes one great."

Luke is frustrated, proud, and hopeless. He cannot find his image of a Jedi warrior and master. Luke flunks his first test of humility. He is still filled with childish attitudes and adolescent fantasies. More ominously, he is full of pride. As Obi Wan says, "he has too much of his father in him." He is still an unhealed, fatherless adolescent looking to typical patriarchal symbols of status and power. He is full of fantasy.

Yoda says he's only a boy.

At first, Yoda denies his help to Luke. As he says, "The boy has no patience! He is not ready. He is looking for excitement. That is not a Jedi." Just looking for adventure is not the motivation needed for maturity. The Evel Knievel syndrome is a terminal disease in the eyes of an Elder. Unbridled passion is a recipe for disaster. Proving manhood only by overpowering is ignorant.

Yoda finally takes Luke as a disciple for the sake of the galaxy. Luke is an orphan, forcefully separated from mother and father, aunt and uncle.

He has been separated by unfortunate circumstance, not by an Elder. Luke suffers from his father wound and has not had a strong fathering foundation to prepare him for an Elder. As Yoda says, speaking of Luke's father wound, "there is much anger in him." Luckily for us, an Elder can make up for our lack of preparation once we humble ourselves and drop our patriarchal expectations. Yoda is very tired after 900 years of life. And Luke does not seem ready. Yet there is a crisis in the whole galaxy and Luke seems their only hope, for he is of the family of Skywalker.

Luke symbolizes the next adolescent generation, the next generation that needs the Elder's guidance in order to eventually rule wisely. Elders are always concerned about the following generations. Yoda represents a thousand generations of Jedi warriors still concerned about the future of the galaxy. They are concerned "with peace and justice," the values of the other side.

Elders do not fight the battles. They prepare young men to battle for what is right, based on values beyond self-aggrandizement. Elders are like grandfathers who are no longer concerned with the trappings of manliness, yet have a great concern about their grandsons. They are not like patriarchal generals who safely send men to company wars to retain their own status. Elders often end up suffering greatly to show their novices the way of wisdom.

What Yoda tries to do with Luke is what all Elders do. He talks of the Force and its values. He tries to teach Luke of unseen, transcendent power that can work through Luke himself. He tries to give Luke a sense of the call within himself. He witnesses to another reality that gives meaning to all that is happening in the galaxy. He gives Luke the greatest gift one man can give another: the vision of a new and truer sense of self.

The Elder Within

I have talked about the Elder archetype emerging, even untriggered, in the form of questioning the status quo and perceiving the flaws in the garment of society. The Elder voice also comes up as a pang of conscience.

The Elder within speaks words that make us uncomfortable. Yet we know he speaks the truth. And we know if we embrace that truth our perspective and our lives will change immensely. This voice of conscience is also the voice of the Elder within. When the deeper conscience speaks, we are called to deeper change. The Elder, like the conscience, tends to speak from a place that is unconcerned with common ideas of success or normal ways of behaving. He calls the adolescent to be unconcerned with peer approval. He has little patience with competition that leads only to dominance. The Elder will call one to pursue deeper values, regardless of the probability of success. The Elder voice will seem odd, though he cares not for odds.

Sometimes a man will start having dreams of an older man who seems contented, peaceful, and wise. This man will often be quite a paradoxical figure as well, something like a Yoda or a Mr. Miyagi, the janitor in *The Karate Kid*. He will often seem inconsequential in the dream. He will seem small. But his image will somehow persist in the waking hours. It is important to give this image attention in our imagination. He will have things to say. His wisdom is for our good, our deepest good. He will often tell us things we already know to be true, but have been afraid, or too busy, to take seriously. He will tell us things that have to do with our initiation.

One valued Elder that appeared in my dreams was quite unusual. He had some facial features of the pope. He was wearing the pope's white, steeple-like hat. However he was about 3 feet tall. He had a gnarly face with a huge under slung jaw. He wore plain, old clothes on a very stocky frame. He just stood there and chuckled, not walking or moving. He looked like a jolly old troll with a miter. He seemed to care little what I thought of him. He seemed to care about what I thought.

I often talk to this man I call John Paul. I ask him questions when I am stuck, just like I speak to my young boy or my adolescent. I ask for perspective when I am down or confused. He often chuckles before he answers, like he is seeing a great cosmic joke that I am not aware of. His answer is usually earthy, often reminding me that I am taking myself and a situation much too seriously. He reminds me of more important values while keeping me humble. He often shows me how I am worrying about the wrong things. He seems to have the best of the pagan and Christian traditions inside of him. I get solace from him. He has helped me with this chapter.

Some psychologies call the inner Elder a wisdom figure. Others call him the inner knower or the higher self. Popularly, there is the idea of intuition or gut feeling, a sense that seems to come from a place beyond ourselves. The ancient Greeks talked of the *daimon*, or guiding spirit, that each man possessed. The ancient Romans called this spirit the genius. Native Americans saw this Elder spirit in totem animals as well as ancestors.

The Elder within is often symbolized in fairy tales by a man similar to John Paul. He is the little old man, troll, elf, beggar, cripple, dog, snake that nobody takes seriously, nobody except the young hero who is out of other answers. The young man or woman, often adolescent, usually has little social power and standing, and even less resources. The insignificant Elder will have the answer to unlock the riddle of the young hero's quest. This wisdom figure is a crucial component of the hero's quest. As we will see, this Elder has been waiting for a very long time for someone humble enough to listen.

I always encourage a man to start an imaginary dialogue with his inner Elders. The dialogue with the Elder is for the purpose of getting in touch with archetypal wisdom that is needed on the personal path. It is also for the purpose of getting motivation to take the next steps. I have worked with many men who have benefited from these internal talks. Finding this inner voice is a big step toward manhood.

It is important to know that the Elder guides us to a sacred place but is not a god. The Elder within is the archetypal knowledge that there is a greater wisdom, a wisdom that we can partake in. This voice draws us to the place where we can confront the source of the wisdom. This voice draws us to the place of initiation.

The Elder in us will have a voice that is countercultural. His voice may be opposed to the patriarchal voice. He pushes the adolescent toward the wilderness, exposing the limitations of the marketplace. He will always bring up a conflict in us. Often the true Elders in our society who have followed their Elder voice come across to us as men of conscience. They seem to do what is right rather than what is acceptable. They disturb us, as they confront our dark inner voices. They are disturbing as they shake up our lives and awaken the Elder within.

Enough

The voice of the Elder within can be a lifelong guide to our deepest identity as men. Just as this Elder will lead us to initiation into the initial Ordeal of manhood he will lead us to the many other transitions we will go through in our entire lives. His voice is enough. Though an external Elder often triggers the conscious step into Ordeal he is there to ultimately introduce a man to his Elder within as I am endeavoring to introduce this wise man to you. I will talk more about the outside Elder in future chapters. However the Elder voice inside a man will be his ultimate guide through initiation and an indispensable counsel for the rest of his life.

Facing the Bull

There is a Spanish proverb. "It is not the same to talk of bulls as to be in the bullring." The Elder, one way or the other, pushes us into the ring. Reading this book or others like it can raise Elder energy and consciousness. However, it is still just talk of bulls or even bull shit. I now encourage you to move toward the bullring by listening to the Elder voice inside. Hopefully he encourages you to read on.

Chapter 12
Death

"Your time has come to die!" Tomme's father, as chief and Elder, has just yelled that at Tomme. The other Elders are also present and in agreement. The suddenness is ominous, as are the prospects. This happens in *The Emerald Forest*.

This will not be a very happy topic. The paradox of the initiatory journey becomes most acute at this time. The young man is not yet a man, though his body is manly. The adolescent within, though needing friends, finds deep aloneness. The middle boy within, who has needed a father, now is faced with other older men, strange Elders. The youngest boy within, who at times still feels he needs a protective mother, finds nobody to protect him.

I will talk now about pain, loss, and death. I will talk about entering the bull ring. I will talk of entering the Ordeal. I will talk of entering the wilderness.

According to the world, and the consensus reality that we live in, this topic will be absurd. The message is crazy. There is profound paradox here. Carl Jung exemplified this paradox in his therapeutic insight. When a friend would tell him good news, about a promotion or a financial windfall, he would usually reply, "I'm sorry to hear that. If we stick together we can get through it." However, if a friend would talk of supposedly bad news, like being laid off from a job, he would say, "Let's open a bottle of wine. This is wonderful news; something good will happen now."

From the view of the marketplace, pain is something to be avoided, loss is tragedy, and death is a defeat. If manhood is based on the assumption that a true man is always on top and feeling good, then this journey to maturity starts to feel like a farce. So here we come to a very mysterious place. Here we come to the great divide between boyhood and manhood. Here we come to the place where pain cannot be avoided if manhood is to be attained. Here we come to the place where death is part of the transition to a changed life, where the pain of loss is the gateway to transformation.

The stakes were so high here that indigenous peoples around the world incorporated their most serious rites to represent the change that was about to happen. It was vital to leave the boy behind. Any remnants of boyhood were considered too dangerous to the new man and to the tribe. Men were needed as fathers and Elders, guaranteeing the physical and spiritual survival of the tribe. Boys had neither the strength, wisdom, nor the courage for this responsibility.

To these people, the harshest, most total symbol of change was death. In death, the old disintegrated. The spirit fled. Old relationships no longer had meaning. Old desires felt corrupted. Old rules no longer held. Nothing was as absolutely finished as something that died. Death was also the symbolic entry to the other side. That is why the boy had to die.

Loss

In aboriginal times, the boy, who would become a man in initiation, was forced to experience death in its many guises. His first death was separation from the community: from his family, village, boyhood pleasures, marketplace goals and successes. Gone were his old routines and schedules. Gone were the familiar sights and sounds of everyday life, the sounds of his mother's food preparations, the sights of commerce in the marketplace, the chatter of his friends. Gone was the familiar anchor, his bedding place that he could return to every night for a sense of stability.

The initiate experienced the loss of his very boyhood, for he would not be treated like a boy again. The immediate boyhood loss he experienced was the loss of nurturance. He had no mother to take away his pain or even sympathize. Nobody to give him a hug. He had no father to share his pain or teach him how to handle it. He experienced the pain of his aloneness. This emotional pain far outweighed the physical pain of facing the elements or evading dangerous predators.

This aloneness, in symbolic death, was often characterized by being painted white, the indigenous people's color of death. If any villager did happen to spy an initiate, or come upon him in the wilderness, they were to treat him as dead and invisible. He was considered a ghost or disembodied spirit. He did not exist in the eyes of the community. Villagers ran from him or ignored him.

The initiate was often sent naked into the wilderness, his physical protection taken away. Sometimes, as happened to Nouk, he had just a loincloth. Even more harshly, his social face, his persona, his way of showing any connection to the community, was destroyed. He did not wear clothing that would identify him as a member of the tribe. He was a nobody, a nowhere man. It is interesting to note, here, that in sleeping dreams where the dreamer is naked the symbolism of nakedness is the loss of persona, the deprivation of role.

The initiate also experienced the death of his boyhood goals. He no longer had his father's goals to shoot for. No longer would his father give him direction and motivation, to structure his life by rules and expectations. He could no longer draw strength from his father's presence. He no longer had a father to cover his mistakes in the hunt, or in the marketplace. He could no longer depend on his father's resources for survival.

To enter the Ordeal he was often taken to the bush where he was taught that he could be killed or devoured by the gods or their animal spirits. The gods were depicted as terrible, mysterious creatures. The gods lived on the other side, close to death, and close to manhood. The gods were revealed to show the process was sacred. They were introduced to show that the journey of manhood ran through the community of the gods. The gods were the gatekeepers of manhood, and death was the gate.

Death was in his aloneness, in the absence of protection, in his deprivation of nurturance, in his confusion about how to survive, in his facing the terrifying gods. For the first time death and manhood became intertwined. Death mysteriously held the secret to his manhood.

Modern Wilderness

It is understandable why a boy decided to face the death experience in an Elder culture. There was the social pressure of family and friends, but also the meaning that initiation held for a boy's future life. There were fathers and Elders to prepare him and explain to him. There was a clear and satisfying sense of manhood on the other side. The boy saw men walking around him who were proof of the efficacy of the process.

But what about today? Why would any man willingly leave the modern village to take this terrifying psychological and spiritual journey? Leaving boyhood doesn't make any sense by today's village standards. Our society has no guidelines that consciously bring a man to inner manhood, painful or not. There is no definite demarcation symbolized by death. Our culture, except through the witness of our religious traditions, recognizes no reality beyond the village, no power beyond the marketplace. If somehow a man finds himself at the village boundary, feeling unsatisfied and alienated and confused, he can spend the rest of his life stuck there. He will stay an emotional adolescent at the crossroads, or he will regress back to the boy's world of his mother's dreams or his father's rules.

As I said, the Elder points the way to another reality. Even though there is death, there is also the promise of a whole different life. The Elder declares there is another reality that is actually more real than what is in the village. This other reality is represented by the wilderness, the other side. Yet the other reality today, as in the aboriginal mentality, involves giving up most of what a man formerly knew to be real. In modern times it means giving up what a man thought manhood to be.

An important modern Elder, Thomas Moore, author of the book *Care of the Soul,* has written, "Care of the soul requires acceptance of all this dying. The temptation is to champion our familiar ideas about life right up to the last second, but it may be necessary in the end to give them up, to enter into the movement of death."

From a more secular viewpoint, yet showing archetypal dimensions, Ken Burns, the famous documentary filmmaker, has said that "regardless of the progress of things, the essential human experience is of loss." He goes on to say that "there can't be any human equation, any truthfulness, without the awareness of loss."

The modern wilderness is in the geography of the inner life, which some people, such as Thomas Moore, call the soul. The modern Ordeal brings one face to face with the wilderness of one's own soul. This wilderness is the other side of the reality we see outside, in the physical world. The father's voice speaks of the outer life of the village and marketplace. The time comes when we need to listen, instead, to the Elder's voice, and give up the voice of the father. The Elder speaks of the reality of the soul and the spirit.

Up to this point in a modern man's journey there is nothing that has alerted a man to his inner life. He has not been introduced to his own wilderness within. When men are forced to look within, thrown into the inner wilderness by a separation experience, most see very little topography, and feel only emptiness. This is why the inner wilderness is often first depicted as a desert or a void.

Men are little prepared for the Ordeal of exploring their inner life. So most men have little idea of what they really want and need, outside of what is expected of them. They do not know what would satisfy their souls or their inner longings. Instead they often recite the routine formula for happiness: a "good job" and "taking care of my family." Or a younger man will talk of finding the "right woman" to love him. These goals are not bad. They are good goals in themselves. However they have no imprint of the wilderness journey. A modern man will often recite his goals with little enthusiasm or inner conviction because they don't come from his soul. They don't ignite his passion, and true passion comes from the soul.

When I speak to a man who talks of his "duty," or his "responsibility," or about doing what is "right," I know I am in the presence of an uninitiated man. He will be a good man, a sincere man. Yet he will parrot the patriarchs, not separating enough to be his own man.

To Carl Jung, the wilderness was the unconscious, including the collective unconscious. His message was clearly that we had to descend into the wilderness within if we were to find real life. A book title of his describes this journey, *Modern Man in Search of a Soul.*

The modern Ordeal of initiation involves moving voluntarily into the wilderness within. The pain of modern man's Ordeal involves the pain of the inner journey. To most men this inward journey means facing feelings and thoughts at the very edges of awareness. To most men this journey means exploring very alien territory.

It is interesting that both ancient Elders and modern depth psychologists, as well as those in the mythopoetic men's movement, talk of going down as the way of going in to the wilderness. We need to go down into our feelings and intuitions to find our manhood. We have to go down into our emotional pain. We have to go down into the confusion and terror of first facing the feelings we were taught to ignore. This is invariably a terrible, frightening place when we first descend into it because the first feelings we face are the fears that have lurked in the shadows of our consciousness for a very long time.

I am struck by the dreams of men in the middle of this struggle. Men at this time often dream of going down into caves or basements or sinkholes or over cliffs. It is often a frightening experience. Sometimes, when they see these images in their dreams, their dream self is afraid to go on. At other times they find themselves in the underworld against their will. Luke Skywalker had this going down experience when Yoda sent him into the cave filled with snakes, insects, darkness and his shadow self, Darth Vader.

This down place is especially frightening to men who were prematurely thrown into the Ordeal as children. Premature separation is terribly traumatic. I talked of mothers who couldn't consistently nurture because of their own depression or physical illness. These are traumatic childhood separations. To these men the Ordeal holds little hope, the inner life symbolizing tragedy. It is especially difficult to talk to a man about going down to his inner life when he associates this inner life with so much trauma. Men is this state need a great deal of preparation before they are ready for this Ordeal so that they are not retraumatized.

For most men this going down is unnerving and terribly uncomfortable, but not traumatic. Forcing oneself into the presence of feelings and ideas that are foreign and unforeseen is not fun. Facing the loss of one's manly persona is very daunting. Starting to realize the losses of the past that have been stored away, unfelt, bodes a great deal of pain. Looking at the possibility of future separations brings no consolation. Looking at life without former structures seems overwhelming and terrifying.

Depression

Most men experience the start of the emotional Ordeal as a decline. They react to this initial part of the Ordeal with depression. They are depressed because they have just consciously suffered a loss, a death. They feel victimized. They feel cut off, out of touch with their normal life and the life of the community. They are also depressed because they are at a loss to know how to handle this tangle of feelings they have fallen into.

Though depression is endemic in younger and older men, men rarely recognize depression in themselves. Rarely will a man say he is sad, never that he is depressed. One reason is that the word depression for men represents some kind of weakness or defeat. To admit to sadness or depression is considered unmanly.

Also, depression is painful. It is the first pain of the Ordeal. Men are not taught how to handle inner pain. The uninitiated boy inside will always feel that pain is unnecessary or shaming. The boy, who is unprepared for the Ordeal by good fathering, will always instinctively run from the wilderness and the Ordeal. He will run blindly without thinking. He will run from his depression and anyone who reminds him of it. Later, there will be many rationalizations for his flight. Some men will say that their pain is caused by someone else, possibly a wife or boss, and it's someone else's problem to fix. Others will talk of a long series of misfortunes and their need to find some relief rather than more pain. Others will say they just can't take the pain any more.

A man who is depressed is very confused and often angry at his own confusion. Men aren't supposed to be confused. A real man is supposed to be in control and on top of things. He doesn't realize that confusion is part of his necessary depression. He doesn't realize that confusion is a natural reaction to the Ordeal, and being at a loss is where he's supposed to be.

Most men, instead of accepting their confusion and loss, will rage against it. I talked about rage when I talked of addictions and rageaholics. Rage is the uninitiated reaction to pain. Rage medicates the pain while blaming it on somebody else. Rage is a retreat to the masculine persona, instead of feeling the powerlessness of the Ordeal. Rage is a last resort.

In terms of the Ordeal, rage effectively keeps a man a boy by blocking his path to the wilderness. Rage silences the Elder voice within and effectively stops any process of being with feelings. Consequently, many men end up alternating between the rage of fighting off their Ordeal and the numbness of being cut off from their inner life. However, below every man's rage lurks his depression and confusion. Just at the other side of his rage stands the boundaries of the wilderness. Within the rage is a frightened boy yearning for a wise masculine guide to explain his pain. If he found this guide he wouldn't rage. He would cry. He might then use his healthy anger to voluntarily set boundaries, separate, and explore the world beyond the village.

It would be easy to just pity the young, helpless, mother's boy if he weren't in a man's body. Unfortunately, a rage reaction to separation is dangerous. This man/boy can do a great deal of damage in his rages. Since an uninitiated man won't own his inner pain and accept his separation, he will believe that others are causing his pain. This produces a kind of paranoia. A man will then try to destroy, in a childish way, anything that he feels causes the pain of the moment. Unfortunately this includes loved ones and other innocent people.

If a man has some fathering, enough to dutifully hold his rage inside, his rage will often go into his body. Rage turned inward fuels a deeper depression. Most men will experience this deep depression as fatigue, physical powerlessness, and lack of motivation. This is a sign the depression is going deeply into the body. The pain can then turn to illness. This may explain why men live on average 5 years less than women. Paradoxically, the men who live a shorter time are often the ones who are more responsible about their anger. I have talked to many sensitive men whose responsible, unguided frustration is slowly killing them.

I mentioned that women can admit to depression much more easily in our culture. Because of this, for a long time women were seen by the dark patriarchy as the only emotional weaklings who were depressed. As a result, the definition of depression and its symptoms have been feminized. Even in psychological circles, the definition of depression describes feminine depression. Therefore, another reason a man does not realize he is depressed, is because he is observing the wrong symptoms. Where a woman strongly feels melancholy, a man will feel only emptiness. Where a woman may react to depression with silence, a man will often react with irritability and anger. Where a woman can have an illness that keeps her from working, a man feels only a deep fatigue while he is working. While both may feel a lessening of sexual drive, to a man this is a sign of loss of manhood or loss of love, unrelated to depression. It is easier for a man to lose his depression in addiction, and more accepted. And for a man, his lack of motivation and direction may have been coming on for most of his adult life, making his depressive situation feel normal.

This last condition, a chronic, low level depression, is endemic in our society. This is the depression that Terrence Real, in his book *I Don't Want to Talk about It,* talks about when he estimates that 50-80% of men have a hidden depression. This "normal" depression goes unnoticed, like water is unnoticed by the fish. Real talks of men's depression being covered over by addiction or rage or numbness, therefore unnoticed and untreated. He calls this omnipresent condition "covert depression." The clinical name is disthymia.

I believe this covert, disthymic depression is caused primarily, not by genetics or brain chemistry, but from the lack of any guidance in the psychological initiation process. Depression is separation with no next steps. This low level depression is existential, not a result of trauma or genes. It is loss without a leader. Initiation with no Elder. It is stuck grief, grief below the radar. This disthymic depression is the foundation for any deeper depression that will result from sudden separation as an adult.

Men who come in to my office are often extremely depressed. These men have been prematurely thrown into the Ordeal with little or no preparation from fathers and Elders. Their rage has been spent with no results. They are confused, alone, and terribly sad. They experience a great deal of fatigue. They have little motivation for anything. They have a hard time concentrating on work. They paradoxically have sleep problems, most often insomnia. They have often lost their appetite and many pounds. These are the classic signs of a clinical depression for men.

These men have been separated from the familiar with no warning. They never realized this could happen to them. They never realized this should happen to them. They are going through a death experience. They feel dead. Their pain is the only sign they are alive.

Turning the Tragedy

I have talked of the tragedies of separation that men experience. I have talked of these deaths. I have talked of these losses, but let's go over some of them again.

Some men's death is the involuntary separation from a mother object. They have just lost a wife or lover. Many are reliving a former separation that was so traumatic they want nothing to do with the wilderness again. They have had little if any fathering to prepare them for the Ordeal. They feel like the very young 6 year-old, suddenly lost in a big, dark woods. Their rage is spent. They feel like crying.

Other men's loss is in the marketplace. Some have been addicted to work and have lost a job or an important position. Their whole manhood depended on their work status and it has been involuntarily lost. They have used work much of their life to keep from experiencing their inner pain. They have been unconsciously separated from the father's world and thrown into a wilderness they knew nothing about. They are depressed.

Still other men have been a success and found that success has not gotten them what they thought they wanted. They are slowly losing a dream that has sustained them through their whole adult life. They are losing the adolescent fantasy that had sustained them through an unguided, unhappy adult adolescence. Theirs is a slow, insidious depression.

In fact, a depressive reaction is normal for a death. The healthy reaction to loss is grief. Separation naturally brings sadness. The loss of boyhood pleasures and dreams should bring mourning. A man is much more authentic mourning than raging or resigning. We must learn as men to accept our depression and make it overt. Then we can deal with it without shame. So do all the modern Elders who are familiar with the soul. Without depression a man is stuck on his road to manhood. By not accepting depression a man will not accept his loss. By not accepting depression a man will not accept his initiatory death.

Depression in response to confusion is also normal. Carl Jung said that depression is the natural reaction to the ego confronting the unconscious. To the small ego the unconscious seems overwhelming. The ego wants a map of this wilderness when there isn't one. The ego wants a guarantee when there isn't one.

The Elder says paradoxically that this is the way and you're not supposed to know the way. Rumi, an Elder and Sufi poet, said, "Sell your cleverness and buy bewilderment." A friend of mine, Reverend Peter Monkres, has written of this wilderness of the soul. In speaking of the entrance to this wilderness he says, "It is important to note that there is nothing wrong or demeaning about one's fear in entering the inner realms. Rather than repressing our anxiety about inner journeying or denying it, should we not suggest plainly that since no traveler knows exactly what to expect, such feelings are natural?"

One of the great Elders of our time is Robert Bly. Bly was one of the first men in our time to explain the need for men to go inside to do their men's work. He explained depression as a form of grief. He talked of men's work as primarily grief work. He explained to modern men that grief is the conscious act of descent, a conscious going down. Bly said that men had to go down into their feelings to find themselves and grief was the doorway to their feelings. Bly pointed out that grief was also the doorway to the Ordeal of initiation and the exit out of their lifelong numbness.

Bly's message, of the necessity of conscious grief and deep masculine initiation, spawned the men's movement. He reminded men that pain was necessary for growth. He talked in the story of Iron John of finding the wild man, our true masculine self, at the bottom of the pond of our soul, by draining the pond cup by cup. This draining was the slow, laborious inner work of the Ordeal. Coincidentally, a drained pond forms a depression.

Dealing with Depression

What I try to do with a man who is depressed is tell him it is not unmanly to be depressed, to feel impotent, to feel defeated. I try to tell him that he needs to go into the depression and find his answers there. I tell him I can't and won't try to take away his pain. But I will stand by him in the pain and try to help him understand it. I appeal to the man's hardwired sense of mission. I explain his new initiatory mission and why it is so important. I try to awaken the latent warrior energy inside him.

The warrior part of the ego is no longer intimidated by the wilderness when he knows the new parameters of his mission. Men who learn the inner mission make remarkably fast progress. All they need is some King/ Elder energy to define their purpose. They then are able to move with their warrior energy into their inner wilderness.

I encourage a man to stand in his confusion while not impulsively acting to relieve it. I encourage him to stand his ground like a warrior in battle, guarding the turf of his Ordeal. I ask him not to retreat under pressure or pain. I show him the direction: down, into his feelings, into his unconscious, into his soul. I tell him the journey is hopeful and necessary. I tell him it is normal, actually healthy, to feel sad and confused and wonder why things make no sense. I recommend Elders to read and study. I talk of other men going through the same experience, of men's groups and friendship. I tell him the mission is absolutely necessary for himself, his family, his community.

I sometimes relate the story of how people in Malaysia catch rice monkeys, a delicacy for them. Malaysians know these monkeys love rice. They also know these monkeys can decimate their rice fields. What they do to catch these monkeys is bore a small hole in a coconut just big enough for a monkey to get its hand inside. Then they half fill the coconut with rice and tie the coconut to a tree. The rice monkeys will find this coconut very quickly. They spy the rice and reach inside for a handful. Their problem is once they have a handful they cannot get their hand out. They are stuck. Nine times out of ten the villagers will find the monkey there, holding the rice, ready for capture. Rice monkeys cannot let go of what they have, even though there is more food than they could possibly eat in the wild. We can be like these monkeys by not being willing to suffer the loss of something that will lead us to our destruction.

Robert Johnson talks of men he counsels who are so depressed that they are suicidal. They are at the same place we are talking about, overwhelmed by the Ordeal. He tells them that they do need to commit suicide, *without harming their bodies*. He then talks of the voluntary emotional death that we have been talking about. He relates advice of Meizumi Roshi, a Zen master in Los Angeles, who once said, "Why don't you die now and enjoy the rest of your life?"

There is another Zen saying that I try to remember: "Die while alive and be completely dead. Then do whatever you will, all is good."

Luke's Death

In the Star Wars myth, Obi Wan is the second father that shows Luke some of this mystery of death. In order for Luke to escape Darth Vader, Obi Wan returns to fight Vader. In the prelude to the fight, Obi Wan warns Vader that if he is killed he will come back more powerful than ever. Vader ignores this paradoxical statement. Obi Wan is then killed.

It seems Obi Wan lets himself be killed as soon as he knows Luke has escaped. Obi Wan shows Luke about death for a higher purpose. As a second father he shows Luke that he no longer needs to fear death. By showing Luke his death Obi Wan models the behavior that Luke will eventually follow to save his father's soul. In the meantime, Obi Wan returns to Luke after his death. He is now an Elder through his death transformation. He returns as inspiration and insight, giving Luke the encouragement and wisdom he needs to overcome the forces of darkness. He repeatedly encourages Luke to trust the Force and his own calling. This is how Obi Wan becomes stronger. He becomes the Elder voice in Luke, to help Luke face his own death.

Luke does not finish his training with Yoda but leaves to rescue his friends. In fact, Luke has failed Yoda's test in the underground cave where he meets Darth Vader. He hasn't yet learned from his depression. In the depression of the cave Luke attacks Darth Vader and cuts off his head. He has given in to hate and anger, unable to handle his depression. His rage is uncontrolled. He then sees himself in his father's helmet, the shadow self that could follow the Vader voice.

It is upon leaving that Luke hears from Obi Wan. Obi Wan tells Luke not to give in to hate. Hate, modern rage, is the doorway to the dark side. It is the anesthetic that dulls the pain of depression.

Luke finds Han and Leia at the mining colony of Lando Calrizzian. There, Darth Vader is waiting for him. Again Luke attacks in an effort to save his friends and save the galaxy. Luke has grown significantly in the tools of the warrior and he has a good warrior's heart in his compassion for his friends and the community. However, he has still not completed his Ordeal. He does not know how to handle the dark father voice.

Darth tries to be a second father to Luke. He tries to get Luke to follow his patriarchal program. Darth tells Luke he will complete Luke's training. He tantalizes Luke with the temptation of joining him in overthrowing the Emperor and ruling together.

Darth then devastates Luke with the message that he is Luke's father. Darth follows by tempting Luke to power while honoring his father. They can rule as father and son. Luke is terribly torn. He has a hardwired loyalty to his father, even though Darth is a dark father. I'm sure he also wondered how much like his father he really was. I'm sure Luke also questioned his motives, his values and his strength at this point. His confusion was overwhelming. Father loyalty is one of the strongest emotions any man will feel.

It is at this point that Darth cuts off Luke's right hand because Luke resists his father voice. This cut is the symbol of Luke's father wound, as well as a show of dominance by the patriarch. Darth understood only power and was losing confidence in his ability to win Luke's loyalty. In the hands of an Elder this ritual wound would be ultimately uplifting. In this context it is merely a show of hierarchy and control. The right hand was Luke's hand of dominance. Darth was showing who was boss.

Most of us would have given in at this point. Here was the promise of power, possibly for some good. Here was the saving of his friends. Here was reuniting with his flesh and blood in a way that honored and showed loyalty to a father he had always admired. Here was his dream, since his father could make him a Jedi warrior. Here were all the symbols of manhood that the patriarchy bestows.

To return to his father would mean giving in to the dark side. Luke had once failed this test in the cave on Degoba. Giving in was yielding to the patriarchy. It was honoring his father. It was being a realist. It was getting with the program. It was protecting his friends, being responsible to his new family. It was all that a man rationalizes to himself when he says you can't fight the system.

Luke's only other choice was to go down, way down to certain death. The promontory he stood on was lonely, dangerous, and utterly desolate. To let go seemed certain death. Luke's only hope was the Force. There was no other tangible way of escape. He had to totally trust the Force, letting go of every security. There was no plan. There was no agenda. There was only overwhelming uncertainty and radical separation. Luke chooses death over the patriarchy. He lets go totally. He accepts the fall of depression.

Wilderness

When a man lets go of anger, faces his depression, stops causing pain, and lets go of his patriarchal script, he reaches the threshold of the Ordeal. In Luke's case his Elders have now done most of their job. They have brought him to the point of voluntary movement to the other side. He has entered his final Ordeal. He has entered the wilderness.

Chapter 13
Humility

L ast chapter I talked about death, loss and depression. I talked about the other side, outside the village. The place beyond the village boundaries, the wilderness of the ancients, was a mysterious, terrifying place. The boy had to grow up a great deal even in taking those first few steps into the wilderness. He had to have great trust in his Elders and great faith in the ultimate benevolence of the universe. He had to go through most of the journey alone and with no clear direction. He had to face death, a symbol for risking everything. When he stepped into the world of men he left the childish boy behind.

Hubris

When stepping into the wilderness, there was another form of death that the boy had to face. This death involved suffering humiliation by allowing himself to be humbled. This suffering had to do with the death of his pride and the loss of supremacy of his own will. It had to do with renouncing the swagger of the young adolescent. It had to do with renouncing the dark side of the ego.

The Greeks had a name for this pride, they called it *hubris*. They understood that if a man fell prey to hubris he would start acting like a god, thinking himself perfect and powerful. The man with hubris would start to feel above the rules of mere mortals. He would rise up instead of going down. The man with hubris would feel no responsibility to anyone or anything higher than himself. He would reside in the heights, not the depths, safe from pain and the compassion that pain engenders. He would be cool. He would be a narcissist.

The Greeks also understood that uncontrolled violence and passion could come from hubris. The man with hubris would be an arrogant ronin, using his warrior energy only for his own self-interest. This man would be a threat to the web of community, including gods and men.

The Greeks believed that any man acting with hubris would eventually draw the jealousy of the real gods, and dire consequences would follow. Nemesis, the goddess of righteous anger, would eventually strike down that man in the name of all the gods, for no mortal had the right to act like a god. The Greeks understood that a man needed to be humble in the presence of gods, instead of trying to usurp their power. They understood that the more a man made himself his own god the more destructive he would be to himself and the community.

Humility involves losing our pride, our hubris. It involves submitting our egos to something greater in the personality. It involves losing adolescent fantasies in favor of manly dreams. Humility involves moving from will to willing, willing to be open to a greater wisdom, a higher power, and the needs of the community.

Ego

This is a time to talk more about the ego. For this is the time in a man's journey when his relationship to ego needs to transform. Here, again, is the need for change and the loss that change entails. This is the time when the ego wants to go one way while the initiate must go another.

I mentioned ego in previous chapters when I talked of the ego in relation to warrior energy and the father. The time of the father is the time of the boy's emerging ego. The wise father bolsters his son's ego by acknowledging his talents and strengths. The father helps a boy find his ego strength and warrior energy, the strength he will need to endure Ordeal.

I also talked of an ego injury when the ego confronts the mystery of the unconscious. This is the beginning of the adolescent's initiation and the genesis of the older boy's necessary new stance towards his ego. This is the time of father separation, where the wilderness rather than the marketplace is the teacher. Depression is a consequence of a humbled and wounded ego. Ego injury is then the start of the humiliation that leads to manhood.

But what is this ego that needs to be humbled, that needs to experience a death? In lay vocabulary the ego is often interchangeably used with the word self. The self in selfish or self-centered is often understood to be the same as the ego in egotistical and egocentric. This interchangeability of self and ego in lay vocabulary leads to confusion. For example, is self-love good or bad? Does it relate to self-esteem or selfishness? What is self-control?

Should we control the self? Why would it need controlling? Is becoming selfless a virtue or psychic suicide? What is a healthy ego? Is it good to have a strong ego? To be egotistical seems bad, but looking out for number one seems good. Is it good to act like one has no ego?

For purposes of this discussion I will use ego to mean our conscious will and conscious motivations. The ego in psychological terms is that part of our psyche that we consciously have control over. It is the I we think of when we make a decision or act on one.

The ego really begins to exercise its strength in adolescence. It is the ego that starts to build a unique persona. It is the ego which starts to act more independently, after borrowing strength from the good father. It is the ego that starts to build a history of choices that makes us a distinct personality.

Ego strength has a lot to do with warrior energy. It has a lot to do with getting things done and keeping to one's goals. We need ego strength to struggle against regressive addictions, to stop acting on irrational moods of rage and blame, and to fight the tendency to give up because of pain. The ego makes the choice of goals and then sets boundaries to protect them.

The ego, like the healthy adolescent, is an important part of us that we will need our entire lives. However, like the unguided adolescent, the ego can make choices that ignore everything but its own regressive needs. Unless it is fathered and Eldered well, the ego can be preoccupied only with pleasure or power and so can be easily manipulated by the dark patriarchy and become stuck in that darkness. The dark side of the ego then gives birth to a dark pride.

Indigenous peoples, like the Greeks, knew that a man with an unhumbled ego was a dangerous man. He would start acting like an autonomous, renegade rather than submitting to the harmony of the community. This is why these people submitted their young adolescents to initiation so early. Otherwise there could be chaos and destruction in the village, as the egos of their young men would submit to nothing besides their own testosterone driven desires.

When I talked in the last chapter of the death of the ego I was talking of the movement of the initiate into a space where he is not in control, and his ego is frustrated. During initiation his ego needs for pleasure and his ego needs for status and power are frustrated. The adolescent, by moving into the wilderness and away from the marketplace, is forced to assume a very lowly position. He loses any semblance of a strong persona. Lacking the status and power that the marketplace can give, he is lost and powerless. He has no clothes signifying power or rank. He is a nobody, unnoticed by the rest of the village. The Elder has purposely put the boy in a space where he is ritually humiliated. He has done this to teach him humility.

Indigenous peoples saw this humiliating experience as essential to a man's growth. They saw that the ego needs to be put in its rightful place before the man can emerge. Notice that the ego is not meant to be destroyed or seriously wounded. It is only forced out of the center of the personality. The ego no longer stays an independent warrior, but is being readied to find more significant values. The warrior ego is being readied to find his King.

In psychology we call the over-identification with one's ego a form of narcissism. A narcissist is the stuck boy who only worries about his pleasures and his manly image. He is really weak and confused from his father wound. His only answer to the feeling of weakness is to work on a mask and illusion of strength. He is obsessed with ego needs and the fear of being unmasked.

When a man feels a blow to his ego, we call this a narcissistic injury. This is a boy injury. An uninitiated man will always feel a narcissistic injury as a dark humiliation. His pride will be hurt. His ego will feel naked and weak as his mask is punctured. Like a wounded animal, this is the time he is most dangerous. For example, a man may not get the promotion he thinks he deserves and has worked for. Or his children do not treat him with respect, not listening to his warnings or advice. His wife or lover might make comments that point to his addictions or weaknesses. His wife or lover may question his job or his career direction or his work addiction. Maybe, like Rodney Dangerfield, he feels he gets no respect at all.

An uninitiated man will see these injuries as humiliation only and as a tragic defeat. He will often react with rage or neurotic depression, his ego out of control. When all a man has is his boy ego protected by a fragile persona, a narcissistic injury feels fatal. Some men totally collapse here. Others will call on any ego strength they have left to wield power through violence, and even war, over those who are weaker in order to feel the illusion of strength. Neither will use their inevitable wounding as initiatory.

Ritual and Humility

In ancient initiation, a boy is purposely and ritually humiliated. His healthy adolescent boisterousness and cockiness is confronted. He is shown that the world does not revolve around his pleasure needs as in the maternal world, or his power needs as in the paternal world. He is shown that his true power and identity resides beyond his own ego control and needs. His natural ego development is pushed to the next level.

The humiliation can take many forms. In one form, the boy's clothes are taken away and he is forced to go around naked. His lack of status is emphasized by having nothing to hang stripes and medals and a power tie on. Clothes symbolize our social role. As is said, "Clothes make the man." Clothes communicate our persona. By going around naked the boy is forced to be only himself without pretense and without pride and without persona. He is stripped to the essentials. He doesn't have a preconceived role in this land outside the village.

Men in counseling often dream of finding themselves naked in an unusual situation, feeling embarrassed and humiliated. This type of dream can be a form of Elder warning, telling a man he needs more humility and less ego. This dream can also tell him he is deeper within an initiatory experience in his life. It is a benevolent warning from the Elder within that he is on the threshold of inner transformation and needs to pay attention. He needs to get his ego out of the way.

Another form of initiatory humiliation involved the boy being forced to submit to a painful ritual. This rite taught the boy humility, as well as the proper place of pain in his life. Even today, in one tribe, the boy is told to look up while the Elder takes a hammer and chisel and suddenly knocks out a tooth. Later whenever a man feels the hole in that part of his mouth he is reminded of his new role and the humility he needs to fulfill it.

Submission to the Elders by accepting these indignities brought a boy to the threshold of the new experiences and new learning that will make him a man. Submission precedes mission, as Michael Meade reminds us. Here the adolescent submits to Elder energy. Here the ego submits to the wisdom of the Elder within.

Dark Humiliation

The problem with the egotistical older boy, and the narcissistic man, is that he has not been ritually humiliated by an Elder. In other words, he has not consciously been taught the meaning and importance of submitting to the wisdom of Ordeal. He has not learned that humility is a most important part of his journey toward manhood. He has been let down by the older men in his culture.

We all have an archetypal need to be humbled by a wise Elder. The archetypal need endures whether it is satisfied or not. Men constantly, yet unconsciously, look to satisfy this need. In the wrong hands this humiliation can be a form of brain washing. It can use archetypal energy to create an inhuman, demeaning experience. The humiliation can be used to subjugate rather than liberate. Shame rather than natural curiosity becomes the prime motivator. The modern patriarchy is based on this type of dark, negative humiliation.

We are mostly a culture of dark Elders who have come up through the ranks, believing in the inherent motivation of shame. This cultural system is able to function only through the work of humiliated drones out to prove themselves as men by humiliating others. Our culture is based on winners and losers, on dark competition, on domination and dark humiliation. From being a dying cockroach in boot camps to being demeaned as the low man on the corporate totem pole, the idea is taught that the only good place is to be on top, while nice guys finish last. The place of pride is always to be first. Even a man or a team that is a close second is a sorry loser. The system works on the motivation not to lose, not to suffer another shame.

As I said, the need to be humbled by an older man is hardwired in every man. If a boy's father is weak or absent he will unconsciously look for someone else to submit to. If there are no genuine Elders around, he will look to any man who takes an interest and promises him manhood. This could take the form of the military, a gang, a political party, a corporation, a religion or cult. It always amazes me how strongly some men can feel bonded to an institution like the army or a corporation. Because of hardwired need and dark Eldering there is a short distance between corporation and cult. The cult is just a starker example of manipulated loyalty through dark humiliation.

Consider the humiliation that medical students go through in residency. There are long hours, little pay, harassment by older doctors, all in the name of professionalism. No wonder many doctors are then seen as arrogant toward others, and rarely admit to mistakes. Witness the hazing in many fraternities, the empty ritual of humiliation that creates the leaders of tomorrow. Witness the humiliation of boot camp, often an empty initiation into the art of humiliating and intimidating others.

When a boy is initiated by an uninitiated man, he is humiliated for no higher purpose. He then unconsciously takes on the negative values of his initiator. I have often talked to men who have come to the embarrassing conclusion that they tend to act under stress just like the father that humiliated them.

One of the greatest obstacles to a man seeking help from an Elder, including counselor Elders, is the feeling that he will go through another dark humiliation and be shamed. Coupled with this fear is the lack of respect for an Elder who has relatively little social status. This situation is one of the most vivid tragedies of an Elderless culture. A true Elder, like Yoda, is first seen as irrelevant and powerless. A man is taught to submit only to those who have more power in the patriarchy. He is used to this type of humiliation. He is willing to go through the shame only because he is promised patriarchal power. Submitting to a man with little patriarchal power is seen as ludicrous. The counselor, or other wise Elder, is considered the janitor in the basement, while a man looks for manhood in the executive suites.

Humility and Counsel

When a man comes in for counseling I realize that this is one of the hardest things he has ever done. Often a man will make a remark to that effect. I tell him I recognize his courage which I genuinely honor. I then try to Elder him by talking of how this first step of humility is the key to the answers he is seeking. And I tell him honestly, as in all initiations, that he is not submitting to me. He is submitting to something bigger than both of us.

In counseling I try to show men that feeling powerless is a normal part of growing. The object of growing is not winning or being perfect or being in control. Embracing error and humiliation is on the road to something much more satisfying. I also try to show him that the shame he feels is needless. There need be no shame attached to admitting confusion or making a mistake or feeling powerless. Shame is the result of a dark humiliation, the work of the dark father. Accepting powerlessness in the realm of the soul is a sign of wisdom.

In counseling I talk of healthy examples of submission and ritual humiliation. One of the most powerful examples is in the 12-step process. This process started through Alcoholics Anonymous in the 1930's. The AA movement has a lot of similarities to the initiatory process and is one of the healthiest and most vibrant parts of our culture. Scott Peck says, only half-jokingly, that the most important function of most churches is to have AA meetings in their basements.

The first four steps of the 12-step process involve ritual submission to a higher power. Jung called this submission part of a spiritual cure. The alcoholic admits he is powerless in dealing with alcohol and vows to rely on a higher power to combat his disease. He forsakes his egocentrism, his prideful reply of being able to quit on his own at any time. He then humbly goes about the next steps, rigorously finding and admitting to previous errors and trying to make amends for them. He doesn't promise not to make mistakes again. He makes a good faith commitment to stick to the process of submission and humility. These are hard but very courageous steps.

Christianity, and the Abrahamic tradition, stress ritual humiliation and the power of redeeming pain. Christ "emptied himself and took the form of a slave," not relying on a powerful persona to convert or intimidate. He "did not grasp at equality with God" as a form of narcissism and ego inflation. He talked of the "humbled being exalted," walking that talk. He suffered the overwhelming humiliation of the crucifixion. He accepted death as the gateway to transformation. He said "not my will but thine be done," humbling himself before the God of the wilderness

The prophets before the time of Christ were continually called by God to humble the kings of the Jews, many of whom suffered periodically from hubris. They did this at considerable risk to themselves. To most, the risk was so considerable that, like Jonah, they ran the other way. Yahweh had to humble them first before they learned to humble kings.

Vader and Humiliation

In the Star Wars myth, Darth Vader tries to initiate Luke to the dark side by humiliating him. Luke's ritual wound, cutting off his right hand, came when he would not submit to the dark power. Darth desperately wanted Luke to become angry and cynical through this wounding. He wanted him to rage. He also wanted to trigger Luke's hardwired need to submit to an older, stronger man.

Back to the promontory, the heart of Luke's test of father separation: Darth tells Luke he is his father. Luke is devastated. He had idolized his father. His father was the motivation for his life. Luke suddenly suffers a life shattering betrayal. It would be so easy to submit to the man who has humiliated him, the man who seems so crucial to his initiation. He still loves and honors his father. And his father is asking him to join him in ruling the galaxy as father and son. Luke could do much good as ruler if he submitted to his patriarchal father. As Darth says, "Your destiny lies with me."

Luke is in the grips of a strong temptation to egocentrism and power and misguided loyalty. Darth tells Luke he can "end the destructive conflict and restore order." This is a good end, even though the means are questionable. He need only submit to his father's lead, to the dark humiliation, for stability to return, especially the stability of the marketplace. How many cultures have sold their soul for the sake of supposed safety and stability and marketplace gain? There is such a parallel here to Christ's temptations in the desert. Power and pleasure would be given in return for loyalty to a dark force. And the power is promised for good ends.

Obi Wan had previously warned Luke that this high road of dark submission and uncontrolled anger was the road of hate "that leads to the dark side." Yet Luke was hurt and angry. He was angry at Obi Wan for not telling him about his father. He was angry at Vader for his devastating humiliation. He was angry and miserable and ready to take his anger out on someone. Vader had him where he wanted him. The combination of filial loyalty and humiliation seemed to be working. Anger was turning Luke. Separation from father meant only death. Submission meant survival for both Luke and his friends.

How many men, in Luke's position, have felt their only choice was to submit to a system or a boss that they couldn't believe in? Maybe they thought they could right the wrongs later, when they achieved more power. Maybe they felt they had no choice because of their need to provide for and protect their families. In any case, they felt it best to submit to the dark patriarchy, feeling they couldn't fight the system. How many then took their anger out on subordinates in frustration and self-contempt? How many more men succumbed to a numbing, devastating depression? In many ways this dark submission is at the heart of most male depression.

It is not good or appropriate to judge these men, for they are us. We are all struggling with these depressing choices. We have all made choices we are ashamed of, or had to live with choices that depress us. Like Luke, we have been confronted with great pressure to submit to a dark patriarchy that we may not believe in. Our egos have been sorely tempted. The up side seems so ego satisfying, the down side too intimidating or too humbling.

Luke does courageously separate. By dark patriarchal standards he becomes a fool. He gives up everything that is important in the father's world. However, by the standards of the Jedi warrior, he has started the final stages of his initiation. He has contained his anger. He has submitted to the death that Obi Wan and Yoda had taught him about. He plummets down into the abyss, out of control and out of answers. He jumps into a void. He moves to certain death. He risks everything for a higher purpose that he has only heard about from his Elders.

Beyond the Ego

The power of initiation is to submit to something beyond the ego and the patriarchy. In the initiatory process the egocentric man dies and is replaced by the humble, self-aware man. This emerging man is humbled before new realizations and wisdom beyond his ego. He doesn't need to pretend anymore that he is important and manly. He doesn't need the respect of the marketplace or marketplace success. He is open to lessons of the wilderness. He moves from will to willing. He is ready for the heart of his Ordeal.

Chapter 14
The Other Side

W
e are now ready to move onto traditionally sacred ground. Sacred ground, the other side for indigenous peoples, contained the mystery of who they were as a people. It was where their wisdom resided. It also contained every man's answer to the mystery of who he was as a man.

This was the place where their Creator still dwelt, including the creator of their manhood. It was a timeless place. It was a dangerous place. Death was all around. So was new life.

As I speak about this place, and the modern wilderness within, I will be talking more and more with the words of monks and mystics and shamans, philosophers and poets and priests. These are the people who have been exploring this realm for thousands of years. Psychology is in its infancy compared to the masters and priests of all the religions of the world and countless mystics who have chosen to journey unaccompanied within.

As we move forward, I will stay grounded in the science of psychology, as psychology is what I know. Yet the closer we come to the Ordeal, the closer we come to the traditions of spirituality, even in terms of answers to the question of manhood. Scott Peck realized this mysterious conjunction in his book, *The Road Less Traveled*. He saw "no distinction between the process of achieving spiritual growth and achieving mental growth." I cannot go that far in this book; however, I realize that achieving both psychological and spiritual manhood requires the same leaps of faith into the death experience, the same renunciations of former attitudes and lifestyles, and the same humility toward a wisdom and energy source greater than one's own. This is why I call this journey toward manhood a psychospiritual journey.

The similarity between great spiritual traditions and the journey of psychological manhood is close enough that the tools and descriptions and insights of the great religious traditions can also be used here very fruitfully. So I can use the terms wilderness and other side, wilderness within and inner life, psyche and soul interchangeably. For they refer to the same place. And this place is where the Ordeal takes place. This place is where the transformation from boy to man happens. Indigenous peoples knew that, mystics have known that, humanistic psychologists like Scott Peck now know that.

For modern man, the other side is more clearly inside. The Ordeal happens within. Sacred ground is deep within a man's psyche. The mystery is that the deeper a man goes inside, the more he feels a power from the outside. It is this power that he will need to complete his Ordeal. It is this power that sustains him in facing his Ordeal, and will sustain him throughout his manhood. It is for each man to answer for himself the mystery of whether this power is wholly inside or comes from the other side. In many respects it doesn't matter. The important thing is for every man to move to this sacred ground, and to stand his ground.

Men's Church

It always interests me that when men get to this time of Ordeal, as part of their therapy, they often feel like they have to get away into nature. Sometimes they need to take long walks alone in woods or into mountains or on beaches. Sometime they need to camp and think. Sometimes they go fishing for long periods of time. Most, though fearful, feel the need to be alone to do this. I know one man in therapy who started walking a nature trail loop every Sunday morning to gain insight and peace. A friend called it his "8 mile church."

To many men, nature feels more spiritual than church, as they move into their initiatory search. I believe that men are showing their hardwired need for wilderness Ordeal through these actions. Walking reflects the journey into the unknown. Nature reflects the wilderness. Aloneness is the necessity of the Ordeal. The search for their own manhood, in this emerging sacred ground, often feels like the most spiritual thing they have ever done, as it was for our ancestors.

I believe sportsmen who fish and hunt are responding unconsciously to this same hardwired need. Hunting and fishing may reflect the sense of primitive survival of the Ordeal. Men have told me they feel most themselves and most at peace lying in wait in the hunt or quietly watching their line. These men usually don't know that they are experiencing the effects of feeding their souls. They don't realize they are unconsciously trying to find the peace of the psychospiritual Ordeal and the serenity of ancestrally sacred space. They don't realize the spiritual aspects of what they are doing.

Sometimes a spouse will bemoan a man's lack of interest in religion. She will feel he is not spiritual because he doesn't go to church. I try to convey to her that he may very well be meeting his soul's needs in the cathedral of the wilderness. He may be finding spiritual meaning in the bible of nature, as the Taoists have for thousands of years. He may be finding answers to his deepest questions in the wordless silence of his forbears. He may be searching for spiritual answers deep in the solitude of the wilderness within and without.

It often happens that men in the middle of their Ordeal, while in therapy, will come in to a session with poetry. Poetry seems to have the form and words that most express their feelings. Poetry seems to be the nonlinear, non-rational expression of the soul beset by intense feelings. As one of my clients in the middle of his Ordeal wrote to me: "I honestly on one level do not want to exhaust myself with these projects but find I have no choice. Nothing will happen for weeks. Then when riding in the car, lines of poetry will 'pop' into my head out of nowhere and I feel compelled to go home and finish the poem. I know this is not what I should be doing from a conventional sense and I am sure my wife is upset that it interrupts my job search."

Some men just need to be alone for a while, whether in nature or not. I find it a very healthy sign when a man finds the need to be alone. This need for aloneness, as long as it isn't a code word for not facing engulfment fears, shows a man has dealt with many of his separation issues and is already approaching sacred ground. Wanting space can be very healthy if a man is not running from or toward a mother object. Wanting distance can show that a man is not afraid of looking at his life as a whole and separate individual, instead of as an extension of other's dreams. Spouses and partners need to understand this need as healthy and as a challenge to their own initiatory needs. I will talk about this extensively in a following chapter.

I once asked the men in my men's group when they felt most themselves and the most at peace. One man, John, said he felt most himself when he was alone, especially walking in the twilight on the golf course near his house. Most of the other men agreed that they felt most themselves when alone, especially in nature. John asked quietly if I felt there was anything wrong with this. I suddenly felt the presence of shame in the room. Aloneness is surely countercultural in our society and even a mark of oddity. I assured John that to a maturing man this centered sense of aloneness is good and normal. Being in nature, even on a golf course, can show a hunger for sacred ground. It is a sign that the Ordeal is working.

I also find that men at this stage of initiation and therapy start talking about God. (I use capital G because in our monotheistic society most men see God as singular and unique.) Men spontaneously talk about needing God, or some higher power, to complete their journey. Some men have been introduced to the idea of a higher power through a 12-step process. Others have returned to a possibility of God's help from their earlier, forgotten religious training. Others have lived with their God as companion all along, without connecting God to their inner search.

Carl Jung felt all people were formed through the collective unconscious to believe in and seek God for an answer to adult problems. He felt we all had the archetypal urge to relate to a higher power. He called man *homo religiosus*. He never claimed that he could prove there was a God. He did say that men routinely act as if there were a God.

He also felt that most people over 35 could not heal without recourse to some "religious answer." The God most men talk about, and the religious deity Jung talks about, is not necessarily the God men meet in church or in studying religion. This is a God they feel could be anywhere. He is more the God of the wilderness, not the God of the civilized edifice. He is the God met face to face, not the God heard about. He is the God of paradox, not the God of logic. He is the God met beyond the mores of the village.

All men are hardwired to move toward Ordeal and maturity. All men are hardwired for the mission leading toward the wilderness. That is a solace I often dwell on. We are made for the wilderness without and within. In a sense we crave Ordeal. We are also looking for the holy and sacred. The sacred is another word for the most important inner values in a man's life, the values that make him a man from the inside out. As we will see sacred is another word for the life path the initiate finds in his soul.

Standing Ground

At the time of Ordeal, men sometimes need outside Elders, different kinds of priests and ministers, to explain some things and point us in the direction of the sacred wilderness. As a counselor, I feel the need to take up an Eldering role with men because most of male society has defaulted on this obligation. I feel the obligation to be the one to explain and help any man who comes to me through his Ordeal. This should be the job of priests and patriarchs. Unfortunately, it rarely is. As in myth, Elders come from the unlikeliest places. One of the unlikeliest is the counselor's office. As one of my clients put it, "I was looking for a great, wise guru someplace; instead I found an ordinary man in a Sears polyester suit." (Actually, I rarely wear suits.)

An Elder has no answers. He can talk of the process of Ordeal. He can talk of how the best men have handled Ordeal in the past. But he can't give answers to the man's deepest questions. What he can do is witness to the reality of the other side. In the secularized world of the marketplace he can speak to the sacredness of the wilderness. The elder can "hold space" for the initiate until he recognizes that sacred space himself.

There is an old Zen mystery expression that holds here. It goes, "If you meet the Buddha on the road, kill him." Part of this expression has to do with someone holding himself out as having the answers to another's spiritual quest. If you meet an Elder who says he has the answers, you have gotten the wrong Elder. You have gotten an Elder who has not been to sacred ground himself.

The most important thing a modern outside Elder can do is encourage a man to stay within his death experience, with its depression, loss, confusion, humiliation, and emptiness. The middle of the Ordeal hurts. The Elder is there not to explain the meaning of the hurt, but to explain that the hurt is meaningful. The Elder explains that pain is part of the reality of the wilderness, that pain does not mean that he is in the wrong place. The Elder encourages a man to stand his ground.

An Elder must witness to the necessity of walking the wilderness.

Sometimes a seeking man will approach Ordeal many times, then return to the comfort of his addiction time after time. Many times going back involves a relationship that was unsatisfying but provided relief from the abandonment pain of the present. An Elder is there to tell him this repetition does not mean that he can't eventually fully separate and complete his initiation. An Elder is there to witness to the need for the next attempt, for the next foray away from the village. An Elder encourages him to return to that sacred place of confusing feelings and unanswered questions.

Hurry Up and Wait

With or without an outside Elder a man at this point in Ordeal feels in a situation a lot like the old Army dictum, "hurry up and wait." After all the separation work a man does, and having stood his ground, he is greeted with the need to just wait. He is given no trophies or medals. He doesn't make the newspapers for the substantial, draining work he has already done. Because he is outside of the patriarchal reality, few people notice or understand all the work he has done. His ability to be humble is sorely tried.

Like being in the Army, a man in the wilderness has no control over his time. And time then starts to hang heavy as nothing seems to be happening. He is really in another time, a sacred time. Here there are no production goals or timetables. A man cannot work his plan because he cannot create one. He can no longer measure himself by his accomplishments. Marketplace skills are useless.

What he needs to do is wait, humbly, for a plan beyond his ego. An outside Elder sometimes points this out. At other times the Elder within sends through a man's intuition the message to stop and wait. Yet waiting seems highly inefficient. If time is money, as in the marketplace, then this is financially disastrous. Waiting for the plan seems a great waste of time and money. Not being productive is at best uncomfortable. At worst it feels totally deflating.

Sometimes the wait is quite a while. At times the biggest pain is boredom. A man is not used to living in a limbo between past and future. He feels the need to plan, to strategize, to do something to relieve the boredom. To be masculine means to act. To act at least gives the illusion of control. Instead the whole experience starts to feel like he'll be stuck in this place forever. That thought is frightening. That thought is normal.

Malidoma Somé, at his initiation, was told to sit in front of a tree in the wilderness, to watch and wait. He was given no other instructions. After the first day he impatiently made up a meaningful story about the message he supposedly got. The Elders unhesitatingly sent him back to wait some more. He waited in front of that tree night and day for three days while nothing happened.

The Buddha decided to make his stand under a Bo Tree. He vowed to either reach enlightenment or die right there. His facing of initiatory death was profound. He fasted and waited a long, long time. He knew he had to.

In the great manhood myth of Western civilization Parsifal roams the alien countryside for 20 years looking for the Grail in the Grail castle. The Grail represents those sacred answers to identity and manhood. Robert Johnson, in his book *He*, talks of this Ordeal time as the dry years.

Here, waiting, a man is in sacred time. With men I see, like any Elder, I try to help by telling them their feelings of discomfort and disorientation are normal for the culturally abnormal experience of Ordeal. I explain that the wilderness has different rules than the marketplace. It is a different place with a different kind of time. I try to appeal to their hardwired sense of the healthy warrior, holding ground sorely won, ground that makes no present sense.

An Initiatory Experience

I cannot emphasize enough how countercultural the Ordeal experience is. A man goes against all he was taught about manliness. Instead of acting, he is asked to wait. Instead of setting goals, he is asked to let them find him. Instead of standing up for his beliefs, he is asked to admit he doesn't know what they are. Instead of being in control, he is asked to give up control. Instead of making himself feel good, he is asked to allow himself to feel lousy.

I have found that giving a man the formal opportunity to have a sense of initiatory space and time can hasten the maturing process. This experience can then give a man the understanding and courage to continue his initiatory process. I call this an initiatory experience, not initiation. Full initiation takes a much longer period of time; however, this experience can trigger or hasten the process.

In structuring this initiatory experience, I act as Elder. As opposed to indigenous Elders I talk to a man about voluntarily trying an initiatory experience. By this time many men have set significant boundaries and understand the need for separation. I explain that this experience incorporates many elements of a traditional Ordeal time. I offer this proposal to a man, as Elders do, when I feel he is ready. I give him the choice of the circumstances. The intensity of the experience can vary, as can the length.

There is a Hasidic saying, "There is another world and it is in this one." The other side is always just around the corner, or just the other side of our own heart. This is why a man can consciously experience the other side in ways that indigenous people do. The most important elements of this other world are voluntary aloneness, being in unstructured time, and listening.

This structured experience can last from one afternoon to one week or more. It involves taking oneself outside of one's ordinary lifestyle, preferably to a place one has not been before. The place must be one of privacy where a man's boundaries will be respected. Most of the time I recommend finding a place to stay where a man can be alone and not know anyone around. This could be anyplace from a hotel room to a cabin in a State Park to a room at a retreat center to a tent in the woods. I usually recommend someplace where there is access to nature for walks and seclusion, although being in a strange city does have both the sense of aloneness and the invisibility of the initiate.

Aloneness involves being in a situation where there is no interaction with significant people in one's life. Preferably, there should be no interaction of any significance with any other person. This ban on interaction also includes any reading or other media: no books, radio, television, computers or cell phone. What interaction is allowed is a writing instrument and paper to record thoughts, feelings, experiences. The aloneness in a strange place is the doorway to the experience of the other side.

The other side has a feeling of timelessness beyond the past and future. I recommend removing one's watch and putting it away, as a symbol of entering this timeless place. We contact this world by removing our schedules, our time bound habits, our planning for the future, and the points we scored in the past.

Most men start feeling uncomfortable just thinking about this experience. That feeling alone shows the sacredness of the space. Most men feel an archetypal fear of going into this experience and entering this space. This fear is normal. Young men have experienced it for thousands of years. Traditionally, any experience of the sacred evokes death and its terror.

There is a feeling of unreality in the Ordeal. Living only in the present, and in the disconnection of loss, brings a weird feeling of timelessness, like being lost in space. Myths and fairy tales try to give this same feeling, telling us we are in a different psychological time. They often start "once upon a time," speaking of a time different from our everyday time. The Star Wars story begins "a long time ago, in a galaxy far, far away." These are the code words for talking of the inner life, the other side, myth time and its timelessness.

The feelings of timelessness, aloneness, emptiness, disorientation, and free-floating discomfort are signals that a man is entering an Ordeal experience. He is starting to experience the other side. This is when the pull to regressive addictions will get much stronger, even though he has worked hard on separating from them. This kind of regressive pull invariably happens when anyone takes a growth step. This is something an Elder must explain. The pull to regression, and sometimes succumbing to that pull, is part of the maturing process. It never stops, even after Ordeal. Maturation depends on how we handle these inevitable regressive pulls.

Talk of the regressive pull leads me to explain other elements of this initiatory experience. Addictions are banned. No sex, drugs, or rock 'n' roll. No sex includes any sexual experience, including masturbation. No drugs means no mood altering substance of any kind, especially alcohol and pot. Not essential, but recommended, are abstention from the drugs nicotine and caffeine. No rock 'n' roll means no music or other taped messages of entertainment.

Work habits are banned. No work planning or work projects. No work planning means not thinking about or writing down any work related ideas. A man in Ordeal will inevitably think about his work accomplishments or work plans as a kind of orienting comfort. There is nothing wrong with thinking of accomplishments as a way of feeling confidence in one's ego strength. Holding on to one's identity as a marketplace worker is regressive.

No work habits means no scheduling the day or setting goals for the experience. These schedules will always be counterproductive and take one back to everyday, time bound reality. Planning is ego work not the work of the self. Schedules cause us to focus away from very important realities that will hold a key for us. Often schedules are the result of work addicted warriors with no Kingly direction. The warrior will have plenty of meaningful work, including schedules, to do once the King is found.

Fasting is another part of the Ordeal that is not essential but very helpful. Fasting not only mimics the survival reality of Ordeal, but it also frustrates a possibly addictive and pleasurable side of ourselves. Fasting intensifies the separation experience from comfort. It has been a traditional way of contacting the other side for millennia.

Fasting also intensifies the feeling of the timelessness of the other side. Many of us use meals as a scheduling technique that orients us to the security of time. When schedules are disrupted in other ways, such as in vacations, retreats or workshops, most people unconsciously start to talk and think about securing the next meal. Meals become the connection to everyday reality and our familiar schedules. Food is also a primitive comfort when feeling disoriented. Fasting can be for one or two days as long as a man drinks large amounts of water or juices and has no complicating health problems.

The most important part of the initiatory experience is the same as in indigenous initiation, to stay within the wilderness, survive and listen. I act as Elder and the only person the initiate can contact. My job is to encourage the man to stay within the experience. Most men will quickly start feeling overwhelmed by the disorientation and separateness. Their discomfort level increases substantially. The purpose seems to get lost. My job is to remind a man of his original purpose, to help him start to understand the meaning of his experience, and to uphold his warrior.

Indigenous people stayed in the wilderness until the sense of meaning and direction arose. The experience described here is less intense and full. Yet, often the elements and structure of this experience jump start the maturing process. I have found that the experiencing of the other side in this conscious way changes a man today as it has changed men for a long time. The intentionality and particular structure of this experience seems to bring a man toward a different sense of his manhood. He starts to feel differently from the inside out. In the absence of cultural rite of initiation, an initiatory experience, like I have described, tries to get as close as possible to a full and conscious rite of male maturity.

Many other processes have elements of this rite and allow a man to contact the other side. Counseling, spiritual direction, guided meditative practices, 12 step work are some other ways. Denise Linn, in the first half of her excellent book *Quest,* describes in detail much these same initiatory pieces in the context of the Native American vision quest.

There are also other opportunities for experiencing a structured initiatory experience. These are sometimes called vision quests, initiations, transformative experiences. The Mankind Project is a national organization that can be trusted to give a man the opportunity to experience an authentic initiatory situation. I can be contacted for information on other groups that I know can do the same.

Most men have already experienced the other side intensely because of a premature separation experience. They have experienced the aloneness, unreality, disorientation, and inner pain as a tragedy they never want to return to. As I have mentioned they have been traumatized by the experience because of the absence of fathers and Elders to prepare, explain and support. Because of this trauma many men are understandably resistant to go there again, especially voluntarily. An initiatory experience can be a crucial part of preparing a man to see his larger initiation through.

Starting to See

When a man perseveres in his Ordeal, things start changing inside. There are very subtle changes at first. Friends often see these changes before the man realizes the shift. After a while a man realizes that he is seeing the world differently. He also notices he is feeling the world differently. He is more comfortable in confusion, comfortable enough to start to notice the village from the viewpoint of the wilderness. He also notices his comfort in the wilderness, itself. He can stay within his feelings and pause to understand them. Instead of acting out, a detour around feelings, he acts in, moving deeper into them. He can stand his ground. The wilderness holds less and less terror and even starts to feel reassuring. He realizes he has given up the familiar for his freedom. Freedom, even with some fear, starts to feel exciting. Feeling starts to feel exciting. Fear and anxiety begin to be memory. He has faced his biggest fears and he is still standing.

He is, as they say, not out of the woods yet. And he moves back and forth between nostalgia and excitement, between anxiety and anticipation. He is in the middle of Ordeal, yet he is still alive and feels alive. He is much stronger than he ever felt he could be. He has a quiet, healthy pride in that. He has gotten the confidence to stand his ground and see it through.

Chapter 15
The Call

'm reminded of the famous words of Stan Laurel, "It's a fine mess you've got us in, Ollie!" Towards the end of the initiatory process, it often feels like a real mess. The young man is looking for manhood and wisdom and he finds himself more miserable than he has ever been. He is slowly losing any motivation. In many ways he has forgotten why he is doing this to begin with. Perhaps the one thing that keeps him going is the confidence and vision of his Elders.

Yet like everything else in the wilderness, there comes paradox. As the initiate loses confidence and motivation, he gets closer to his goal. As he feels most alone, he starts to feel less lonely. As he feels most humiliated, he starts to feel a new dignity. As things feel more and more uncertain, he feels a growing comfort with confusion. As he stands on foreign ground, it starts to feel like home.

Slowly, he begins to see things differently. New thoughts enter his head. He begins to see the world around him with different eyes. Instead of his mother's eyes or his father's eyes, he starts to see the world through a man's eyes. In many primitive cultures, especially in the Native American tradition, he has a vision, perhaps a kind of holy hallucination. In other cultures, he has an altered state experience. Luke, on Dagobah, described a feeling "like living in a dream."

These visions or experiences tell him that he has come in contact with another power and another place. Within the experience are many messages, all vital to his manhood. Scared becomes sacred. The wilderness becomes home. Pain leads to purpose.

Manhood and Identity
And purpose leads to manhood...

Indigenous peoples believed that one's identity and life work were sacred gifts from the gods. They did not believe that these things were arbitrary.

These people were not existentialists, like modern man, believing that they could create their own identities, or arbitrarily create a satisfying life direction. People for tens of thousands of years humbly believed that their deepest identity was there even before they were born. A power had already created a purpose. A power was calling with this purpose from the other side. At the same time, they believed that their action in the world was their purpose and identity playing out in their lives. They believed their role and work continued the work of a higher power, like the Force, if they kept attuned to that call.

North American Indians' experience of initiation seem most significant here, not only because of their particular search for meaning, but because their experience is so close to our own history as Anglo-Americans. The Sioux Indians' initiation is a good example.

Leaving father and mother, the young Sioux boy went out into the wilderness alone. He would carry only a blanket and a prayer pipe. The boy was looking to find a vision given to him by the Great Mystery, the Great Spirit. He would stay in a sacred space, usually a sacred circle that he would construct at a place in the wilderness he found to have significance. For three days and four nights, alone, he would fast and pray, not even drinking water. He would have to stay up all night and only doze during the day. His prayer would actually be a lament or cry to the Great Spirit for a vision. The prayer was called a lamentation. The experience was called a Vision Quest.

The vision would be the bestowal by the Great Spirit of the boy's role in the community, giving the direction for his life's work. Often, the boy would get this vision or message from Nature. Nature being analogous to the Word of the Christian bible or the language of the Holy Spirit. The boy would have to be extremely sensitive to all that went on around him because the message could come from anywhere. Every activity around him of birds, animals, wind, clouds could have significance. The boys knew they were constantly surrounded with messages and signs from the spiritual realms, and the Vision Quest allowed them to be still long enough so that they could listen intently to these messages about their identity.

When he returned from his quest the initiate would explain to his Elders all that happened to him. His Elders would then interpret for him anything he did not understand about his vision. From the significance of this experience, the boy would be given a new name by his Elders. This name was a sign of his new status in the community, as well as a guideline for his new role in society. With his new name he would start his new life. His new name would symbolize his new identity, describe his life direction, and point him to his life work. His identity would be forever linked to the fate of his community. His identity would be linked to his responsibility to his community.

Malidoma Some found his life work through initiation. His name means "make friends with strangers." His Elders interpreted that he was called to bring his people's message of manhood and spirituality to western culture. He was to be a missionary of sorts. He came to Europe and the Americas to teach men these truths of his people. He discerned this through initiation. His Elders confirmed it.

Call

The old Christian word, vocation, comes to mind here. The word vocation, at one time, had the connotation of life direction. The word vocation comes from a Latin word meaning to call. To have a vocation in Christian circles meant to be called by a higher power to a sacred identity. The call was always personal and powerful. The assumption has always been that a person was given this identity by his God to fulfill a purpose that would be for the good of all in a divine plan.

James Hillman, in his very significant book *The Soul's Code*, brings this mystical and spiritual idea into the realm of psychology. Hillman talks of the archetypal pull from beyond the ego. He describes this pull as feeling like a call. This call seems to pull out of us a yearning for a destiny we had, seemingly at birth. He calls this innate viewpoint the "acorn theory." Just as the acorn has the potential for the oak inside from the beginning, so "each person bears a uniqueness that asks to be lived and that is already present before it can be lived."

The point Hillman makes is that this call is not a consequence of nature or nurture in the traditional sense, not a consequence of good or bad parenting or genes. The call is deeper and more unique, from a place beyond personal history. Yet, in the history of the world, "only our contemporary psychology and psychiatry omit it from our textbooks."

Indigenous people knew that a person came into the world with a unique mission. Elders often talked with the fetus to discern the talents each child brought to the community. In Classical times the Romans understood a higher self, or maybe an internal guide, that came with each human life. They called this being the genius. The Greeks called this being the *daimon*. Native Americans called this being a nature totem. This guide acted, like the Christian idea of angel, as a personal intermediary from a higher power to bring one to a continuing awareness of the call.

I named my men's center the Christos Center because of the meaning of the Greek word *christos*. The meaning signifies being blessed or anointed for a purpose. Similar to call, the word conveys the insight that every man, and woman, has been sent into this world with a sacred purpose and a sacred set of talents and visions.

It should be noted that individual free will is always in play here. A man is not forced to answer a call or follow a fate. And a man has the opportunity to follow many paths under the umbrella of his fate. Deep identity can move in different directions. But the price to pay for ignoring or not even recognizing a call is the endemic depression most men live with.

Soul and Spirit

The word mission comes from the Latin words meaning to be sent forth. Mission begs the question who is sending, as call begs the question who is calling. Clearly these ancient concepts assume the existence of a power beyond the individual and his ego that has a sense of the bigger picture and our place in it. Whatever one thinks about the identity of this power or entity, the idea has been around for thousands of years that this sender resides on the other side. Hillman, as well as indigenous peoples through millennia, would say that it is this sender who has the most influence on who we should become, not our parents, not our culture, not even our Elders.

A man's highest calling is intimately related to his deepest identity. In finding ones' true self, one's essence so to speak, a man does a mysterious and sacred thing according to most great religions and spiritual beliefs. This is the nexus of calling and identity, where psychology and spirituality meet. This is also the place where soul and spirit meet.

Carl Jung had a name for that part of a man that contained his identity, as well as the place that opened onto a higher power. He called it the Self. The Self is an archetype of the whole man, consciously using all parts of his personality. To Jung, the Self, by including the depths of the unconscious, connected to a life seemingly beyond himself, certainly beyond his ego. Through contact with the Self, a man found a deeper identity and deeper meaning in his life. Jung believed that the Self had an innate sense of a higher power and deeper wisdom, a religious sense that was not identified with any religion. The Self acted like a soul looking for spirit. As a scientist, Jung would never venture to say that a higher power existed, only that the Self acted like it existed. *Philosophy of "as if"*

A mature man seems to know that a higher power, at least a higher *mystic* wisdom, exists because he has experienced it. Through initiation he has learned more and more of the topography of his inner life, the terrain of the Self, the wilderness within. This is the place of the soul. He has found that soul yearns for otherworldly answers, as a boy yearns for manhood.

Indigenous people saw the wilderness as the place where their higher power, their Great Spirit, dwelled. Initiation not only introduced a boy to his soul, the message from his Elders was that his soul was intimately connected to Spirit. Elders experienced Spirit, assumed Spirit, taught about Spirit. Part of the initiatory experience was the explanation of how their people came to be through the action of Spirit. Elders always taught this spiritual context, the myth of their people. In the Elder's eyes, their people were continually upheld by Spirit, as each man's life would be connected to Spirit starting with initiation.

I believe that a modern man going through this Ordeal of transformation takes a psychospiritual journey that finds both the potential of soul identity and the existence of something sacred beyond the ego's ability to understand. This something is sacred because it has the effect of bestowing a goodness to a man's life.

It is up to every man to go on this journey alone, to find out for himself. Then he can define Spirit for himself. As a psychologist, I can talk of the steps that a man has to take to painstakingly get himself ready for the wilderness. As an Elder, I can tell a man he is meant for the wilderness. As a counselor, I have observed that most every man who has struggled with Ordeal has emerged with a spiritual sense. As a man, I can attest to the Spirit that dwells there.

This Spirit is not the Spirit that is automatically found in a church or in a religion, though this power can also be there. This is a bigger, more powerful, more mysterious Spirit who cannot be contained by one church or one religion. This is a Spirit of paradox. This is a Spirit who seemingly doesn't go by his own rules. This is the Spirit who teaches the mystery of transformative pain. This is a Spirit only accessed from deep inside every man, from his own soul.

The paradox, here, is that a man does not have to be spiritual to complete this journey. He must merely be radically open to the life beyond the ego, beyond the village, beyond his rational understanding. He must be willing to risk everything for a good beyond what he intuits the village can give.

A mature man has learned the difference between soul and Spirit. If he doesn't believe in Spirit in some way, he can too easily feel that his small self is the highest good. He can make himself the center of his universe, deifying his own existence, his own ego. He can more easily fall victim to hubris, psychologically suffering from inflation. This is why his humility is so important. His soul life is meant to work in resonance with Spirit, not take its place. Ego is meant to surrender to Self. Soul is meant to submit to spirit.

Enthusiasm and Passion

Whether or not a man believes in Spirit I believe a man will still find that his deepest identity contains his deepest sense of peace and even joy. There seems a benevolence here. Who we really are makes us feel the most alive, the most passionate. What contains our deepest yearning and passions has the secret to who we really are. In fact, in his book *Callings* Gregg Levoy states it is "better to ask whether a call will give us a feeling of aliveness which, as mythologist Joseph Campbell argued, is more important than even meaning for people to experience."

When thinking of the characteristics of a mature man the word enthusiasm comes to mind. This word comes from two Greek words: en, within, and *theos*, god. The mature man has found meaning and a higher purpose on the journey within. This changes everything. His soul, resonating with Spirit, has a life that overflows with passion and enthusiasm.

The mature man is enthusiastic in his approach to life because he has an important, sacred purpose. He has braved the wilderness of the soul and faced his deepest fears. He has gone to the brink of death to find himself. He is now free, because he is fearless. He is no longer driven by his fears of abandonment or engulfment or lack of manly approval. He is no longer driven by his need to control by using money or status. He doesn't need to feel like and act like a god in order to feel safe and comforted. He takes pleasure in life but does not look for a life of pleasure. What he has can't be taken away by anyone else, or given by anyone else.

The mature man lives in paradox because he has his feet in two different worlds. One foot is in the village, the other in the wilderness. One foot is in pain, his pain and the pain of his community. The other is in a peaceful place of wilderness awe and detachment. He lives a two-tiered life. As Robert Johnson's book portrays, he lives between heaven and earth.

The mature man learns to live in many worlds at once. He can be in the wilderness of his own soul, then in the marketplace of his job, then by the hearth (or small business) with his soul mate.

A man's major Ordeal immunizes him to the despair of the world. His Ordeal lessons keep him from being cynical, or worse, desperate. Desperate men are dangerous men. Instead of despair, a man finds hope because he has faced a most desperate situation in Ordeal and has not only survived but found new life. This is not a new life devoid of pain or confusion. It is just that pain and confusion are not the final chapter, for himself or for his community.

Intuition

A man is hardwired to feel the call deep within himself. He hears the call in the wilderness of his own soul just as his ancestors heard the call in the initiatory wilderness. Carl Jung calls this "knowing" intuition. This is a non-rational way of knowing similar to a hunch or a gut feeling. This is a direct knowledge, skipping the steps of everyday logic, making a quantum leap into a more meaningful logic. This is knowledge gained in the wilderness about the truths of the other side. This is soul knowledge.

Intuition is not clear like an e-mail or a verbal command or a very personal letter. It doesn't come from the logical head but from the feeling heart. It is an inner knowing that comes through that part of the Self that is in touch with the world beyond the senses. Just as we cannot hear radio waves without a radio we cannot hear the call of the other side without intuition.

Intuitions of the call kind keep coming around if not heeded the first or second or third time. This cosmic insistence is another proof of the validity of an intuition. Important intuitions seem to hang around, nagging and nudging. They have a "should" quality but without the guilt.

A man needs to recognize the process of his deeper way of knowing. He must learn of his own internal truth meter. He must learn the signals of when he is inspired.

Another word similar to intuition is inspiration. The word inspiration means to have the spirit within. A man must learn when he is truly being called by spirit or guide. Or in Christian terms called by the Holy Spirit. He needs to learn to be open to inspiration. He learns about inspiration in the Ordeal. When he is inspired, he is called. When he is called and listens he is inspired.

Intuition is most needed during Ordeal. Often insistent intuition is the only thing that keeps a man in Ordeal. Ordeal makes no worldly sense. And it is an affront to the senses to say the least. How does a man explain the urgings of the Elder within? How does a man explain his yearning for something he has never experienced? How does a man explain the dogged persistence of standing his ground when his reasons are groundless?

A man who learns the feeling of deep rightness about a truth or an action will hear his call. The call sometimes comes in an instant of insight. It sometimes builds over months and even years. But it never goes. Men may numb themselves to the call. They may depress the call. Yet the call continues to speak from the shadows of the Self to a man's heart.

Luke

Luke had a passion to be a Jedi warrior from a young age. This passion was in itself antithetical to the culture since Jedi warriors were "all but extinct" and espoused a philosophy at great odds with the Empire. He was a good pilot but that was the extent of any noticeable Jedi talent. Yet his passion burned in him continually though his talents lay dormant and unrecognized. His passion seemed mere fantasy. Luke didn't even know what a light saber was when Ben Kenobi handed him his father's.

Through Obi Wan's good fathering Luke starts to find his Jedi talents. Luke is drawn deeper in to his identity through his passion and talent. He also starts to realize that his talent is strongly connected to his cooperation with the Force. His identity and the Force are inextricably entwined

Luke's following his call of deeper inherent identity leads inevitably to the start of his initiation and his mission. Like most men following their call Luke, though not fully initiated, felt his whole life was preparation for confronting the Empire in the form of the Death Star. It felt like fate, a sign of the call. When other pilots thought of the mission as doomed and hitting the target "impossible, even for a computer" Luke talks of times he used to "bull's-eye womp rats in my T-16 back home."

Some men like Luke know their passion and have a sense of their talent from a very young age. Often these men are naturally intuitive and even artistic, such as writers, photographers, painters, designers. Yet, being uninitiated, they are confused as to how to use their talent. Often they have no second father or mentor to hone their skills and encourage them to go deeper into the risk of initiation to find a meaningful place for their talent. These are men who do not fit easily into the patriarchy and have an intuition that their path may be contrary to the patriarchy and marketplace values. These are men who live fairly chaotic and unhappy lives in their teens and twenties and even thirties, feeling adrift and invisible. I have worked with these talented men frequently. These are men who, if they persist in their inner journey and humbly reach out for Eldering, often find their mission and satisfaction in early midlife. These are late bloomers whose talent is often extraordinary.

Some men have found their talent but because of a lack of a meaningful mission have little passion. These are men numbed out with a great deal of warrior energy but lacking in King energy. They are successful in the patriarchy but feel little aliveness. Talent, and even passion, in themselves cannot provide direction. Initiation for these men gives a new set of values and a deeper understanding of service to community. These men often feel alive in a way they have not felt before, as if they were always meant to do this work.

Other men find their talent and ignite their passion only in the midst of initiation. These are men who have often not had much recognition either from the patriarchy or their peers. Neither have they had the pleasure of exercising a natural talent. As a result of initiation the rightness of their mission joins with the newfound pleasure of experiencing their talent.

Luke, even though successful in destroying the Death Star, had not gone deeply into initiation to find the intersection of his passion, talent, and deeper mission. As we will see, he needed to find the meaning and values associated with his mission, the inner strength and direction that would ground him in his purpose. He had experienced second fathering, gaining recognition of his talent and passion. He also got a taste of how mission and Spirit bring life to his talents. Now he needed to continue to follow his call. His intuition, and his second father, was leading him to a paradoxical place. He needed to go to Dagobah.

Chapter 16
Return

D agobah. There Luke learns about the Force. And unlearns certain
rules of the village mentality. Unlearning is part of initiatory loss
and also part of deeper learning. On Dagobah Luke learns the spiritual
values of inner peace and unlearns macho anger, fear, aggression. Here he
also learns that his talents can be used negatively. He can be seduced as
his father was. Yoda almost predicts this.

Luke's initiation is not complete yet he returns prematurely to his
community to serve his friends. Yoda can only give his last teaching: "don't
give in to hate." What Luke acts on is his instinctive learning of the connection
between mission and community. Whether he is ready or not will be seen.
But hopefully he has learned the values of the other side, the perspective of
serving the world for a higher good represented by the Force. Initiation brings
a new spirituality based on serving the good of the whole community first,
even risking one's death in the process.

So Luke returns.

Third Step

As a result of initiation, the boy who begins his life in the village as a boy,
returns to the village as a man. His journey has changed who he is and what
he does. A man's journey starts in community and ends in community. Yet
all his relationships are changed. This new man is given a new name by his
Elders. His community recognizes him by a new name because he is a new
person to them.

The initiated man returns with a boon, often described by his name.
This boon is his newfound talent and vision he finds in his Ordeal. The
boon is for the renewal of the community, which can atrophy in patriarchal
rigidity. His gift, as well as giving his life meaning, is also meant to transform
his community. Indigenous societies waited excitedly for the new man and
his boon.

This is the beginning of the third step in initiation, the return to the community that badly needs his presence. For the gift of initiation is ultimately given for the good of everyone in the initiated man's community.

If a community is not open to his gift, as happens in an Elderless, modern society, his message can bring estrangement, ridicule, even danger and death. For instance, modern societies do not particularly want mature men. Mature men are not blindly obedient.

The mark of an initiated man is a deep peace in the face of scorn that could be described as otherworldly. This is the peace that the Bible says passes understanding. This is Yoda's calm. There is a detachment that seems like despair. Actually, it is a detachment that comes from a vision that the community does not yet understand, especially a modern community. It is often a vision that patriarchal cultures scorn.

A man who started writing poetry in his therapy described the mature man he could glimpse in his own life:

> *Nothing is the same anymore. He is quiet now and does not*
> *need to drink on Friday evenings or worry about market volatility.*
> *Something greater is pulling him now and he realizes he is no longer*
> *in control. Just a pulsating flow of energy passing through the body*
> *from a source that cannot be described.*

The Common Good

As I have said in the traditional Western myth, as outlined by Joseph Campbell, the hero returns with a boon that saves the community from outright destruction or prolonged harm. The boon, like a medicine, rejuvenates and renews the life of the community. The Sioux have a belief that a mature man always acts with the awareness that his actions will either benefit or hurt the next seven generations. Their community spans time as well as space.

The valuable boon of a man's Ordeal is the gift he gives others. A man who strives for maturity must eventually take responsibility for the good of the larger community. He must put his personal ego needs in their proper place, as the Ordeal has taught. This sometimes means taking on the pain of the larger community and showing how the pain must be endured and transformed. Sometimes that pain can result in personal death, even while the community is being transformed. Jesus, Gandhi and King provide high examples of such witness. Most often the pain is feeling misunderstood and alienated, until the rightness of his vision is recognized. But the mature man has already been in confusion and misunderstanding. He has been immunized by his Ordeal.

It is very hard for a man to think about the public good, and see the world through an Elder's eyes, if he still yearns for pleasure and power. In Yoda's word he is too easily "seduced." The temptation will be too much for him, as he gets the attention of women and the adulation brought on by power. He will not have been immunized against the corrupting influence of power, including sexual power. Our own American politics is a testament to many immature men unable to handle the responsibility of power. The whole issue of sexual harassment is a symbol of men who use power to get pleasure. Corruption in government or corporations results from men putting their boy needs above the good of the community.

The uninitiated man finds it too hard to discharge his responsibilities well. Often his unguided adolescent will sabotage his career, either publicly or privately. His immature adolescent within, hidden by his polished persona, will take over periodically. The power of sexual excitement or the sexual excitement of power will overcome his persona. There will be no healthy Self to restrain the ego. The community suffers instead of being saved.

The mature man takes on the pain of the community instead of indulging his own pleasure. This is the time the mature man can use his anger, the anger of his warrior. This is the time he turns his rage at injustice into just anger. I am often asked by men what they are to do with their anger. I first talk to them about using their anger to set boundaries and let anger give them the energy to endure Ordeal. However another use of anger is in motivating work for those who have been unjustly treated. This is the anger of the Seven Samurai, the anger of Jesus in the Temple.

Working for justice is part of a mature man's mission. Anger at injustice in his community is his motivation. The warrior in him, when under the control of his Kingly self, becomes fierce in defense of the undefended. But the answer is not violence that destroys, although it may involve measured physical force. More often the real answer is the confrontation of injustice even in the face of personal pain. As Aaron Kipnis says, "in the vision of masculinity we are moving toward, a man expresses his rage through empowered and compassionate action. This is the anger of the good warrior, the anger of the warrior practicing bushido."

In Native American tradition a man is judged by how he handles the fruits of his talent. His manhood is judged not by how many riches he accumulates but by how much of his belongings he gives away for the benefit of his whole tribal community, especially to those with the least ability to take care of themselves. This is the virtue of the potlatch or the giveaway. A person who claims more than his just share is looked on as selfish. A man who feels responsible for even the least of his brothers and sisters is honored.

I am not suggesting men leave their families to become gurus or hermits. I don't believe that we have to give our IRAs away to become mature. But I do feel that a mature man must go the painful route of separating from the values of the patriarchal world of self-aggrandizement. I do espouse that a man listen seriously for a call to mission. I do strongly suggest that a man, once having faced his Ordeal, will find the fullness of his call and his life by authentically serving his community.

I encourage men to live continually in both worlds, the village and the forest, realizing his marketplace mentality must be secondary to the values he learned in the wilderness. I know that a man who finds that call and uses his gifts will naturally want to serve his community. He will not have to be reminded. And he will do it with an enthusiasm and peace that only he and his initiated brothers will understand.

Work and the Father Wound

For many men the call, where boon, talent and mission intersect, is to their work in the world. Since mission always means service to community, the third big step in initiation often involves a man's work in the community. This work often involves their job. Many men find that their initiatory talent is not used in their job. Some find that their talent is used by the patriarchy but for dubious ends.

I believe that today much of the depression that men experience can be traced to problems with their job. The arbitrariness and lack of meaning in most men's jobs demoralizes them. Consequently, men's lives are a hectic search for something or someone to make up for the hours of pain and discontent at their job. This is where addictions or the pursuit of power comes in. High salaries are meant to compensate for low satisfaction. Golden handcuffs belie the reality of job imprisonment. Poor work quality is assumed if workers are not strictly monitored. The marketplace job world becomes one big Dilbert cartoon.

In a sense, lack of workplace morale comes from lack of moral direction. At best, marketplace values are amoral, leaving the good of the community to churches and non-profits. At worst marketplace work tears the fabric of community apart by teaching the good of the greedy ego. Modern marketplace work doesn't make sense to an initiated man and depresses any sensitive uninitiated man. Modern marketplace work is merely a lifeless job where a man is abused for a paycheck.

My father's generation probably represents the low point in this downward spiral of the meaning of work. Coming out of the Depression and the continuing technological changes following the Industrial Revolution, the generation coming out of World War II looked for any job that could pay enough to raise a family and live a normal life. These happened to be mostly industrial jobs, following the continuing shift from agricultural work. The farm itself was even becoming industrialized, as agribusiness was born. As Robert Bly points out, not long ago there was a profound connection broken between men and the land, and men and their sons. This situation would be a kind of hell to indigenous peoples. They would be out of contact with the natural world and their initiatory direction. Thus, they would be out of contact with the other side, the soul side that gave everything else purpose. They would have nothing of purpose to get from their Elders, and little legacy of meaning to give to their sons.

My father picked a career in engineering because it paid decently and there was a need for engineers after the war. He never thought of his own satisfaction or a higher meaning. He was from an immigrant family where any paying job was enough. My grandfather came to America at 14, because there was little opportunity in his small town in Italy. He was thrown, like so many other immigrants, into a terrible initiation, with no Elders to help him. My grandfather was a janitor, an intelligent, hardworking man with no opportunity to use his greatest talents. Amazingly he provided enough to send my father to college, so that my father did not have to work 14 hours a day in backbreaking work. He wanted my father to have choices. Education was his legacy. Unknowingly, his legacy did not include the call of meaningful work.

My father took the first job that came along after college and World War II. He stayed with it for 43 years. He stayed in a job he didn't like because he didn't want to risk his family's welfare. He had choices, but he was afraid of the risk. He was increasingly unhappy at his work. He did what it took to be a man in his time, just as my grandfather did. He suffered for a higher purpose. He also gave me a legacy of choices. It is sad for me to realize I was given choices at the expense of his spirit. My father was able to hide his unhappiness from all of us siblings growing up. Like many of his generation he suffered his wound courageously and silently.

Though a man may not able to change from a job to his initiatory work it is important that he realizes the cause of his depression. He is not the problem. He is the victim of marketplace abuse and the victim of a father wound. The awareness of the origin of this abuse and betrayal can be the first step in walking his initiatory path.

Work and Play

Work is not supposed to be merely a paying job. It is much more than putting food on the table though, like my father, I honor men who have the courage and warrior energy to endure marketplace abuse for their family. I am sad at the waste of talent and the pain of lost promise.

An initiated man can witness to a whole other world of work. An initiated man risks much to find the work of his initiatory call. This work most often involves a severe pay cut. Or, as we will see, he does unpaid work because he must live out the values he has gained through initiation.

I said earlier that the work addicted man looks like the mature man, because of the hours spent in dedication to the task. Yet here is the difference: essentially, the work addicted man is trying to find his manhood through his work. And not knowing manhood inside, he is desperately looking for outward verification that he does things that men do. The immature man says "I am what I do." Persona is enough.

The mature man says, "I do what I am." The initiated man doesn't have to do his work to create self-esteem. He is not working for rewards. He does it for the feeling of rightness and for the community he is a part of. So many great men and women have said that they did their work because it needed to be done. Their motivation resided in their person.

When a man wants to do what needs to be done for the community, with no thought to reward, he is coming upon his own manhood and his initiatory call. Then the work is not responsibility in the traditional sense, not a burden or a duty. Work becomes a sacred play, even when there is pain involved and there are serious stakes in the community.

Mircea Eliade talks of what happens to a man when he finds a life work. He refers to this life work as sacred or sanctified. This work has qualities that give it a specialness that mirrors a high that others seek in dark ways, such as addiction. He talked of the volunteers in Mahatma Gandhi's liberation campaign who "could work 16 and 18 hours a day, singing, laughing and shouting out of sheer joy."

He said in an interview in the Spring, 1976 issue of *Parabola* that "any type of labor that is undertaken for an ideal such as defense or liberation of one's own country, preaching a religious, social or ethical message, and so on, can be performed in a kind of 'ecstatic' enthusiasm – one might also say 'outside of time.' Notice the buoyant and otherworldly quality described in this kind of life work. Signs of the other side. The sense of being periodically invigorated is surely a mark of what is sacred work for each of us.

Again the word enthusiasm, even joy. The mature man finds joy in his work, as well as in his life, even though there is pain and frustration. Maybe peace is a better term. Some men have found the precursor of this feeling in fatherhood. In healthy fatherhood there is no pay, not much status, and a lot of work and pain. Yet the peace that can come from nurturing a young, growing life is indescribable. The view from the other side does cause everything to look different.

I often talk to men who realize that their work does not have the meaning it once did. Some realize that their work never did have meaning. They have often outgrown their jobs. I believe that most men who have started initiatory work will find that their job starts to feel stale. This is because most men will still be working for someone else's vision, be it in a company or corporation. They will be following a father that they start to realize has nothing more to offer. They will find that they have their own vision of work that doesn't coincide with their corporation. This will be a crossroads for many men, and the substance of their Ordeal. Their Elder within will not shut up!

Most men at mid-life need to either direct a company and incarnate their vision, be freed by a company to follow their own vision by finding a new voice in an old job description, or leave the father company to follow their own meaningful work. Otherwise, when they return to the village with a boon, they hide it away for nobody to see or use. Work is the way most men give their vision to the community. A man must be free to pursue his own vision or he is perpetually a son and a boy.

Downsizing has thrown many men into their initiatory Ordeal. Some have been destroyed by this separation. Many others have used their Ordeal well. Most men I have talked to, who have survived this Ordeal, have said that the pain and stress of their transition was worth it. They came out the other side with a new sense of purpose in their lives and a great deal more job satisfaction. Most also admit that they wouldn't have believed this outcome was possible when separation first happened.

Nontraditional Work

The work a man finds himself doing after initiation does not always coincide with his job. Sometimes a man finds that his job allows him to carry on his true vocation with the rest of his time. This can often happen with men who have found a calling through their midlife Ordeal. They may not be called to change careers, but called to bring the focus of their lives to another meaningful work. I once gave a workshop for men studying to be permanent deacons in the Catholic Church. These were men who were married and had families, all at midlife. They were preparing to be ordained ministers in the church, while still following their careers and their families. As one man said, "I have a job, but this is my vocation."

As a man matures the line between a job and work tends to blur. Men can turn their job into a sacred work with the right intention of service and love for community. Men can also turn their sacred work into what looks like a passionate job. Indigenous people could not tell the difference. All work was service.

In other traditions mature men devoted their lives to their community in a more conscious way after serving their family and community as householders. There is a model of masculine maturity in the Russian countryside that comes out of their Orthodox Christian tradition. Catherine de Hueck Doherty, an expatriate Russian baroness, writes about it in her book *Poustinia*. The process starts with a man experiencing a call, similar to the call experienced in Ordeal. He could be any age, but usually in his 30's or 40's (women who were called were usually much older). His call would be to go to an isolated, secluded place, usually in the forest. The word *poustinia* means desert in Russian. The word also has come to mean any desert-like place, similar to the isolated places that the Desert Fathers went to in the 4th century.

A poustinik could be anyone, a peasant, a duke, a member of the middle class, learned or unlearned, or anyone in between. The poustinik would leave his earthly possessions behind, wearing the normal dress of a pilgrim, a linen shift with an ordinary cord tied around his middle. He took along a linen bag, some tea, a loaf of bread, some salt, a gourd of water. The poustinik would go to the outskirts of the village. He would pray in the forest until he would be led to the place he would dwell. There he would build his poustinia, a small, simple hut. Here he would pray and enter into "the great silence of God." He would take on the pain of the world, voluntarily, especially the pain of the poor. Out of his pain and prayer he would find the wisdom of God.

Poustinikki are different from hermits. Hermits would be shut off from the world. Poustinikki opened themselves to whoever came to them. They would always offer the meager, material hospitality they had, usually tea and bread. Many times they were sought after for their counsel, in matters both spiritual and social. Other times they were sought after for physical help, like getting in a late crop that could was threatened by weather. The poustinik was there to pray and to serve. He lived off of whatever was given to him freely. He consoled, he understood, he loved—and he asked nothing for himself. As of 1967, the forests of Russia were still peopled with many poustinikki.

Good work can take all forms, paid or unpaid, formal or informal, seen or unseen. The call can involve finding new work, changing one's job into meaningful work, or finding meaningful unpaid work while keeping one's responsibility as householder. The absolute necessity for every man is to honor his initiatory call to his community. The absolute necessity is for a man to believe in his boon.

The Twelfth Step

There are also some specific works that all men are called to. All men are called to be fathers and Elders to the following generations of men. By fathers I do not mean necessarily biological fathers. I mean soul fathers. We will not finally be a wise, Elder culture unless every man individually becomes initiated and takes up his role as father, and then Elder, to the next generation.

Aaron Kipnis talks of "Twelve Tasks of Men." His Twelfth Task: "Reach out to other men and continue awakening masculine soul together." Older men today are the only hope of the next two generations. For this work there will be no pay. There will be little recognition. But it is one hell of a good mission.

Elderhood is probably the greatest boon a man can give. Sharing of his wisdom and knowledge, gotten through Ordeal, is ultimately the key to the meaning of life. Indigenous peoples knew this in their bones. The renewal of our society will only happen when enough men become Elders and make commonplace the journey of initiation.

In the hero myths and many fairy tales, when the hero returns from initiation, he most often returns to take his rightful place as a ruler or king. Through the Ordeal he has found the strength and wisdom to overcome the present ruler who has abused his office for personal gain, leaving the kingdom in chaos. The hero overcomes the dark patriarch. The new king rules with the idea of the greater good of the community, immune to temptations of the ego. He then is free to Elder the next generations.

I want to close this chapter by giving you words from the shaman, Petaga:

> *I did not ask for my office. My work was made for me by the other world, by the Thunder Beings. I am compelled to live this way that is not of my own choosing, because they chose me. I am a poor man; see how I dress and the house I live in. My whole life is to do the bidding of the Thunder Beings and of my people and to pay heed to what the Grandfathers tell me.*

Chapter 17
Patriarch Light

A s we all live longer than previous generations we go through more stages of life, sometimes an elongated older stage, sometimes a whole new one. There now seems to be a new stage and archetype that has been lost for thousands of years in Western civilization. This is a healthy patriarchal archetype that emerges in men's psyche and a new stage that emerges in the wider culture. This healthy patriarch can only emerge after the appearance of the initiated man. This is the stage of the enlightened patriarch I sometimes call patriarch light.

This archetype emerges in modern men most often in his 50's and 60's. Modern men have an extra 20 to 30 years of health and power that previous generations have not had for thousands of years. This time calls for a new and formal initiation process as well as a naming and description. Instead of a time of retirement or sunset walking this should be a time of extended vibrant manhood. This should be a patriarchal time in a man's life.

For most men this is a stage that calls for a formal patriarchal initiation. Because most men have not been initiated, the entrance to the healthy patriarchal stage requires an amalgam of initiations containing the Ordeal of manhood and the Ordeal of patriarch. For the uninitiated this is a particularly intense time precipitated by the crisis of loss with no previous Ordeal experience to fall back on.

If a man has completed the Ordeal of manhood initiation when younger this patriarchal initiation is often less intense than its predecessor. Previously initiated men would have found their talents and honed their skills through their sacred initiatory calling and served their family and community well. For these men the patriarchal archetype would start to emerge in a man's psyche as a responsibility and desire. The template of initiatory transformation would be present. The patriarchal Ordeal with its disorientation and movement into the unknown would have a familiarity.

Any loss is felt as a trigger for needed personal change, not a tragedy. Anger at injustice is felt as a motivation not a complaint.

Men not previously initiated often have a history of marketplace success but little sense of meaning and purpose. The good news is that they have many honed skills based on seasoned talents. The good news is also that they are good and sincere men. The bad news is that they have neither the meaningful context of service to exercise those talents or the consciousness of a calling that initiation brings. They are not receiving the call or the message. These are men of goodwill who are still searching for the peace and fulfillment of manhood. They are often stuck in an initiatory depression with no idea why the golden years feel like fool's gold. Yet the opportunity still exists to finish initiation and find their patriarchal purpose.

For both of these men finding the vocational context for their talents often goes beyond personal service. Besides serving the community on a personal level this initiation often adds the crucial mission of using patriarchal power to change the wider society. This stage moves beyond nurturing family into a stage of nurturing a community of families. This is a time of understanding the cultural systems, especially of marketplace values and dynamics, in order to transform these systems in ways that reflect the values found in initiation. This is a transformation that requires a wider view and deeper understanding of the flawed dynamics of the dark patriarchy.

The patriarchal stage is all about power, its use and misuse. The dark patriarch is about power over others, a form of self-serving manipulation. Its key word is obedience. Shameful behavior is questioning how the dark patriarch's power is used. The dark patriarch endeavors to create a community in his own image. His talent is used to compete and overcome. His need for power, even more than money and sex, becomes his addiction. There is never enough power. The victims of this power lay at his feet, in adulation or numbness, never knowing their soul self or calling.

The dark patriarch practices a dark power. This kind of power over others results in a steep hierarchy where the resources of the community inevitably move toward the top. The invisible hand plays with loaded dice. In the dark patriarchy wealth and power are in themselves signs of a deserving and blessed man. Dark patriarchs are seen as deserving of the fruits of power because of their wisdom at holding power. In this paradigm those that don't have power don't deserve the wealth and are seen as less than men.

The healthy patriarch, a kind of patriarch light or patriarch of the light, uses power to empower. These men would fight for new ways of structuring society that efficiently brings social justice and power to all. They would strive to create social norms that nurtured boys and girls in obeying their inner calling instead of the dark patriarchy that calls them to obey an external command. These healthy patriarchs already serving the community move to creating communities that serve. These patriarchs strive to build an economy and community that reflects psychospiritual values instead of an unguided economy that creates its own dark values.

Another way of looking at this emergence of the patriarchal archetype would be viewing men moving from early to late adulthood. Early adulthood includes the first initiation of manhood, carrying the most important lesson of living from a center of wisdom beyond the ego. This is wisdom of Spirit and soul that seeks to find a spiritual mission and identity. This first initiation will form an inner template of transformation for a man that he will use as guidance for the great and small initiations he will go through the rest of his life.

The new man in early adulthood finds his mission in using and refining the talents that initiation has uncovered. The mission and consequent recognition of talents are not random or arbitrary. These are talents the community desperately needs to serve everyone's life journey. And for an initiated man the giving of his talents is also the way to his deeper sense of peace and fulfillment.

For a man initiated in late adulthood the talents are the same but the role can be different. Late adulthood is a time when there is an initiatory calling to take a wider responsibility for the entire culture, the whole community. This man has more time take this responsibility as the demands of fatherhood and family wane. A healthy patriarchal voice, similar to the Elder voice within, grows insistently pointing out systemic injustices that get harder and harder to ignore. This archetype has tried to right systemic wrongs for millennia. Modern initiated man now has much more time to address these issues and the awareness to know how uninitiated men are victims of a greater wrong. In the past this archetype incarnated as the enlightened king or the compassionate chief.

The Return of the King

The enlightened patriarch is a channel of King energy. And healthy King energy usually matures past mid-life. This is when a patriarchal man emerges who has the strength, talent, and vision to wield healthy power. His initiatory humility keeps him honest about using power. The enlightened King uses his power for the good of everyone in his kingdom. He feels responsible for those on the margins as much as those in the middle, at the bottom as well as the top. He is especially aware of the poorest and the most vulnerable. The integrity of his whole kingdom rests on the well-being of the least. For example, as I mentioned earlier, in many Native American traditions the goodness and effectiveness of the leader, the chief, is measured by how much he gives away, especially to the poor and elderly and disabled, not how much he accumulates. In a healthy patriarchy if the least are taken care of those who have more, even a lot more, are also respected.

Actually the enlightened Patriarch knows that he is the conduit of power much greater than himself. His initiations have taught him this truth. He embodies archetypal King energy. This energy emanates from the higher power spoken about in Alcoholics Anonymous. This is the energy of "Creator" or "Source" or "Great Mystery" that Native Americans speak of. This is the sacred power coming through an initiated man called grace or intuition or the Tao. It is also the archetypal energy and wisdom deep within the psyche of every man.

The enlightened patriarch as King brings order in the form of justice throughout the community. This is a divine kind of justice where everyone has an honored place in a divine order. Good King leadership is like a coach who recognizes the talents of every player and places each in the team structure where he will contribute the most. This coach is also able to confront a player who has an inflated view of his talents and a skewed recognition of his value to the team. He instills humility without dark humiliation.

A man with this King energy may or may not have formal authority, may or may not be a boss. What is important is that he uses that energy as it is given to him. He must have the humility to recognize his initiatory talents and the talents of others. He must risk using his talents and risk blessing the talents of those younger. He must take up leadership when there is an injustice and promote justice wherever he is. He must be a bulwark for psychospiritual values even at the risk of his own reputation and lifestyle. And, if called, even at the risk of his life.

A man with King energy is often called to use political power for the common good. He is called to change systems. He may not be a politician but he knows how to use the levers of power. He is often called to use his power at the local community level. His initiation has given him a vision of a better harmony within a community. He does not strive for leadership or power in itself. In fact he has a natural skepticism concerning the use of power. He promotes his sacred vision not himself.

Separation

Most uninitiated men nearing the patriarchal age will face a major crisis of loss with little preparation or support. Besides the losses that manhood initiation brings the loss in this patriarchal initiation is often the loss of work through retirement, downsizing, or economic downturns. Others may lose a job through loss of motivation. To an uninitiated man the loss of work is tantamount to loss of identity. Most successful uninitiated men are more or less work addicted. Loss of work triggers an intense time of withdrawal worse than any drug withdrawal. Withdrawal is Ordeal with no initiatory meaning. Retirement, forced or unforced, can lead to interminable painful addiction withdrawal. The waning of motivation for dark patriarchal work often leads to the depression of quiet desperation. Without an Elder to explain and hold space this pain of loss has no meaning and turns chronic.

What is often hardest is the loss of respect and even adulation that successful work can bring. Downsizing can feel like a repudiation of talents and legacy. Self-esteem dependent on marketplace success and power can erode quickly.

For some older men who never achieved their marketplace goals and consequent respect the loss can be the loss of dreams. Addiction to dreams can be just as insidious as addiction to any substance. Dreams, even if unrealized, provide some sense of aliveness and motivation. Dreams lost can haunt a man. This field of dreams can turn quickly into nightmares.

These uninitiated and separated men desperately need Elders to convince them that it is never too late. The next 20 years and more are a field where initiatory dreams can unfold and motivate. It is not too late to find a new set of values that bring inner respect, a new set of values the culture desperately needs. And not too late to find new and deep meaning to one's life.

Return

Men will find themselves in patriarchal Ordeal whether they have previously been initiated or not. A successful Ordeal brings a new work with wider ripples, a work of public service. Often a man will find this new work, paid or unpaid, in an organization that mirrors his newfound values and life direction. These are often non-profit or governmental organizations. These are organizations that are not obsessed with the bottom line but, hopefully, have a mission of creating service systems that are value driven. Of course not all non-profits have values that mirror Spirit and merely mirror the marketplace culture. But an initiated man quickly discerns those that deliver what their missions espouse.

Marci Alboher has written a book called *The Encore Career Handbook*. The subtitle is, "How to make a living and a difference in the second half of life." She reminds us that the in the past 100 years the average life span in the United States has expanded from 47 to 78 years. This book is a great how-to about using that patriarchal age to find a work that truly creates an Elder culture. As she says, "Growing numbers of baby boomers are rewriting the narrative of twenty-first-century midlife by crafting a new stage of work: an encore career for the greater good."

The healthy patriarchal stage is also one that spawns new and innovative delivery systems of service. Old patriarchal systems often have merely momentum going for them. As Bill Plotkin mentions in his book *Nature and the Human Soul* the emerging patriarch feels the need to devise new delivery systems for serving the community needs. He talks about this time in a man's life as the Artisan stage. A man who has mastered his craft is needed to change or refine or update its usefulness in light of changing cultural situations. He must ask questions such as how can his skill set best serve the community and how can this skill set be taught to others.

This is where leadership leads to new and more appropriate social service structures. This is where the levers of healthy patriarchal power are used.

Teaching skill sets to others is also a major mission of the enlightened patriarch. Every man who goes through a patriarchal initiation also is called to use his experience and talents as mentor for younger men. A mentor is a person who has a love and passion for a sacred work and dedicates himself to pass on this knowledge and experience to those having the same talent and passion. A mentor is a second father. A mentor and mentee contract on some level to develop and advance that craft. This relationship is similar to the medieval concept of master and apprentice. A healthy patriarch guides a man with a similar calling, like a son, and sees this as a sacred mission.

I am reminded of elephants here when speaking of mentoring the young. When a young adolescent elephant reaches puberty he is thrown from the herd to live in what's called a bachelor herd apart from mothers, siblings and assorted other relatives. If there is no older male, actually called a patriarch, around them they often become aggressive and intimidating to any elephants weaker than them. They can destroy the harmony of the whole herd. These adolescents, like modern city gangs, use their newfound power of bulk and muscle to selfishly get whatever they want, regardless of how it affects the whole herd.

The bull patriarch mentors them by literally showing them how to be civilized and live within the harmony of the herd. He uses his power and bulk as an enlightened bully, not for his own gain but for the good of the whole herd. He must sometimes physically confront rogue youngsters using warrior energy to make a point.

The enlightened patriarch is a needed mentor for those coming out of manhood initiation. He is also a guarantee that public service systems are truly service to the public. An Elder holds a space of initiation where talents are found. He then hands an initiated man to a mentor. A mentor as healthy patriarch helps refine and mature these talents while witnessing to a life of service.

The Enduring Elder

It is never too late to be an initiated man. It is never too late to volunteer to work the second shift of our calling. There is always a mission waiting and a passion to be lived. There are always those who need the benefits of our power. Hopefully the boy we all were eventually becomes a man then a patriarch then an Elder, all the while guided by the Elder within who never gives up. The Elder within persistently whispers to us of sacred possibilities because he is also the voice of the sacred.

Chapter 18
Pain and Purpose

A man who moves through Ordeal in humility learns to see pain with new eyes, Elder eyes. He learns to accept pain, to stand his ground in pain, if it leads toward his own transformation or, as a necessary part of his return, leads to the transformation of his community. A man in Ordeal learns to endure pain for a higher purpose—one of the most important lessons of male maturity and male spirituality. He learns that his call often means absorbing the pain that the uninitiated can create in community without returning the pain in kind. He becomes a witness to another way of handling pain, both the existential pain of life's vicissitudes and the unconscious pain that members of his community visit on each other. He becomes a witness to what masculine love means.

Neurotic Pain

In moving through modern initiation and initiatory pain, a man will start to see that his emotional pain was necessary. He realizes that he couldn't go through the transformation to manhood without it. As in a chemical reaction, the heat had to be increased significantly for a new substance to be formed. Pain is the heat. A man will start to see that enduring initiatory pain will continue to be necessary. It will be a part of the rest of his life, if he is to continue his growth. Yet he will feel less afraid of the pain, even befriending it.

An initiated man will also be able to see the difference between necessary initiatory pain and the unnecessary neurotic pain of staying in the village too long. This neurotic pain is the one accompanying any addiction. It is the inevitable pain that a man brings upon himself for not dealing with his inner life. It is initiatory pain not faced. "Neurosis is a substitute for legitimate suffering," observed Carl Jung.

The paradox of life is that we can run from pain or we can run toward it. But we can never ultimately avoid it. Inner pain cannot be avoided. The young, unguided boy instinctively runs from pain and from his manhood. He runs unless he finds an Elder to help him stop running. Most modern men's pain is the pain of running from pain. This is neurotic suffering. It serves no useful purpose to the man or his loved ones.

Before the initiatory experience, a man will not understand what I am talking about. One man I worked with was incredulous when I mentioned that the goal of life and counseling was not the wise pursuit of pleasure. He could see no other reason for living. I understood his feelings, as he was in a lot of neurotic emotional pain. Pleasure seemed his only release from emotional as well as physical pain. He did not realize that the emotional and physical pleasure he sought from his wife would not bring him satisfaction. He did not realize that the rages he would go into toward his wife were really a very young boy's frustration with his mother object. His intense frustration was the cause of his pain, not his wife. His rages dulled the pain toward numbness without getting himself one inch closer to the peace of manhood.

The price of neurotic pain is often the catastrophic payment of a heart attack, a stroke, liver disease from the late stages of alcoholism, chronic fatigue. Or the price is the estrangement of family and friends because of rage or withdrawal. All this because a man was not able to pay the initiatory price.

Legitimate Pain

A man in the latter stages of Ordeal starts to realize that his manhood and deep inner satisfaction comes from finding purpose, not pleasure. He realizes that manhood does not consist in avoiding pain. He sees that the pleasures that he strived for no longer have meaning. Addictions have lost their allure. He realizes there is no right woman that will make life bearable. There are only fantasies of women. He realizes that manhood does not come from protecting a woman or that initiation does not come from her adoration. He will have grieved these losses and begins to leave his neurotic anxiety behind.

This man will also realize that his manhood and deep inner satisfaction comes from purpose, not power. He will see that status and money do not make him feel more like a man on the inside. He will see that the respect of uninitiated men is meaningless. He will see that all the power he has will not allay the anxiety he feels about losing the trappings of manhood. If he does choose to take on power in a corporation, church, or club, he will do this to fulfill a greater purpose, his call, and not to prove his manhood.

The man in the Ordeal will start to realize that the measure of a man is not how much pain he can render but how much pain he can endure for a higher purpose. Here we come to the mystery of initiatory pain. The existential pain of initiation, choosing to transform pain rather than transmit it, makes not only a new man, but a new ideal of manhood.

If a man cannot get past his boyhood, he cannot bring his son and his brother's sons to manhood. He cannot find peace. He cannot give peace to those he loves. Yet, the peace of his manhood is paradoxical. This peace includes pain. And the pain is OK. This paradoxical pain has meaning. It goes somewhere. Unlike neurotic pain it somehow changes the universe instead of being swallowed uselessly into a black hole. This is pain with a purpose. Only the initiated man and woman understand this.

An initiated man is then able to experience a further mystery of initiatory pain. He has become someone who can transform the neurotic pain in the world. Instead of retransmitting the neurotic pain directed at him, he has learned to transform his community by absorbing this pain. He is like a carbon rod in a nuclear reactor, absorbing neutrons of negative energy that cause critical explosive masses of anger and emotional destructiveness in his community. He has learned to absorb pain, both his own and the neurotic pain around him, for a higher purpose of transforming it into compassion. By doing this he creates compassion in the world.

It is interesting that the word compassion means to suffer with. An initiated man will voluntarily suffer emotional pain as he realizes that joining in the suffering around him, rather than transmitting or internalizing it, can be as healing to the community as it was for himself. He will become a transmitter of the lessons of pain, while walking his talk.

A man, toward the latter stages of initiation, starts to find how his pain has started to make him a different person, a person he likes much more. He also starts to realize that he couldn't be that different person without the lessons from that pain. Pain becomes another Elder, teaching him important lessons about how a man moves in the world. Through enduring pain for a higher purpose a man transforms pain into the highest good, both for himself and for the community he is a part of. He goes from a hellion to a healer.

The transformation to manhood brings a man to a willingness to suffer pain for the next generation. It is purely voluntary. The motivation is not shame or ego or status or respect. It is a man's need to fulfill what he has learned and what he has become through his Ordeal.

Groundhog Day

I am thinking of the classic movie *Groundhog Day*, one of my favorites. The writer and director, the late Harold Ramis, called it a very spiritual movie. It is also quite entertaining. This movie is about neurotic pain, the other side, initiatory pain, and transformation.

A very narcissistic television weatherman, played by Bill Murray, comes to the town of Punxsutawney to report on the Groundhog Day celebration there. In the process of living Groundhog Day he exhibits a lot of negative boy behavior. He is selfish, ego absorbed, and addictive. He tends to use people for his own ends and to satisfy his own needs. He is stuck.

His stuckness in neurosis is soon made clear when he wakes up the next morning to find out he is starting a painful Groundhog Day all over again. He repeats his neurotic behavior and gets the same painful results Groundhog Day after Groundhog Day. His anxiety increases. He continues hurting others and himself. His only answer is to continue to live the same day over as most men stuck in their neurosis recreate, daily, their pain and their painful situations.

Most men who are stuck will then blame the world for their problems. Their frustration is rationalized as not their fault. They feel that the world is out to get them. They are unable or unwilling to look inside.

Actually, the world is out to get Phil. The universe is trying to initiate him. Phil is separated from all that orients him. He is in a strange town, in a strange time. Nothing makes sense. There seems no way out. The wilderness, right there in Punxsutawney. The Ordeal, without notice, comes unbidden. Actually the other side has found him, like Elders in the middle of the night.

This movie shows a fine representation of the other side, the timeless side, the eternal present. This is the mythic, psychological time I have talked about. This is the surreal time that men feel in the middle of Ordeal. The movie depicts, paradoxically, both neurotic time and initiatory time.

Phil is forced to deal with his inner life or be stuck forever. This is the place every man will come to in his life, usually right in his own home town. The questions arise. Will he step in the same puddle every day, or will he become aware of his destructive habits and lifestyle? Will he accept the pain of change and separation, or will he forever rail at the unfair world? Will he deal with this inner world or be stuck in the outer world?

Eventually, Phil becomes seriously depressed. He has tried a number of adolescent ways to feel good, and he only feels worse. He decides to face death. Unfortunately the death involves the death of his body, not initiatory death. He tries a number of ways of committing suicide only to wake up the next day. He stays stuck because he will not face his initiatory depression. Suicide is his desperate attempt at eternal numbness.

Eventually, Phil starts to deal with his internal pain and frustration. He accepts his separation. He gives up his former striving for pleasure and status. He allows the Ordeal to start to transform him. He eventually learns that he cannot change the day, but he can change the way he relates to the day. He realizes that he does not have to be stuck in his old narcissistic ways. He doesn't have to step in the same puddle every day. His consciousness dawns slowly.

For most men the transformation takes a long time. Ordeal takes many months, sometimes many years. Yet the peace I talked about also grows apace. So the Ordeal takes on the quality of painful peace as it progresses. There is this sense in the movie. During the day, Phil is continually faced with the narcissistic behaviors that lead to his unhappiness. These repeats finally sink in. He is changed through his aloneness, confusion, frustration and depression. He starts to be aware of other's needs. He finds strength. He finds peace. He finds compassion. He starts to realize the gifts that he can bring to the small town community he is now a part of. He voluntarily starts to give of himself with no ulterior motives. He seems oblivious to the respect he receives. He has found the peace that passes understanding. He has found it through Ordeal and return. There is no other way.

Holy Teachers

The greatest model of manhood in western civilization, according to Carl Jung and many others, is Jesus Christ. No matter if a person feels Jesus

221

was divine or not, his life has profoundly influenced western civilization. And his message shows a profound answer to pain, mostly to those who have started to learn the lessons of initiation. Christ, though he arguably had the power of the universe at his disposal, chose to suffer pain rather than inflict it. Why would a man with all this power choose to suffer so horribly? As St. Paul said, this crucifixion was a scandal to the world, meaning the patriarchy of his day. In the words of the gospel, Christ suffered that others might live. Living meant living from the inside out, from finding the "kingdom within." Living meant absorbing pain for the good of others.

Christ refused to listen to the patriarchal voice of power. Both in the desert and on the cross he refused to listen to the voices that said, "If you are so strong and godlike do something powerful and show us." Just as today the patriarchal voice will always say to us, "Do something powerful to show them you're a man, or else you're a wimp." Christ modeled the manly life we are talking about. He was called Rabbi which means teacher. He came to teach us about pain. He, who could have had all the pleasure and power he wanted, suffered instead. The cross is a symbol of voluntary suffering. He suffered for the higher good of the community and to show the gateway to the life of the soul. He suffered to teach that there is purpose in life, and in pain.

As I have mentioned, the Buddhist tradition has a similar model in the Bodhisattva. This person would choose to go back into the suffering world after finding enlightenment and peace. The Bodhisattva paid his dues. He has done the work of separating and detaching from the hearth and village. He has detached himself from the illusions of worldly satisfaction and gone through the pain of that separation. He has also separated from the karmic cycle of causing pain and yearning for pleasure. Yet he chooses to stay in this world as a model and guide for the human community, until all have reached the same enlightenment.

Luke and Pain

An answer to pain and the freedom of manhood is also depicted wonderfully in another man. In the Star War myths, Luke learns the secret of the Jedi, the secret of a mature man. He finds it in his final Ordeal. In his final struggle with his father, in the presence of the Emperor, after being tempted to destroy his father violently, through hatred and anger, Luke puts down his weapon. The Emperor has tempted Luke to violence and hatred because of a good cause. The Emperor tries to lure Luke back into the patriarchal violence of outer control instead of the inner struggle of transformation. He tries to lure Luke away from Yoda's message that "a Jedi uses force for knowledge and defense—never attack." He tempts Luke to create patriarchal pain for the good of his community.

Instead of defending himself in righteous struggle, Luke tells the Emperor that he refuses to fight. Luke tells the Emperor he will have to kill him first. Luke refuses to save himself by causing others pain. This is madness. It is also the mystery and strength of initiatory pain. The Emperor starts to destroy Luke in front of his father. Luke endures a great deal of pain, and is at the brink of physical death. His father seems unmoved because of his loyalty to the Emperor. Even when his own son pleads for help, he does not respond. Right in front of Darth Vader is pure witness to the powers of both light and dark. Luke is witnessing to the mystery of inner power and the humble acceptance of initiatory pain. The Emperor is witness to the prideful illusion of exterior control, and the destruction it causes. One is causing death, the other is humbly accepting death. Both face their fate on the Death Star.

Somehow Darth's heart is moved. He suddenly picks up the Emperor and throws him into an abyss. Darth then turns back into Anakin, his original Jedi name. He tells Luke, while dying, that Luke has already saved him by his witness. He has seen the power and rightness of Luke's witness, and he could die as a man again, not an unemotional machine. Darth remembers the forgotten truths of the Jedi warrior. He takes off his helmet, which symbolizes the artificial life of his narcissism, to see his son with human eyes. He is again a Jedi. Then he dies.

Luke has not only saved his integrity through his voluntary suffering, he has saved someone he loves very deeply. Soul has spoken to soul. Transformation has led to transformation. Compassion has led to healing. That is the mystery of initiatory pain.

The Wounded Healer
Initiatory pain has other lessons to teach. One of the most powerful and instructive archetypes in the human psyche is the wounded healer, first

written about by Carl Jung. The message of the wounded healer is that the power and wisdom to heal another resides in the wounds of the healer himself. The wound is the teacher. If a man can endure consciously the pain of his own wounds, experiencing them as part of his initiatory pain, he will find the wisdom and power in this painful experience to Elder other men going through their initiatory pain. He will recognize this call as being that of Elder healer. From his own woundedness and initiatory healing comes an understanding of the healing process itself.

In a similar context, in many indigenous cultures the shaman or medicine man discovered that he could not heal any serious condition unless he had already suffered and healed this condition himself. The shaman's healed wound gave him an archetypal power as well as permission to heal.

In fact many men were called to be shamans through what is called a shamanic illness. This was and is an Ordeal of shamanic initiation. This illness was a sacred woundedness signifying a call to be a shaman. If a man in humility answered the call the illness would spontaneously heal. If he didn't acquiesce to the call he could suffer this chronic illness or even succumb to it, the victim of neurotic pain.

Looked at another way initiatory pain produces compassion triggered by similar wounds. A man must feel his own pain before he can feel other's pain. Compassion can connect a man in a meaningful way to all other men suffering from the same feelings of abandonment or engulfment or isolation or chronic depression. This connection is what happens in a men's group when men share their pain and experience the relief of feeling understood. This feeling of connection through similar wounds in itself can start the healing process. Often out of a man's particular pain the passion to help others with the same pain seems to well up. It may be no coincidence that the word "passion" means both suffering and intense motivation.

Pain can make us or break us. We can transform it as a wounded healer, hold it in a neurotic embrace, or just pass the pain on to someone else. Only the first choice liberates both a man and his community.

Chapter 19
Alone Together

Freud talked of the two most important issues in a man's life being love and work. I have talked of work and purpose. I have talked of the separation from the problems of uninitiated men in relationship. I now talk of committed love, that love two people must learn about for them to find the wonder of loving community, and to support each other in their missions. Notice I have talked of initiation and mission first. The order is important. Mission before marriage holds the best hope for life and relationship happiness. Yet this culture holds the opposite to be true and most men and women have not found their purpose before committing themselves to each other.

However, all is not lost. Boys can become men and girls women within a relationship if they both understand the necessity of their personal initiation. That they cannot be initiated together. That their partner cannot initiate them. That there is a time when they must be alone together.

Tomme

Before Tomme, our protagonist in *The Emerald Forest*, could marry, he had to go through initiation. His indigenous culture took marriage too seriously to let immature boys marry. As Tomme emerges, finally, from a deathly dunk in their river of life, his father as Elder yells, "The boy is dead. The man is born." Tomme is now ready to marry.

Most of us, unlike Tomme, enter into a committed relationship before we realize that we haven't done the emotional work of maturing. We find out after commitment that the initiatory work of finding our calling and true identity still needs to be done. Since we are not in an Elder culture, we usually discover this more toward midlife, if we find it at all. I mentioned in a previous chapter the dilemma of becoming initiated while within a committed relationship. I want to talk more fully in this chapter about the complexity of dealing with this dilemma.

Most of us look at relationship as a cure for our loneliness, a salve for our lonely hurts. To most in our culture, loneliness is the symptom of the disease of aloneness. The medicine prescribed is romantic connectedness. Psychologically, many of us see a committed relationship as life's goal and the cure for diseased aloneness. Certainly the entertainment media portray the romantic love relationship as the focus and goal of life.

For example, many people still feel embarrassed to sit alone at a movie theater, haunted by the romantic ideals in the very movies they wish to see. A romantic relationship seems the obvious cure for this disease. Anyone who suffers from the disease is assumed to be a failure, not having what it takes in the most important endeavor of life. A man who has this magic relationship is assumed to be initiated, automatically reaching manhood, just as the damsel brings manhood to her knight. This relationship then relieves a man of the fear and challenge of facing his initiatory aloneness.

A Second Chance

Most men who come to counseling have been ambushed by strong feelings they never knew they had. The relationship that they thought would give them happiness has betrayed them. Separation, or the threat of separation, has triggered the initiatory archetype inside. Buried feelings of abandonment rush to the surface, where they erupt into consciousness. The boy is being yanked from the village. He is overwhelmed by being thrown into the wilderness alone. His aloneness is frightful and shocking. The initiatory depression is overwhelming.

It is entirely understandable that most men in this extreme condition will instinctively look back, pulled by regressive forces. Many a man will feel a deep nostalgia for the very relationship that bored him the month before. A man will feel the tenderest feelings for a woman he has been angry at for years. In his desperation, he will look at this disintegrating relationship the same way the boy looks longingly back at the village.

Some men get a chance to go back to a separated relationship. Others have the relationship permanently taken away.

Most yearn for a second chance. If a man who is given another chance will not minimize the memory of his initiatory terror, he can start to take his initiation seriously. He can use the relationship to further his growth together with the growth of his partner. A committed relationship can be part of a path to initiation and maturity. However, this path still involves all the initiatory pain and loneliness of the solitary man.

The realization that relationship is not a shortcut to happiness is one of the first realizations of the initiatory path of relationship. It is also one of the hardest initiatory losses to face. Adolph Guggenbuhl-Craig, a Jungian psychiatrist, speaks to this issue when talking of the purpose of marriage. In his book *Marriage, Dead or Alive*, he says that "the central issue in marriage is not well-being or happiness; it is ...salvation." By salvation he means the sense of wholeness and maturity that comes from the inner journey.

Salvation is a good word to convey the soul work of the initiatory path. If the reason for a committed relationship is indeed initiatory, then a healthy commitment involves initiatory suffering, not instant comfort and identity. If relationship is initiatory, the initiatory suffering involves death and loss. The first, and perhaps hardest loss, is the death of many of our romantic ideals of relationship itself. Probably the hardest ideal for a man to lose is the assumption that the romantic relationship will automatically and immediately bring happiness and satisfaction. The right relationship is assumed to cure all life's wrongs. The honeymoon will last forever.

The next hardest loss is the ideal that the right relationship is a shortcut to manhood, and the path to instant self-esteem.

If Only She'd. . .

Our cultural answer to the problem of an unhappy marriage is to assume there is something wrong with the relationship. The timing was wrong. The two people are not suited for each other. This was a case of mistaken identity. An uninitiated man will often start fantasizing about another woman at the first signs of deep dissatisfaction in his present relationship, feeling that the right relationship should not be this much trouble.

Even if a man feels he is with the right person, an uninitiated man will assume that any problems lie with his partner. His partner obviously doesn't understand or accept him. His partner has serious problems. His partner is being irrational or hysterical. For whatever reasons, the answer lies squarely in the other person's domain.

This is the typical feeling in a marriage counseling situation. Usually each member of the couple will feel that once his or her side is understood the counselor will straighten out the partner. Each partner is sure they are being unfairly treated. Each partner feels the other has some serious problems. This is typical of thinking before initiation. The uninitiated man will always look outside himself for an answer. And he will always see the problem outside himself.

If a man continually feels that the problems are mostly with his partner, and concentrates his energy on changing that partner, he is really trapped in the village. For he will be unconsciously acting like the spoiled boy looking for the right parent, really the mother, to finally understand him and treat him right. He will be stuck with the notion that the right woman, in effect, can initiate him.

For most men in our culture, a committed relationship is not an initiatory path but a Grand Detour. It is a way to stay in the village while seeming to be a mature and initiated man. Who can question a man who is a good provider, having a good job and sharing his fortune with his family? In our culture a committed relationship, especially marriage, has become a pseudo-initiatory rite, a responsible way to avoid the painful initiatory path. Because of the lack of Elder consciousness, our whole society unconsciously believes this.

Separation

As I have said before, often a man will come to some dim realization of an initiatory need, beyond a relationship, at the time of a relationship crisis. His normal world has been taken away. Sometimes his partner has withdrawn any positive feeling, possibly talking about separation or divorce. She may say she no longer loves him. Perhaps he has already been kicked out of the house. Or maybe his partner has been indifferent for some time finally realizing his unwillingness to relate and grow.

Sometimes, the initiatory archetype has started to stimulate him into realizing his need for inner fulfillment. The Elder voice within becomes more compelling. A man starts to change enough inside to see his relationship differently. In other words, he has started to look inside, while withdrawing regressive expectations from his partner. He is moving unconsciously toward Ordeal.

This is where a man finds himself in a dilemma. The unhealed 6 year-old boy in him, especially if the woman is separating, will go about trying to please the partner, most often the wife, as a way of getting her back. He will be frightened of mother separation and in need of comfort. He will long for the village of his former life. He will be desperate, pulled strongly in the wrong direction.

The unhealed 10 year-old within may not be so afraid of mother separation, but more afraid of the social disapproval of the patriarchal father voice. Responsible men don't divorce and leave their children or their fortune. Responsible men keep commitments. According to the patriarchy, a responsible man must play by the rules of duty, the patriarchal mission that cannot see beyond the traditional father role. He will not be able to bear society's disapproval if there is separation for any reason. (He is also ripe for an affair. The patriarchy actually winks at this behavior, as long as a man is not caught and supports his family.)

The unhealed adolescent within, possibly the one having the affair, will be looking for a friend, without the commitment and responsibility of an exclusive relationship. He wants his freedom, yet he is not yet ready to find the freedom that only initiation can bring. He sees the possibilities of commitment, yet he is missing the emotional tools of manhood. He also has not had his vision yet of what his manhood will be. He is not yet ready for true emotional commitment, yet he is still in a committed situation. He will be terribly afraid of any new commitment, yet he will constantly be in some relationship, fearing aloneness.

On the other side of the dilemma, the emerging man, who is now in the older adolescent stage, starts hearing an insistent Elder voice of fuller consciousness. This voice speaks of the need for a whole new way to relate to the world. The voice talks of an answer within himself beyond the patriarchal responsibility of the village. This new consciousness also beckons to a new way of being in a relationship. The Elder voice will always send a man within questioning himself first before questioning his partner.

When a man listens to the Elder voice, and goes within, he instantly realizes he is putting all his relationships at risk, especially the committed relationship he is in. He intuits he will be changed profoundly by initiation. Like any initiate, he wonders if his relationships will survive these changes. He wonders if he can bear the separation involved. He wonders if his partner will stay loyal. He will start to experience the terror of all new initiates, as he waits for the Elder to surprise him one very early morning.

The Elder voice tells him he must separate from the old relationship in order to really test his motivation and his commitment. It also tells him that most of the reasons he has stayed in relationship will no longer work. This voice starts to question the reasons any man stays in a committed relationship. The uninitiated man has only old, outdated answers. The initiate starts looking for new ones. The initiate is ready to risk.

Recontracting

Most of the time when I do marriage or relationship counseling, I talk about the need to recontract the relationship. Recontracting involves uncovering the expectations and assumptions that each partner has of the other. The original honeymoon expectations and assumptions, the clauses of the contract, are universally unconscious. They are assumptions that are not verbalized or understood. Yet they affect every day of a couple's life. One of the first steps in counseling is to try to make these unconscious agreements conscious, in order to see if they still fit the marriage after disillusionment has set in.

Most relationships in our culture were originally contracted with insufficient information and limited self-awareness. In other words, there was not the maturity needed to follow through on a healthy commitment. Nor was there sufficient information about the identity of the partner to make a healthy decision. Most decisions for relationship are made in the honeymoon phase of a relationship, which is always a regressed place. From the male perspective, the boy's fantasies and dreams are projected onto the loved one. So the boy, not the man, ends up choosing a mate. Psychologically, the child ends up making the adult decision.

Most often the unconscious emotional contract involves the woman mothering the man or the man fathering the woman. There are many examples of this unconscious contract depending on how a man and a woman were mothered and fathered. This patriarchal, traditional marriage does seem to work for a while. But the perils of other unconscious mother-father contracts are many.

In one situation a woman will mother relentlessly while the man never takes up his patriarchal role and acts the lost adolescent. He may have little success in the marketplace because of addictions or depression or other boy behavior. He may be a success in the marketplace but an unfaithful adolescent. He will be the *puer aeternas*, the archetype of the eternal boy, the same as the Peter Pan syndrome. She will identify totally with the mother archetype. Both will unconsciously act out these archetypes and find them very unsatisfying. For the boy will not grow up for the mother to feel fulfilled and the mother will never be understanding enough for the boy to feel satisfied and manly. Yet she cannot stop trying to save him and he cannot get beyond the need for her comfort and praise. They are stuck in that contract. Neither has left the hut of the village.

Another situation of this mother-father contract is the damsel in distress contract. The damsel, like a beautiful adolescent girl, looks for a father to give her the self-esteem of womanhood as well as an honored place in society. The knightly man plays a patriarch to save the damsel from her own fragility. She must do what she can to uphold his self-esteem as a man. He must take care of her emotionally and physically in a hostile world. They are stuck in that contract even though as time goes on he feels less and less a man and she feels less and less a grown up woman. They are unconsciously contracted and stuck in archetypes that keep them in the village. (There is an extended discussion of Knights and Damsels in the Appendix.)

Another situation involves children. The unconscious contract can be between two adolescents. Both will have fun, enjoy life, start careers and have little outside responsibilities. Jobs are there to support a somewhat hedonistic lifestyle. Then the woman becomes pregnant. She is engulfed in the mother archetype and can't wait to be a mother. However, the boy adolescent loses his play partner. He feels abandoned as she feels fulfilled. The original contract is broken. He becomes the betrayed spoiled boy. These marriages often last little longer than the birth of the child.

If a committed relationship is to survive, these unconscious contracts must be unearthed and understood. Most couples are shocked to realize they have been acting out of their contract for years. There is hope if each partner realizes their own half of the contract and stops blaming the other. Each partner must then be dedicated to do their own initiatory work to change their part of the contract. Only then can the recontracting begin.

Household Stage

Sometimes the original contract, though childlike and unconscious, meets the immediate needs of the couple. For example, in most traditional marriages each member of the couple takes a stereotypical role. The woman becomes primarily a mother, both to the children and to the man, even though she might have a job. A man becomes the father, both to the children and the woman. The couple eventually relates as mother and father, rarely as husband and wife. In this arrangement, the boy acts out his father script and his masculine persona while getting his mother needs met. The girl becomes a mother, while getting her father needs met by a protector/provider.

This contract works well during the family, or what I call householder, stage. At least it works enough to keep the relationship fairly intact. And it often works well for couples with young children. As long as neither partner grows or regresses significantly, the marriage endures. These are the traditional marriages that have worked by society's standards for thousands of years. This is the patriarchal marriage, and still the dominant model of marriage in our society.

In the case of a working patriarchal marriage, the couple is psychologically ready only to make a life stage commitment, not a lifetime commitment. For the life stage of householding and family building, each partner is clear about the expectations of the contract and has the emotional capability of following through. The couple can often accomplish one life stage together. They can keep their commitment because of clear expectations going in. Their contract is clear because it is the model contract of the day. And up to about 100 years ago, this was the type of marriage that was the model of a total committed relationship.

The householder stage of marriage is still the life stage most people are taught to accomplish. In the past by the time most men were at the end of this stage, they were into old age, or dead. In this case the traditional adult lifetime, and marriage time, spanned two life stages, householding and old age. In very few marriages did both members of the couple reach the end of the householder stage together. Many women died in childbirth, or from complications of childbirth. Men often died in war or from overwork.

The traditional marriage worked for centuries for the patriarchal man. Men lived and died within the father paradigm, finding success with being a provider to wife and children. Men also enjoyed whatever pleasure there was in having social and political control in the marketplace. Success had little to do with finding emotional intimacy with a partner. Success had little to do with calling. There was no vibrant next stage of married life after the householder one.

The negative side of this paradigm, today, is the pseudo-initiation that the patriarchy promises. The illusion of manhood is no substitute for manhood itself. The positive side of the paradigm is that in our culture this is the time a man can get father needs met, and ego strengthened, by being a good father. During this time a man can unconsciously father himself and thus provide a foundation for the next initiatory step. He, sometimes with the help of other fathers, can ready himself for the Elder's call.

The patriarchal marriage still works for many couples today through the householder stage. This is true even if it is a second marriage. Then something new happens. The marriage becomes very fragile and often falls apart, often at the time when the youngest child reaches adolescence. The something new is modern midlife. The waning time of householdership is the time a modern man reaches midlife instead of death. Marriage then often loses its patriarchal meaning to a man. The man is no longer an active father. He is often exhausted or disillusioned by his provider role. Patriarchal motivation is lost. The illusion of manhood starts to become clear.

This is the time the Elder voice starts more insistent questioning. The existing marriage contract starts losing its meaning on many levels. The marriage and the man are at the crossroad between village and wilderness.

Recontracting In the Wilderness

Today, the marriage commitment calls for a true lifetime commitment rather than the life stage commitment of our forebears. Cultural and religious expectations have not changed, even though practice has. Most marriages must go through several more adult life stages if they endure to death, many more than earlier marriages. Each transition to another stage has the seeds of a crisis. Each crisis carries the possibility of initiatory transformation.

The modern committed relationship involves the inevitability of crises over many life stage transitions, as men and women live through more life stages. However, there is a lack of modern Elders to mirror this new reality.

There is little social support in our society to provide a model for a healthy lifetime commitment. There is little social awareness of the cost and the opportunity of a lifetime committed relationship.

If a man is able to realize that his unhappiness is a result of his lack of initiation, and not the result of choosing the wrong partner, he has passed a crucial test in his initiatory journey. He may have chosen a person unsuited to his path, but he will not know that until after he has passed through several initiatory experiences, and been transformed by them.

In Elder cultures marriage is acceptable for men who have been initiated. In our Elderless, modern time most men are not ready for psychological initiation until about 35. Yet most of us make at least one lifetime commitment before that age. If men can use relationship as an initiatory experience, the premature commitment takes on meaning and can work.

Age 35-45 is the time that the traditional marriage crisis happens. It is also the time the initiatory archetype becomes a strong inner drive. These dual crises can provide the terrible opportunity for deep initiatory work that can lead to a true lifetime commitment, as well as to the goal of full manhood. As in all crises there is danger in the opportunity

Recontracting involves, first, an acknowledgment of the loss of the previous relationship. For the inner boy this often means a separation from a wife as a mother figure. Sometimes the wife in a marriage starts this separation by her own maturing process. A maturing wife or partner will no longer accept the expected role of being understanding and amenable. She might no longer accept the male role as the head of the family. Since she is looking less for a father figure, she will feel less of a need to give the lead to her husband.

Sometimes it is the emerging man who will actively separate. For example, a man will no longer accept an angry, frustrated mother/wife and is willing to face the risk of the aloneness of no mother at all. This may be after years of having chosen to "go along to get along." Or maybe the boy was addicted sexually, and refused to give up the high of sexual pleasure and union for the aloneness of separation. Or his addiction to pornography prolongs some illusion of female union. One day he might realize that the mother connection is not worth his pain. He will face his fear of anger as separation instead of enduring the neurotic anxiety of worrying about her reactions.

The initiatory loss of the old marriage will always bring disorientation and a feeling of not having a place. A man will feel married legally but have no sense of a real marriage. Since most often the separation happens emotionally not physically, this is a very confusing state of mind, a sign one is in the wilderness. A man is in the limbo of the other side, where he is neither married nor single. He is surrounded by the paradox of the other side.

Often both members of the couple will find themselves not acting like married couples 'should' act. Neither will know how to act in the limbo of no contract, with the uncertainty of no guaranteed commitment even though they are still together. Depression will follow. This will be both the depression of loss, and the initiatory depression. This depression will often cause disruption of the process for most men, because they will take depression as a sign that the process is not working. Yet a man and a woman need to stay in this initiatory place, sometimes for extended periods of time, for the recontracting to work.

The limbo between contracts always feels like nothing is happening. All feels lost. There seems no well-being or comfort anywhere, since previous sources of nurturing have been taken away with the previous contract, and previous roles have no meaning. Both find themselves in the wilderness. This separation is the time of being alone together. Individual initiatory aloneness is predominant.

The separation doesn't need to be physical, though sometimes it is. For the separation is really happening in the soul of each partner. Each member of the couple is already in the wilderness of their own. This is an initiatory time not only for the man, but for the woman and the couple. The couple will increasingly question the paradox of how separation and aloneness can possibly help two people get closer. Yet, if both members of a couple don't go through a transformation, the couple will continue to flounder, and the initiatory paradox cannot work.

I counseled a couple who were separated physically, as well as emotionally, and were trying to recontract. However, the wife could not get past the idea that her husband needed to come home before they could work on the relationship. Whenever some progress was made, or things went badly, she would angrily demand that he return to the house as the only way to make it work. She was overwhelmed by separation, and the consequent paradox of initiation. Because she could not be alone, she could not be truly together.

Often one member of a couple will feel too overwhelmed to risk separation and loss. This was usually the member who was most satisfied with the previous life stage. This member is not ready to move on, too frightened to take the risk. Usually this member sees no need for the major change of recontracting. S/he is not aware of the danger the relationship is in because s/he is looking though uninitiated eyes. S/he would have voted to rearrange the deck chairs on the Titanic.

This is where Eldering energy is crucial, for both the man and the woman. If both members of a couple can consciously and willingly endure the pain and paradox of feeling intensely alone, while being in relationship, they will allow the initiatory transformation to happen. Both will usually need an Elder/counselor or an Eldering group to help them understand and endure. As Scott Peck says, "ultimately, if they stay in therapy, all couples learn that a true acceptance of their own and each other's individuality and separateness is the only foundation upon which a mature marriage can be based and real love can grow."

Covenant

Even if one member of a couple is stuck in a previous life stage, the other, who feels called, should first do his initiatory work before deciding on the viability of the relationship. Sometimes the continued work of one member will ultimately provide motivation for the other.

On Ground Hog Day, Phil somehow realized that he had to go his own way, while holding his love for Rita. He had gone through night after night of night ending slaps in trying to be with Rita in his old, narcissistic way. He had tried to forget her through a sexual addiction with a hairdresser. He had given up trying to manipulate her emotions in order to seduce her. He was stung by her comment that he loved nobody but himself.

He ended up going his own initiatory way, with seemingly no hope of relationship with Rita. In the process of his initiatory depression, he humbly realizes he is a jerk. He also becomes a person who is genuinely interested in those around him. When Rita asks him to have coffee, he hardly notices the caring attention of others. He casually talks of seeing her later.

Phil has found his initiatory direction. He starts to accept Rita with no romantic strings, but as a person and friend. His adolescent is healed. They stay in the same bed. He makes no adolescent moves. He is content with their closeness. He starts to understand what real love is.

Phil has given up the illusion of Ms. Right. His happiness is in the love of the moment, with no strings and no guarantees. Having grieved so many expectations and regressive needs, Phil is able to love purely in the present. This breakthrough allows the couple to go into the next day with a sense of soul connection that makes for a true covenant.

In fact, any long term relationship will have to go through numerous big and little recontracting times, if it is to be healthy and vibrant. Couples who use their relationship as initiatory experiences are able to see major crises as necessary opportunities for growth. The first major recontracting that a couple goes through will initiate them into a new kind of coupleness. They will come to realize that healthy commitment involves depth of soul not length of time. Soul depth involves a connectedness that transcends many contracts and doesn't rely on the sacredness of commitment to keep it alive. Soul depth turns a contract into a covenant.

The couple will realize that a lifetime commitment is a covenant with a deep sense of soul connection that transcends even marriage. A covenant is open to many transformations and many initiatory transitions that involve risk and change, sometimes even the change of permanent separation. Covenant always respects the individual journey first, but also opens one to the profound affect another can have on that journey. Separation is rare when soul connection has been formed.

A contract works on the status quo and assumes no change. A marriage covenant mirrors life itself, with its many lives within a life. A covenanted marriage welcomes change as a sign of life, and welcomes life wherever it leads. If two people go deep within the wilderness of their own soul, they will also find the key to their coupleness there. After a number of successful recontracts, a sense of covenant will usually form. There will be a sense of calling as a couple as strong as an individual calling. Coupleness then becomes a sacred thing, an intimate part of the personal journey. The question of length of time will seem irrelevant. One lifetime will feel too short.

A paradox often comes into play when one member of the couple starts doing initiatory work, as Phil did. When the initiatory work happens, a maturing person, especially a man, starts needing the other less, but wants the other more. This lessening of need allows an individual to wait on a stuck partner, without the feeling of desperation or overwhelming aloneness. And a man doing his initiatory work will find that he has much less time to obsess about the relationship because he is caught up in his own work. Time and its meaning change. And goals change. As a result, a man may be led to stay in a relationship for good reasons he will only realize later.

But the challenges for a lifetime covenant are enormous and the pitfalls are many. If one's partner is not able to move to the next stage, including recontracting, an initiated man may feel led to separate physically and go a different way. This means divorce or permanent separation. An initiated man will take an active part in this situation, without being impulsive or vengeful. Upon separation he will feel mostly sadness. Heavy sadness, with little anger or desperation, is usually the sign that the man has worked through this separation as an initiatory experience.

However, if a couple is able to recontract they will have built a whole new relationship. They will have achieved an invaluable initiatory step that will also be initiatory for each individual. Marriage will then become a true source of inspiration, motivating a man to continue his initiatory journey to completion.

After his initiation Tomme leaves his family to find his beloved. He is now able to marry. He finds her in her family's compound. She lets him take her away from her family with the mock violence of radical separation. They both separate from mother and father. They are man and woman. They consummate their marriage in the wilderness.

Chapter 20
Just Peace

The journey of manhood is a psychospiritual one that demands modern man's attention. Society's and the world's survival depends on men consciously taking up this mission toward inner wisdom and purpose. Burned out depressed men are unconscious dangerous men, pawns in destructive patriarchal power schemes.

A man, though alone, never makes the journey just for himself. A man's initiation is not a personal luxury. Many are waiting for his presence though they don't know it. Many are counting on him though they've never met him.

This may sound melodramatic. In my experience it isn't.

In returning in service a man often feels he is fulfilling a prompt or desire that is his heritage, like a son willingly inheriting a legacy from a father. The active creating of a healthy community is every man's legacy. The active movement to create a larger, just, caring community comes from the deep masculine, becoming a man's mission. This is the deep masculine that is the reflection of the masculine face of God.

Wisdom of the Ancestors

In writing this book I have consciously drawn on the wisdom of indigenous people and cultures. Studying their puberty initiation rituals became a gateway to learning the archetypal values, customs, and beliefs of many of their cultures. In following my intuition I found much more than I could imagine. I could see the world from their perspective, grasp a bit of their wisdom.

Indigenous people experience this wisdom as coming from their ancestors. At times I felt these ancestors, these ancient Elders were speaking through me. Then I realized how these ancestors could speak through the Elder within. I felt the Elder voice of ancestors speaking with a masculine voice when talking of creating just relations in community. I heard the same masculine voice prompting me to protect Mother Earth.

Of course I have drawn on other wisdoms, on other religious and spiritual traditions that hold universal wisdom. Yet indigenous cultures have embodied and lived out more of their stated values than any I have studied. Indigenous peoples were, and often are, walking their talk. The closest smaller cultures that have lived out their ideals are probably monastic religious traditions.

Yes, many of these indigenous cultures have been corrupted over the recent centuries, many from the dark side of certain religious traditions. I'm sure that there were rogue bands and whole tribes, even from the beginning of humankind, who lived out a dark, destructive lifestyle. Yet even until today, especially today, the ancestors' wisdom is reemerging in teachings and examples that are significantly affecting Western culture. Increasingly these ancient teachings are being studied and lived out in modern ways, heard by many men and women who are going through an ancient initiation in a modern way.

I say all this because I believe that cultures of the world need to return to the values of indigenous cultures, to the wisdom of these ancestors, to literally survive. There is a legacy here. Initiated men and women are the last real hope that we can save the earth and the dignity of every being on her. I believe we are in the middle of a tragedy for earth and its people. And this is a tragedy of our own making. In this case, it is not only men and women and children who are being wounded, even destroyed in their spirit. The earth itself is being grievously wounded.

I see no real hope for the honoring of the spirit of all people and the honoring of what indigenous people call our Mother Earth unless these indigenous values are embraced by modern Elders and taught to future generations.

Paul Hawken in his book *Blessed Unrest* talks of the huge underground movement in the world for social justice and honoring the environment. He speaks of up to 2 million groups in the world operating under the radar where "The quiet hub of the new movement—its heart and soul—is indigenous culture."

Peacemaker

The journey of manhood begins when a man starts to hear the voice of wisdom within, the Elder voice that the ancestors heard, and chooses to listen. From there the inner transformation starts. There starts the journey that results in deep inner peace, the peace that passes understanding. Inner peace is the product of initiation and the signal a man has reached his destination.

I believe that peace in families, friendships, nations, and the world will only spring from the inner peace in every man. The initiated man learns, as most indigenous people know, that his inner peace produces a resonance that triggers potential peace in those around him. And a sense of awe can follow as a man sees the ripple effect of his wisdom, knowing that the source of that wisdom comes from a place way beyond his own ego. Indigenous people intuitively know the symbiosis between personal peace and community peace. They take seriously Gandhi's exhortation to be the change you want to see in the world.

An initiated man will feel in partnership with a benevolent force working for good in the world, a force he has befriended in the darkest time of his Ordeal. In a real sense he will feel part of a team that he can be proud of, a spiritual team that he is willing to suffer for. And teamwork is a deeply ingrained masculine endeavor.

He will know that acting from his own deep identity is essential for the greater good. He continually chooses for those he loves. And the circle of those he loves seems to increase daily. In fact, the more a man grows into his full manhood the larger the circle becomes, beyond his family, his clan, his nation, his religion, his race. He cannot help feeling a brother to all. He tends to be the instant brother wherever he wanders.

Though it sounds an oxymoron, an initiated man will invariably become a warrior for peace. He will not shy away from conflict that he sees in his own life first, then in the world around him. He will not withdraw out of fear but treat an unjust situation as an Ordeal where he risks his safety for the unknown good that he may facilitate. An initiated man is a peacemaker. He is willing to risk even his life for peace. He can risk because he has become used to risk, because he is a warrior.

Indigenous Justice

The warrior of peace invariably develops a sense of justice beyond me and mine. Sharing that feeling with loved ones, men and women, who are also partners for justice is the final piece in the puzzle of inner peace and community peace. There can never be enduring peace without justice. There can never be peace in the world without peaceful men. There can never be peace without all participating.

The third big step of the initiatory process has to do with returning to a man's community with a gift. That gift most often includes an acute sense of the need for justice for every member of his community. He yearns for a peaceful community, yearning to share with others the deep peace he feels most of the time. The initiated man works in whatever way his talents and mission calls for a just community.

But what is justice? In writing this book I am more convinced than ever that indigenous cultures have great lessons about what it means to be fully human, including the meaning of peace and justice in community. They knew of Elder justice, the justice envisioned by initiated men and women who took their call seriously. Theirs was not a theoretical understanding. Initiated men lived justice as they were taught by their Elders and their initiatory understanding. Their witness was then a living lesson to others.

Indigenous justice was based on spiritual teachings. The assumption was that each member of the community was connected in a meaningful way to every other member. Every member had a spark of Spirit in him or her. Most tribes called themselves by a name which meant The People. Each member was a Person with dignity. Each person was assumed to be striving to be a full human being. To be fully human was to be responsible for the well-being of all the People. This was indigenous love.

Justice was connected to a kind of harmony between people. The outer harmony of the tribe was connected to the inner harmony of each member. If one member was out of harmony, with inner conflict leading to destructiveness in the tribe, the first response was invariably how to help the man or woman be restored to inner harmony. Next, the question would be how to restore the harmony of the tribe hurt by the destructive act. Punishment was not a rationale. Redemption and reconciliation was, followed by compensation to the wronged individual or family.

As I have mentioned one of the main values, especially among Native Americans, was the giveaway. This was a ritual and value of sharing any goods that one possessed with the whole community. This sharing was at once a releasing of attachment to the material realm and an honoring of the priority of Spirit. Literally their sacrifice of giving embodied the meaning of the word sacrifice, to make sacred. By these acts the material was seen as sacred. Instead of materialism there was mysticism. If spirit is first, materialism does not become a religion.

Gandhi once said that communism and capitalism are equally dangerous to the human community precisely because both were based on a foundation of materialism. Indigenous people loved and learned from the material world. They enjoyed the fruits of the world and their labor. This natural world of Mother Nature was also how Spirit most often communicated with People. The giveaway was a continual reminder and witness that spiritual values always trumped material concerns.

The giveaway was based on spirituality. As Jamie Sams says, "In native tradition, no one is ever abandoned, orphaned, or left without dwellings, or help. The understanding among Native people is that when one shares all that one has, in order that the People may live, honor and abundance is brought to the giver....Those who are blessed with possessions and food have always shared with those who are lacking." The giveaway is a ritual of faith and trust in being taken care of by Spirit. There was never any justification for some to live in luxury while others of the same tribe starved or lived in abject poverty. If there were people in the tribe who went hungry the whole tribe or clan lost face.

The giveaway was based on spiritual values first. A man who gave away much of what was of value to a tribe was most respected. He would often be chosen as a leader. This was not a game of who can die with the most toys. This was not a value of entitlement where talent gave a man the right to hoard treasures while others starved. This was not an accidental and impersonal trickle down of goods that never quite trickle down. This was personal giving and sacrifice. This was not a rationalization of reliance on a benevolent invisible hand. This was flesh and blood hands creating a just, peaceful community.

The lack of material success was not a sign of the withholding of God's blessing as some religions teach. People were not blamed for their poverty. Material success was not a sign of being saved. Patriarchal power was seen as selfishness. It is interesting that in early American history the giveaway ritual was actually banned by the U.S. government. The patriarchy cannot understand the sacred.

One of the most profound giveaway's of indigenous peoples was how the Elderly would see their responsibility to their people. If an Elderly person became disabled or just frail and ceased to be a perceived help to the tribe he or she would often voluntarily leave for the wilderness to pass over to the other side to not be a drain on the community. This death was a gift to the community as well as a sign of faith in the spiritual foundation of their life. The experience of initiation showed them the reality of the goodness of the other side and relieved them of any fear of that place. The witness reminded every initiated man and woman of their priorities and their initiatory gift.

With spirit first, justice meant a community of mutual respect and responsibility. Each responsible for the harmony of the whole and in service to the inner harmony of each other. The initiated man understands this coevolution and endeavors to live this understanding.

Indigenous Community

Patriarchal community most often sees the individual as primarily serving the community. It subtly ends up being all one way. As such patriarchal values often tend toward totalitarianism, where a gifted few control the structure of life of the many. The proletarian dictatorship of communism is one example. Patriarchal authoritarian actions in the name of national security or the free market system is another example. If the masculine tends to build structure, the dark masculine always moves to rationalize and create social structures that serve the power elite under the guise of serving the whole community.

Indigenous community is the opposite. The community is there to serve the spiritual path of the individual soul. As Malidoma says, "The community thus takes upon itself the responsibility of nurturing and protecting the individual, because the individual, knowing his or her purpose, will then invest energy in sustaining the community."

Spiritual purpose of each man and woman is first. This is the bedrock value of the indigenous person. This is the foundational value of the initiated man. From inner to outer. Spirit incarnating in matter.

In indigenous populations nobody has exclusive connection to Spirit. There is no elite who wield power over the rest. There are no creative individuals who deserve wealth because they create wealth. Wealth for indigenous peoples is finding purpose and living that purpose out in a community of purpose. Wealth is a wealth of spiritual mission and mutual caring. Wealth is a spiritual thing.

If a man wishes to grow to the point of bringing healthy patriarchal and Elder energy to his community he must learn to be very aware of the need of those around him for encouragement and blessing to follow their initiatory call no matter what the obstacles. He also must continually witness to the absolute existence of that call for every individual in his community.

Equality

The symbol of the social construct of indigenous peoples is the circle. In most of these cultures dialogue and decision making was done in a circle comprised of all initiated men and women. All could have a say. Often huts or other shelters were placed in a circle to show the respect and honor of every member.

On the other hand patriarchal symbol is the pyramid. This has its place in a crisis. But top down authority most often leads to a chronic condition of very few being heard and even fewer making decisions for all.

The circle is a symbol that honors the truth of every member of the tribe and each person's spiritual path. Children were taught from that truth and could look forward to their voice being heard after initiation. The inner path of self-discovery was intimately connected to the path of the whole tribe. Any *a priori* ignoring of an individual ran the risk of ignoring spiritual facts that could have a profound negative effect on the community. Nobody, even a nominal leader, automatically had the truth and wisdom for the whole tribe. The leader was most often a facilitator and listener. When he or she did make a decision it was with respect for the consensus of those speaking. Men and women saw themselves as together looking for wisdom. There was a constant search for synergy.

Laurens van der Post befriended and studied the Bushmen of Southern Africa his whole life. These indigenous people had many legends describing their history and relationship with their divine ancestors. Yet he responds that "a plurality of legends is very characteristic of the Bushmen for whom no one person's story or perception of the supernatural, is regarded as inferior to another's—each tells its own truth and can illumine some aspect of the divine." Their political culture reflects this spiritual equality as "they have no chiefs or rulers, and leadership may not even be vested in one individual."

I believe an initiated man will intuitively understand and embrace indigenous values related to peace and justice partly because the Elder within has the genetic memory of this indigenous way, a way lived for tens of thousands of years. So part of any hope for our future lies in the wisdom of the past, in the wisdom of our ancestors. From all that I have studied there was relative peace and prosperity and spiritual connection for those tens of thousands of years. Most accounts of Western people first encountering indigenous populations talk of these people's natural hospitality and friendliness.

It is also interesting to note that many indigenous peoples have decided from signs they have been given that now is the time to share their wisdom with the world. This is true for the Hopi, the Aborigines, Malidoma's Dagara tribe, and many others.

I don't want to untruthfully idealize indigenous culture. It is easier to have peace in the midst of the material abundance of prehistoric nature. It is easier to have justice on a smaller scale. Yet Western culture, in embracing patriarchy, seems to believe that there is little wisdom in those who don't have power no matter what the scale. The dark patriarchal warrior is about dark power, and patriarch is king. This power is about getting not giving. It is about the myth of scarcity and survival at the cost of another, rather than the reality of abundance and synergy with the other. As an example, there is enough food today in the world so nobody need starve or suffer from malnutrition. It is the myth of scarcity and the consequent need for political power that keeps some people impoverished so others have much more than they need. This kind of power gives the illusion of security. Security becomes trust in the dark warrior ego. The sacred is seen as weakness.

Gratitude

The ultimate value of indigenous people all over the world is the gift of gratitude. To an indigenous person all of life is a gift. For example, in Native American tradition the hunted animals they used for food and myriad utensils and clothes were seen to voluntarily give their lives for the good of the tribe. Animals were asked for their life and were thanked and honored when life was given. Animals did not owe human beings nor were they seen as owned by right of some spiritual dominion. All life was seen as a gift from Spirit. The ultimate sin was ingratitude.

The initiated man is full of gratitude. The eyes of humility allow him to see gifts all around without the illusion that he somehow created it all or deserves it. He sees his own life as a gift as well as a giveaway.

Psychologically speaking it is almost impossible to be in gratitude and not be in the present. Depression is often about the past. Anxiety is often about the future. Being grateful in the present is one of the best stress relievers of all to say nothing of the stress relief it can give to those around us!

To indigenous peoples gratitude is only just. If all they needed was seen as a giveaway by Spirit then gratitude was natural. There was no entitlement here, as if the People deserved whatever they got. Even worse, the People have never sought to take or exploit from some sense of ownership of the natural world. Gratitude is always a way of honoring creation, a continual prayer of acknowledgment.

Why the Green Mother?

Indigenous people see nature as the primary source of communication of Spirit and the most truthful reflection of the essence of Spirit. As above, so below. Nature is their Bible. Malidoma talks of nature as "their first home, the home that holds the wisdom of the cosmos." Their lessons are in the behavior of all of mother earth's creatures. In their spiritual understanding respect for nature is the same as respect for Spirit. Most people would be scandalized if the culture talked of using the pages of the Bible for fire starters. Indigenous people are scandalized at how this culture rationalizes the destruction of sacred nature for the temporary warmth of nonrenewable oil or gas heating.

Most men know, deep inside, that the earth is sacred. Most men will go to nature when they are troubled, if they haven't completely lost themselves in addiction. As I have mentioned, many men naturally go to nature as a way of prayer or meditation, reminding themselves of their initiatory path or instinctively yearning for it. I include most hunters and fishermen in this category. Most of these men have an innate respect for nature by respecting the balance in nature that their hunting may provide, as well as preserving the habitat of their prey. This is the natural instinct of the authentic warrior hunter, and the heart of any true sportsman. Hopefully, more men will learn from Elders that this instinct is as much spiritual as hunting savvy. And that their prey also has much to teach them.

Indigenous people see Earth as mother and alive. I believe that a man's relation to the earth and environment tells a lot about his initiatory and spiritual maturity. Does a man see the Earth and its resources as a limitless supply, which can be taken with no return, like an uninitiated boy expecting a mother object to always comfort him or a woman to be sexually used? Or does he feel a strong sense of gratitude at the sight of food on the table or the warmth of a wood fire? Does he take from the Earth based on a world view that when this planet is exhausted humanity will be ready to find another, just as he transfers his mother needs to a new woman? Or does he look on the Earth as a covenanted relationship of give and take, sharing the sacred, continually renewing and growing? Does a man act like a dark patriarch exploiting the" inert" Earth, like his subordinates, only for his own gain? Or does he partner with the living Earth to create a vibrant community?

Indigenous people around the world today are desperately fighting to protect Mother Earth. They see the natural connection between the health of the community and the health of the environment, their mother. Both require the acknowledgment of a vibrant, respectful, even loving, interconnectedness where everyone and every being counts because there is some of Spirit in everything. For the initiated man has taken himself out of the center of the universe and humbly honored his newfound higher power in that place.

I believe the modern initiated man will see his community as more than the people he serves. He will see his community as including the natural structure of the web of life as well as the manmade social ones.

Elder Watch

Elders, men and women, were responsible for the spiritual well-being of their community. They made sure the values of harmony, peace, and justice were honored and followed. They were the mediators and reconcilers. They were the institutional memory of the best the culture had created. They taught this history in the process of initiating the young. They reminded the whole community of this history when important decisions were to be made.

They were close to the other side in spirit as well as age so they were more immune to the petty ego games that all were tempted by. They were so close to the other side they heard the voice of the ancestors. True Elders were not rigid about tradition. They also realized that each new initiated generation had its latest, vibrant message from the other side. They were there to help discern what that message was.

Today we are in such need of Elders instead of dark patriarchs. We need mediators and reconcilers who have found a healthy place for their own egos. We need patriarchs and Elders who don't want power over others but who want to empower others. Initiation is a ritual of empowerment in the context of a spiritual tradition. The spiritual tradition includes the belief in the sacred calling of every person within the larger sacred context of the natural world. Elders hold the vision that if every initiated man and woman follows their call the community will self-guide to harmony. Elders know the dark side of humanity can only be contained by supporting the spiritual vision of every human.

Ultimately authentic Elders of the past knew that all life, especially human life, is connected. They saw all men as brothers and all women as sisters, not just their tribe. They saw this. They felt this. It was beyond belief. Today we need the same kind of authentic Elders. For all of us men this starts with initiation.

Epilogue

Most men are good men trying to do the right thing. Unfortunately, most men are burnt out trying to do the right thing without questioning what is deeply right. Thus, depression is rampant. Numbness is pervasive. Addictions become the default antidepressant. Yet addictions only depress more. The cycle continues as numbness leads to more addiction.

This book has been about the mystery of initiation and the mystery of manhood. Even more it is about the path to the feeling of aliveness. Initiation into manhood is the only real and lasting antidepressant.

The initiatory journey of manhood is perilous and painful, full of paradox and mystery. Men come to me for answers. I talk of mystery and nagging, deeper questions. Men come for pain relief. I talk of the relief of handling pain. Men come feeling misunderstood. I talk of misunderstanding themselves. Most men ask for help in being a success in the world. I talk of the risk of being seen as a failure. Most men want patriarchal instructions. I talk of the wise Elder within. Yet most men stay to hear more because part of them knows that there is truth in this message of initiation.

I have written this book acting as an Elder culture keeper. I have translated the initiatory experience of indigenous cultures into modern terms. I have used the archetype of initiation as a guide for modern man's psychospiritual transformation to wholeness and maturity. I have tried to meld ancient and modern wisdoms. I have talked of other cultural Elders who speak of aspects of the inner journey. I have alerted you to your inner Elder voice, the sacred voice of intuition, the voice of Spirit within.

I have also endeavored to act as an Elder by creating and holding a space where men can sit safely with their questions. I have held and offered a vision of the direction their journey needs to take. I have tried to hold a sense of hope so that men may expect that their journey will bring them answers.

If you have already found your mission through initiatory struggle, remember that you are also called to father and Elder younger men and their next generations. We all are called to reconnect this circle of men from generation to generation. We are all called to make this an Elder culture.

I wish you the peace that this psychospiritual journey brings. Thank you for giving my words and thoughts your attention.

Appendix

Damsels

Has anyone noticed how a great many of the books written about men have titles referring to knighthood. There are *Knights in Shining Armor, Knights Without Armor, Knights in Rusty Armor*. Robert Johnson writes of the knightly myth of Parsifal in his book, *He*. Robert Bly talks of slaying the Red Knight on a man's way to maturity.

It could be argued that the time of the knights started a unique era in the development of men's psyches. This is the time of the 12th Century, the high Middle Ages, when a new cultural myth was born. The knightly quest was actually a variation and adaptation of the aboriginal initiation archetype described by Joseph Campbell in his book *The Hero with a Thousand Faces*. (In the same spirit this book is an attempt to reinterpret this archetype in a modern context).

This new cultural paradigm posited the idea of the common man's individual search for personal identity. The new idea emerged of the man, as knight, going on an individual search for God and self, while serving the community. Just as this era could be considered the beginning of the adolescence of our Western culture, the young knight starting on his quest was, like most adolescents, a sincere but naïve teenager. He was like the older adolescent who is eager for initiation but has little idea how hard the Ordeal, or the Quest in the knight's vocabulary, will be. And he has few tools or guidance to complete his quest. But his intent is noble and his desire shows a growing maturity.

Knights were heroes and heroes could be any of us, not just royalty or clergy. The idea of knighthood introduced the modern ideal of individual emotional maturity. To the knight, maturity involved the endurance of emotional and physical pain for a spiritual good. This warrior had a higher power to be subservient to. Just as all healthy, ethical warriors need a king, the traditional knight's king was Christ. Though few knights or men reached this ideal the template of a personal call to personal integrity and service was formed.

The spiritual good that was sought was the welfare of the community based on the value of love and generativity. The knight's quest for spiritual enlightenment mirrored the adolescent stage of questing and questioning. The knight moved away from his village at this time, moving toward the other side, moving toward spiritual values.

Modern Damsels

Knighthood also introduced the cultural ideal of a healthier relationship to women. The time of the knights marked the beginning of the idea that men and women could have a different relationship than that of master and slave. This was the first time in Western culture that men and women could love each other, rather than just join as an economic unit. The idea that a woman could be a partner and inspiration to a man started at this time, with the concept of courtly love.

Courtly love was a man's non-sexual devotion to a woman other than his mother. This love introduced the notion that a woman could be something other than a mother object. Courtly love brought women into partnership with men on the spiritual journey, helping men to separate from mother and the village. Women gave men the inspiration to take the spiritual journey or quest. They were a catalyst for men to embark on the road to maturity.

Adolescence can bring a man to a new relationship with women, one that is more mature than the young boy and his mother. The knightly ideal of a new relationship with women has some authentic goals for the adolescent to strive for. Unfortunately, the ideal knightly quest was lost as it has trickled down to modern culture, especially concerning a man's relationship with women. Though a man may grow to a new and healthier maturity level in relationship with women, the temptation to get stuck, or regress, gets stronger.

Robert Johnson, in his extremely wise book *We,* talks of the devolution of courtly love. He talks of knightly love, starting as a spiritual pursuit, becoming in our culture the pursuit of romantic love as a goal in itself. On this pursuit by both men and women, men have substituted the love of a woman for their own search for identity. Romantic love becomes a substitute for initiation. Romantic love keeps a man stuck at the crossroads. Romantic love becomes permanently adolescent love.

Harvey Hornstein in his book, *A Knight in Shining Armor,* talks of an agreement a man often makes with the woman in his life at the beginning of a relationship. He will provide for and protect her, in the form of bigger castles and more ornate carriages, as a damsel in distress who is meant for higher things. She will then make him feel like a man by massaging his manly ego in a form of chivalrous adoration. The romance will turn both their heads. Infatuation will bring both to a level of intoxication that feels noble and meaningful. The man will feel like a questing knight who is close to the Grail.

As the infatuation ends (in Johnson's book, this is after three years) the quest for the man degenerates into the competition of the marketplace, as castles are quite expensive. The knight finds that he has never left the village. In fact, he has regressed to the world of the father. He spends his time being paternal, finding his identity in protecting by providing. He then finds that his damsel's acceptance of his castle, and all those gifts and goods, does not make him feel like a knightly man.

Today, damsels as inspiration have become mere damsels in distress. As Harvey Hornstein points out, finding the right damsel has become the end of a man's search for self. Instead of finding inspiration to start the search for manhood, men see women as the means to manhood. And the quest is lost.

Rescuing a dependent damsel makes a man feel strong and manly in an adolescent way. The adoration from a desirable, but naive, damsel can substitute for self-esteem. So the knight settles for this shortsighted adoration and never leaves his castle, just as the adolescent in our society rarely leaves the village, just as the father never leaves the marketplace.

The stereotypical damsel in distress is an affront to women and is tedious to mature men. At least the damsel of the knightly era, though one dimensional, sent a man off to find his manhood elsewhere. The modern damsel, if she wishes to be rescued, ultimately becomes a frustrated queen, whose castle never relieves her distress. She keeps him in the keep out of dependency, she thought was protection. He stays home out of fear. The adolescent then becomes a frustrated father before he ever becomes a man.

A Knightly Tragedy

Harvey Hornstein calls him manservant. Warren Farrell calls him a disposable protector. According to Aaron Kipnis, he is the man trying to be a Hero by protecting and sacrificing for a woman and family. According to Mark Gerzon he is the hero as Breadwinner. Jan Halpern quotes an executive saying, "Women think we are the privileged sex. But have they ever got it wrong. We are the slaves, sacrificing our needs for the company and the family."

The knight is the beleaguered and misguided Don Quixote, with wonderful ideals that just about kill him. Like the Man of La Mancha, this man is trying to find that inside feeling of manhood and integrity that has so eluded him. The sadness is that he is strong enough to sacrifice for a purpose other than himself. He has enough masculine energy to go part of the way. He has reached an important adolescent stage, and separated from the most regressive parts of his boyhood. The modern knight has qualities that are admirable, and he has admirable motivation. But like the misguided Don, he is like a man living in the wrong time.

Often this man gets started by trying to become the hero in the eyes of his mother. She unknowingly becomes his damsel. He starts on the search to give her the dreams that have eluded her. The mother is usually a kind but overwhelmed woman, the original distressed damsel. Often this hero is the oldest boy in the family, a boy with an absent father. Sometimes he is the second oldest if the oldest son absconds under the responsibility. Sometimes, he is the only responsible boy in an irresponsible family. He is usually the most sensitive and compassionate one.

Because of an absent father, this son starts taking over some of the father's responsibilities around the house. If the father is totally absent through death or desertion, the responsibilities become quite large. The boy starts having to act like a man way before he is ready. He becomes the man of the house before he is a man. He unknowingly puts his adolescence on hold, as he jumps to the persona of manhood.

He tries to give his mother what his father could never give. He does this out of caring, less out of the regressive need for mothering. The patriarchy colludes in this misbegotten hero drama by encouraging men to be responsible and protective. The patriarchal voice calls him selfish or wimpy if he doesn't protect someone.

The adolescent boy becomes the ideal of society's values, as he protects his mother. He does become a cultural hero, treating all women with respect. He comes to believe his heroism will make him a man. When this boy attains an adult body, to match his hero role, he will find himself attracted to distressed damsels. These damsels will look up to him for strength and guidance and protection.

By this time his self-esteem will be very fragile because of his lack of male guidance. Yet he will be old enough to notice that younger women's attentions are making him feel manly. The adolescent damsel's adoring eyes are a powerful attraction. The man will feel he can be a hero again. He will feel like a knight. His damsel will make him feel strong and noble. She has already buoyed his self-esteem. He will be her protector. He will provide for her. Unfortunately, he hasn't thought to wonder why she needs protection, or why she is in need of his providence.

To the adolescent knight, rescuing can become a habit and a reward. As Robert Fisher says in his wonderful allegory, *The Knight in Rusty Armor,* "When the Knight business was slow, he had the annoying habit of rescuing damsels even if they did not want to be rescued, so, although many ladies were grateful to him, just as many were furious with him."

Often he will marry the first distressed damsel who finds him attractive. Through marriage, the adolescent finds a way to fit in. The hero mask seems to be working. His damsel treats him like a man. His dark father voice tells him marriage is the manly and responsible thing to do. The same voice tells him that being single is basically selfish and irresponsible.

The poor adolescent wants badly to become a man. This seems to be the perfect route. So he marries. He has children, soon, and usually becomes a good father. Up to this time his damsel has continued to be adoring and distressed. However, as children come the infatuation spell is broken. The castle becomes just a regular home. The damsel finds that the work of motherhood is tough and demanding, especially with no ladies in waiting. The romance of chivalry fades as the knight and damsel become father and mother. Both feel betrayed.

She has started to realize that the armor, the knightly persona, keeps him from being a real person with her. He is a knight not a friend. She soon feels alone with the children, while her knight is out slaying dragons to support the family. His heroism, the basis of his self-esteem, starts to fade in her eyes. As the wife of Fisher's rusted knight said, "I think you love your armor more than you love me."

The damsel also realizes that her white knight no longer relieves her distress. She will start blaming the knight for her continued distress. She will realize that motherhood is far harder than damselhood. Her distress will increase, even though she loves her children. She will start being critical and unhappy. She will talk of him being gone all the time and not helping with the children. She will wonder what happened to her hero.

The knight will wonder, in his own growing distress, where his adoring damsel went. He will wonder why she is complaining about the very things that knights are supposed to do, providing her with a safe, protective castle and lifestyle. He will not understand what she means when she demands to know who is inside the armor.

The adolescent knight inside the armor will start to get angry. He will not know how to handle his feelings. His damsel has been replaced by a witch. He feels that someone has cast a spell on her, not realizing that she is coming out of a spell, not entering one. She has changed. Someone has taken his manhood away. He has no idea who cast the spell, or how to remove it. He struggles with how to get her back. He neither wants to lose her nor does he want to lose his armor. Yet she complains about the very knightly role she always adored about him.

Is there hope for this confused warrior? Will the distressed damsel ever find a life free of distress? Will this knightly tragedy become a nightly tragedy? Is there hope for Camelot?

It depends.

If a knight gets some healthy guidance from a second father and wise Elder, he will start to realize that he does identify with his armor. He will realize that his armor gives him a sense of meaning that seems to cure the emptiness inside. He will realize that he may be more in love with his armor than he is with his wife. As Frank Pittman says, "Most men have a far stronger passion for their masculinity than for their women, or even for their sexuality, but they try to keep that a secret." Masculinity, here, means the masculine persona, the chainmail and breastplate.

If a man can realize that this cultural masculinity is not really masculine, that mail does not equal male, he can start to look for other answers. He can start to be open to other men who have a different message, pointing to a different road. He will then move on from the crossroads. He will realize that the answer is not in another damsel or another suit of armor.

In Robert Fisher's book, the knight and his damsel start to grow toward initiation. They start to take up healthy adolescent tasks. The hero knight finds he is stuck inside his armor and can't take it off. The armor was too much a part of him. His wife sets boundaries and threatens to leave him if he can't take it off. The knight, in despair, decides to go on a quest to have someone help him remove his armor. He starts on the road to initiation. He starts looking for an Elder. The story of his initiation is a good one that will be continued later.

Romantic Love

The drama of heterosexual love starts to unfold in adolescence. Romantic love and sexual feeling is a symptom of the adolescent trying to individuate, to become a separate self. This type of love can signal the need to leave family and the relationship of woman as mother object. This romantic spell, sometimes called infatuation, is also the first taste of the other side. If understood properly, it can be a strong motivation for an adolescent to grow. As Robert Johnson says, "Romantic love has always been inextricably tied to spiritual aspiration." In other words, this love has a lot to do with initiation.

Adolescence always brings with it the yearning for a connection to the feminine. The feminine for men represents the mystery of the other side and the mystery of his own soul. This connection can be healthy for a man if he realizes its real meaning. But it is a path strewn with obstacles. Indigenous peoples realized how regressive too early relationships with females could be, and usually kept the sexes divided all through adolescence. The adolescent was still too close to the mother object to handle women in another way. It was only after initiation that young men were free to interact with women in a serious way.

Our society skips the stage of healthy adolescence. There is great social pressure to fit into the patriarchy by prematurely getting married and starting a family and career. Our culture confuses the individual need for romantic love with society's need for marriage. The need behind romantic love is the need for individuation. It is each man's need. Marriage is society's need. Marriage is much better for the marketplace. It provides a growing, stable market. It also provides motivation for men to produce. Single men are less stable, less procreative, and less obedient.

I have talked to numerous men who speak of getting married because it seemed to be the right thing to do at the time, and everyone else was doing it. This seems especially true for war vets who just want to feel normal again after returning from war. Marriage provided vets with normalcy and a sense of nurturance after the horror and deprivation of war. It also gave men a reason to forget.

Being deprived of a healthy adolescence robs a man of the foundation he needs for initiation and beyond. This deprivation robs a man of brothers and the freedom of experimenting with his newfound sense of self. It also robs a man of significant emotional relationships with women.

Sex

Society is frightened of the individuating adolescence for many reasons already talked about. The patriarchy is also threatened because of the emerging sexuality brought on by adolescent puberty. There is a great fear of sexuality, approaching archetypal proportions, in Western civilization that forms our unhealthy sexual attitudes. This fear is curiously lacking in most Eastern religions and cultures, as well as in indigenous cultures.

The fear of "selfish," "licentious" sex, especially among adolescents, dominates our formal social attitudes. The message we all get about sex is more shaming than uplifting, more about denying it than living it. Healthy heterosexual relations are often stymied or truncated by these shaming messages and structures. Yet, informally, society is obsessed with sex, both by moralizing on it and yet acting it out. Both obsessions act to the detriment of adult relationships.

Actually fear of sexuality is related to fear of initiation. Unrestrained sexual activity is more the action of uninitiated men and women, the blind activity of the sibling society. Malidoma Some talks of the "hormonal invasion" of adolescence being the start of the initiatory process for men. The newfound sexual urge brought by puberty, along with the aggressive energy of maleness, triggers both the adolescent drive and the initiatory archetype. The adolescent urge for freedom is the initiatory archetype being stirred.

Healthy sexual energy is another form of initiatory energy. This stirring is the archetypal need for separation from the prohibitions of father and mother, and the joining with others outside the family circle. In the movie *Emerald Forest* a young Caucasian boy, Tommy, is kidnapped from his father's presence, while his father is working to build a power generating dam in the Amazon basin. The tribe, called by a name meaning invisible people, raise the young boy, now Tomme, as their own. As Tomme grows up, the boys and girls move in different circles under the watchful eyes of Elders. As Tomme grows into adolescence he starts to notice the young adolescent girls and feels the familiar stirrings. One day Tomme, while swimming, moves away from his friends and curiously and playfully reaches for the girl he is attracted to. At that point his father, as Elder and chief, forcefully stops him.

The other Elders of the tribe support their chief. Tomme does not get a lecture about sexual purity or safe sex. Neither is he punished for lusting in his heart. He is not shamed in any way. What the Elders realize is that Tomme is ready for initiation. He cannot bond with a woman, especially in marriage, before he is initiated. Tomme is not ashamed, but he is terrified. The Elders have surprised him and started to take him away. He has no time to prepare. His initiation is to start immediately. His mother wails, "I will never see my boy again!" His sexual drive has signaled his readiness for manhood.

For Tomme's tribe, sex and serious relationship are intimately connected. He must be initiated to have an adult relationship with a woman. Sex is reserved for men, not boys. Sex is a sacred part of manhood. Sobonfu Somé, Malidoma's wife, talks of sex in the same way in her tribe. Her tribal language has no word for sex. Sex doesn't exist for them outside of an adult context. Sex is an essential part of an adult relationship, symbolized by marriage. Sex is an intricate part of an honest, exclusive, transparent relationship.

Tomme's whole life will change as a result of his maturing adolescence. Tomme will never see women again in the same way. He will also experience his sexual urge in a totally different way. If left alone, his sexual urge would bring him into an area that he was not emotionally able to handle. Like adolescents today, he would find himself in a world, including the possibility of parenthood, which he is ill-prepared to handle. Tomme's story of initiation and preparation will continue in the chapter on death.

Healthy adolescence means experimenting with relationships with the opposite sex, experimenting with issues of friendship, equality, and teamwork. These are the same issues an adolescent needs to explore with male adolescents, his peers. Dealing with women as people, like oneself, rather than as objects that give sexual nurturance, opens a whole new world of relationship. When men find that it is not impossible to be friends with a woman, especially one's wife, the realization is a step toward adulthood. Combining sex and friendship then becomes the Rosetta stone for a whole new life of healthy, heterosexual relationship. It is very hard to have exploitative, destructive sex with a friend.

Healthy adolescence introduces an emerging man to the possibility of a satisfying, committed, sexual relationship with a woman, a relationship which most men want to experience in marriage. If society were not stuck in dark, regressed adolescence there would not be such a fear of sex, or the shadow prevalence of pornography. There would be few double sexual messages. The sibling society creates unhealthy sexuality because it leaves men isolated in a regressed adolescence. A regressed adolescent will pair his newfound sexuality with a mother object instead of with a friend. Sexual addiction will follow. This is when a woman becomes a sexual object rather than a person.

Princess Leia

In the Star Wars myth, Luke and Han tried to be the hero so Leia would notice them and prove they were men. However, Princess Leia proves very early she is no damsel in distress. She is unimpressed by adolescent heroes sporting manly personas. As the story unfolds, there is a big surprise for Luke. The woman Luke was romantically attracted to becomes someone infinitely more dear and cherished. He finds she is his sister.

Leia has been a partner in a most meaningful endeavor. She has been friend and confidante. Now she becomes a key to his own self-discovery. Leia as Luke's sister symbolizes the heterosexual relationship of friendship and partnership. She also symbolizes the new family a man needs when he leaves his village family. Luke has ultimately found a new sister and a new brother in Leia and Han. Together this new family will inspire him to continue his initiatory journey.

They also open up to him a whole new type of relationship that a man discovers in healthy adolescence. Every man's wife must also become part sister, the part that is beloved friend and ally. In the knightly myth of courtly love, the knight also keeps his relationship to his damsel spiritual, like a sister. Spirituality is symbolized by no hope of sexual union, because of the connection at a soul and spiritual level. She is inspiration, and her love motivates him to find his own true self. She doesn't protect him from his pain. She does not depend on him to take care of her. She is there out of love for his spirit. Every man needs to incorporate this soul connection into his relationship with a beloved. At this point sexuality becomes sacred and part of the spiritual journey.

These two myths are symbolic of the deep connection of friendship and equality, and yes inspiration, that a man and woman can have. Adolescence can lay the foundation for these kinds of relationships. Men and women can inspire each other to find their own initiation. Marriage and sexuality then become the symbol of the union of two mature, initiated people, as well as the archetypal symbol of psychological wholeness. This is when the knight becomes a king, and the damsel, a queen.

Bibliography

Alboher, Marci. (2013). *The Encore Career Handbook* Workman Publishing: New York. <u>Socio-Cultural</u>. Later career directions for healthy patriarchs that can change the world. An important second chance for baby boomers!

Bly, Robert. (1990). *Iron John* Addison-Wesley: New York. <u>Mythopoetic/Archetypal Psychology</u>. A classic in the men's movement. Bly is a pioneer in the unmasking of the pseudo-masculinity of the patriarchy. Some may not connect with this book because of its literary and mythic bent.

Bly, Robert. *The Sibling Society* <u>Mythopoetic/Socio-Cultural</u>. A book about the dearth of elders in society with the result that we are primarily an adolescent society. More data for the politically inclined. A good insight into our morally leaderless society.

Bolen, Jean Shinoda. (1989). *Gods in Everyman* Harper and Row: San Francisco. <u>Archetypal Psychology</u>. Connection of Greek myth to insights into the dynamics of a patriarchal society. Also a look into the roots of our Western culture in its model of manhood.

Bradshaw, John. (1990). *Homecoming* Bantam: New York. <u>Psychology</u>. Great insight into work with the complex of the inner child. The ages of Bradshaw's children do not correspond to the ages in this book. But the process and principles are very helpful. The ages will take care of themselves if the process is followed. The youngest boy, middle boy, and adolescent will emerge.

Brooks, Gary. (1995). *The Centerfold Syndrome* Jossey-Bass: San Francisco. A look at unhealthy male sexuality leading to unhealthy intimacy. A study of the roots of sexual addiction. For the professional he has also written a good book on therapy: *A New Psychotherapy for Traditional Men.*

Campbell, Joseph. (1949). *The Hero with a Thousand Faces* MJF Books: New York. <u>Mythopoetic</u>. Another classic. Campbell opened up the truth of myth to the larger population. His work undergirds Jung's theory of the collective unconscious and the hardwiring in every man. He studies the hero archetype rather than the initiatory archetype, but the parallels are too important to miss.

Carnes, Patrick. (1983), *Out Of the Shadows, Understanding Sexual Addiction* CompCare: Minneapolis. <u>Psychology</u>. A clinical look at sexual addiction. Carnes is a pioneer in studying and researching this topic.

Diamond, Jed. (1997). *Male Menopause* Sourcebooks: Naperville. <u>Medical/ Mythopoetic</u>. Sound medical basis for the losses men feel at midlife. A description of the 'menopause passage' that mirrors initiation. A mythopoetic answer to midlife struggles.

Doherty, Catherine. (1975). *Poustinia* Ave Maria Press: Notre Dame. <u>Socio-cultural/ Spirituality</u>. A look at Russian spirituality as an insight into an older Elder society. A spiritual look at aspects of the Ordeal of initiation.

Eliade, Mircea. (1958) *Rite and Symbols Of Initiation* Harper and Row: New York. <u>Socio-Cultural/Spirituality</u>. A great scholar of the history of religion and myth. This is a scholarly work for those who want to study initiation in depth from an anthropological and cultural perspective.

Farrell, Warren. (1993). *The Myth of Male Power* Simon and Schuster: New York. <u>Socio-Cultural</u>. A strong case for the toxicity of modern culture for men. Many proofs of how men are as oppressed as women by the patriarchal culture. Be ready for your blood pressure to rise upon reading.

Fisher, Robert, (1990). *The Knight in Rusty Armor* Wilshire Book: Hollywood. <u>Mythopoetic</u>. A short, entertaining allegory written by a successful TV and radio comedy writer. The story of a knight totally encumbered and imprisoned in his own patriarchal armor and how he escapes.

Gerzon, Mark. (1982, 1992). *A Choice of Heroes* Houghton-Mifflin: New York. <u>Socio-Cultural/ Archetypal Psychology</u>. A look at the modern archetypes of manhood and how limiting they are. Groundbreaking at the time. Many examples of how our leaders and heroes are formed and form us.

Gerzon, Mark. (1996). *Listening To Midlife* Shambhala: Boston. <u>Psychology</u>. A wise look at the challenge of initiation at midlife. A hopeful book by a seasoned elder.

Gilmore, David (1990). *Manhood in The Making* Yale University Press: New Haven. <u>Socio-Cultural</u>. A study of modern initiation rituals and masculine mores from an anthropologist's point of view. A look at faulty rituals that have devolved over the centuries. Good comparison to modern American culture with insight into the roots of modern cultural attitudes.

Gray, John (1992). *Men Are From Mars, Women Are From Venus* HarperCollins: New York. <u>Psychology</u>. Basic descriptions of the differences of men and women in the area of intimacy.

Guggenbuhl-Craig, Adolf. (1977). *Marriage Dead or Alive* Spring Publications: Woodstock, Connecticut. <u>Psychology/Archetypal Psychology</u>. A Jungian psychologist talks of marriage as a way of reaching maturity.

Gurian, Michael. (2003). *What Could He Be Thinking?* St. Martin's Press: New York. <u>Psychology/Neurobiology</u>. A book about the differences in male and female neurobiology and its effects on gender attitudes and behavior. This is a field that is shaping our gender understanding in the 21st century.

Halper, Janice. (1988). *Quiet Desperation: The Truth About Successful Men* Warner: New York. <u>Socio-Cultural</u>. An executive consultant for Fortune 500 companies, she conducted over 4,000 interviews of successful executives. Her findings question the myth of happiness that comes from success as well as the myth that corporate culture breeds real men. A good study of workaholism.

Hawken, Paul. (2007). *Blessed Unrest* Viking: New York. <u>Socio-Cultural</u>. A book about the 'largest movement in the world' that relates to social justice, protection of the environment, and indigenous values. A hopeful, motivating book.

Hillman, James. (1996). *The Soul's Code: In Search of Character and Calling* Random House: New York. <u>Archetypal Psychology</u>. An Elder archetypal psychologist looks at the way men and women are called to very specific talents and endeavors. How this idea has been around in Western culture since the early Greeks. A new psychology of "fate."

Hornstein, Harvey. (1991). *A Knight In Shining Armor: Understanding Men's Romantic Illusions* William Morrow: New York. Psychology. A more complete explanation of the damsel in distress syndrome. A book about how men lose in romantic relationships.

Jarema, William. (1994). *Fathering the Next Generation* Crossroads: New York. <u>Psychology</u>. A great book for men who want to be good fathers. A help for men exploring their father wounds.

Johnson, Robert, (1989). *He: Understanding Masculine Psychology* (Revised Edition). Harper and Row: New York. <u>Archetypal Psychology</u>. Johnson is a true elder, wise, humble, caring. His books are short but very dense. He is a man of few words but the words are powerful. He follows in the line of Joseph Campbell in studying the hero myth, but from a psychological perspective. He has also written a book, *She,* about feminine psychology.

Johnson, Robert (1994). *Lying With The Heavenly Woman: Understanding and Integrating The Feminine Archetypes In Men's Lives* Harper San Francisco. <u>Archetypal Psychology</u>. A good study of the anima and how it affects men's lives.

Johnson, Robert (1983). *We: Understanding the Psychology of Romantic Love* Harper-San Francisco. <u>Archetypal Psychology</u>. This is a book that gives some answers to the confusion of romantic love. It can bring a man back to what is most important about his own life and how relationships fit in.

Keen, Sam. (1991). *Fire In The Belly: On Being A Man* Bantam: New York. <u>Socio-Cultural/ Psychology</u>. One of the most readable and understandable books about men. A good understanding of psychology for a philosopher. He puts it together in a way that a man can connect to. Discussion of WOMAN a classic. Good discussion of pseudo-rituals of initiation.

Kindlon, Dan and Thompson, Michael. (1999). *Raising Cain: Protecting the Emotional Life Of Boys* Ballantine Books: New York. Psychology. An excellent book that should be read by every mother and father of a son. A good companion to Pollack's book. More balanced in explaining the role of father and mentors.

Kipnis, Aaron. (1991). *Knights without Armor* St. Martin's Press: New York. Archetypal Psychology/Socio-Cultural/Mythopoetic. Kipnis is a psychotherapist with a large perspective and good instincts. He talks of the need for men to have new missions outside the patriarchy. He delineates twelve tasks that mature men need to accomplish. His analysis of the empty hero myth of our culture is well worth reading.

Krantzler, Mel. (1992). *The 7 Marriages of Your Marriage* HarperSanFrancisco: New York. Psychology. An excellent look at the developmental stages of marriage from a cultural and psychological point of view. Out of print, but can be found in libraries.

Lee, John. (2009). *The Anger Solution* Da Capo Lifelong Books: Cambridge, MA. Psychology. Excellent book on the difference between healthy anger and harmful rage. A good explanation of rage addiction.

Lee, John. (2001), *Growing Yourself Back Up* Three Rivers Press: New York. Psychology. A very good book about regression and how to deal with it.

Levinson, Daniel. (1978). *The Seasons of A Man's Life* Alfred Knopf: New York. Psychology/Socio-Cultural. Still relevant over 20 years later. A long-range, scientific study of mostly professional men's social and psychological development. His stages of masculine development deserve careful reading as they fly in the face of popular conceptions. Good discussion of mentors.

Levoy, Gregg. (1997). *Callings* Three Rivers Press: New York. Archetypal Psychology. Many wise thoughts on the way a man may find his purpose in life.

Linn, Denise. (1997). *Quest, A Guide For Creating Your Own Vision Quest* Ballantine Books: New York. Socio-Cultural. An excellent, step-by-step guide to the initiatory process by a woman elder who has guided many.

Mahdi, Louise, Editor. (1987). *Betwixt & Between: Patterns of Masculine and Feminine Initiation* Open Court: La Salle, Illinois. Socio-Cultural/Psychology/Archetypal Psychology. This may be the first book to reach for in order to understand male initiation in all it aspects. Great background for this book.

Meade, Michael. (1993). *Men and The Water Of Life* Harper-San Francisco: New York. Mythopoetic/Archetypal Psychology. "Meade writes quite brilliantly about initiation, ordeal and the importance of scars and wounds..." (New York Times). Meade is a seminal pioneer in the men's movement. If you like Bly you'll love Meade.

Miller, Stuart. (1983). *Men and Friendship* Tarcher: Los Angeles. <u>Socio-Cultural</u>. A compelling account of one man's struggle with finding men to be brothers rather than competitors. A good look at the obstacles to male friendship and the emotional need we all have for male companionship.

Moore, Robert and Gillette, Douglas. (1991). *King. Warrior, Magician, Lover: Rediscovering The Archetypes Of The Mature Masculine* Harper-San Francisco: New York. <u>Archetypal Psychology/Psychology</u>. A must read book. Important ideas of king and warrior that refer to men's missions and boundaries.

Moore, Thomas. (1992). *Care of the Soul* Harper Collins: New York. <u>Psychology/ Archetypal Psychology</u>. The connection of psychology with a wider look at what it is to be human. Like Bly and Meade but from a therapist's and philosopher's point of view.

Morgan, Marlo. (1991). *Mutant Message Down Under* MM Co.:Missouri. <u>Socio-Cultural</u>. A controversial book, little known. I believe it to be an accurate look into the beliefs and lifestyle of indigenous Aborigine of Australia.

Peck, Scott. (1978). *The Road Less Traveled* Simon and Schuster: New York. <u>Psychology/Spirituality</u>. A classic book that made many ideas in psychology understandable to all of us. Then he connects these ideas to love relationships and the spiritual search. I recommend it to most men starting counseling.

Pittman, Frank. (1993). *Man Enough: Fathers, Sons, and the Search for Masculinity* Putnam's Sons: New York. <u>Psychology/Socio-Cultural</u>. An incisive look at the "male chorus," all the male voices telling us how to be men, that affects all men's life in their search for masculinity. Also a good look at fathers and mothers and how they affect adult relationships.

Plotkin, Bill. (2008) *Nature and the Human Soul* New World Library: Novato, California. <u>Archetypal Psychology</u>. Indigenous sense of life stages and the need for connection to Nature.

Pollack, William (1998). *Real Boys: Rescuing Our Sons from the Myths of Boyhood* Random House: New York. <u>Psychology</u>. A scientific study of how boys are socialized to be patriarchal men, by what Pollack calls "the Boy Code." Answers to how to parent a boy into a healthy male. Also, for professionals, he has co-authored and edited a book on counseling for men called *The New Psychotherapy for Men*. John Wiley & Sons: New York.

Real, Terrence. (1997). *I Don't Want To Talk About It: Overcoming the Secret Legacy Of Male Depression* Scribner: New York. <u>Psychology</u>. Excellent discussion of the widespread hidden depression in men, masked by addiction and violence. Uninformed criticism of the men's movement and the initiatory journey.

Rohr, Richard. (1996). *The Wild Man's Journey: Reflections on Male Spirituality* (Revised Edition). St. Anthony Messenger Press: Cincinnati. Spirituality/Psychology. Fr. Rohr has the unusual ability to wed spiritual wisdom and psychological truth in a way that enhances both. Bring that background to men's issues and you have a powerful book for men.

Rotundo, Anthony. (1993). *American Manhood: Transformations in Masculinity from the Revolution to the Modern Era* HarperCollins: New York. Socio-Cultural. A fine history of how the traditional American male ideology was formed.

Sams, Jamie. (1990). *Sacred Path Cards: The Discovery of Self Through Native Teachings* HarperCollins: New York. Socio-Cultural/PsychoSpiritual. Wise book describing Native American values. The cards can be used as synchronous guidance to wisdom related to specific life situations.

Somé, Malidoma. (1998). *The Healing Wisdom of Africa* Jeremy Tarcher/Putnam: New York. A study of indigenous culture and the making of a man. A look at the roles of mentor, Elder, ritual healers. One model of a spiritually and psychologically healthy society.

Somé, Malidoma. (1994). *Of Water and the Spirit* Jeremy Tarcher/ Putnam: New York. A riveting story of Malidoma's experience of his initiation into the Dagara tribe of West Africa.

Van der Post, Laurens and Taylor, Jane. (1984). *Testament to the Bushmen* Viking:England. Socio-Cultural. Laurens has befriended and studied the Bushmen his whole life. A look into a healthy indigenous culture. He was also a friend of Carl Jung and wrote of Jung's study trips to Africa.

Yablonsky, Lewis. (1982). *Fathers & Sons* Simon and Schuster: New York. Psychology. An enlightened look at father wounds and father guidance. The psychological insight will help any man be a better father or understand his own father.

Zilbergeld, Bernie. (1992). *The New Male Sexuality* Bantam: NewYork. Psychology. An important work about how full sexuality is connected to male maturation. How traditional male attitudes get in the way of full sexual satisfaction. Ways to become a mature lover.

About the Author

My name is Larry Pesavento. I have been a licensed counselor and administrator in the mental health field for over 40 years. I have worked with people of all ages from toddlers to senior citizens. During the last 2½ decades I have been especially interested in men's issues. I have been drawn to these issues the way most men have, through my own life crises. In trying to figure out my own life I came upon many parts of myself that didn't fit into conventional notions of manhood and psychological development. That realization led me on a journey that I am still on today.

The journey was helped along considerably when I attended a men's workshop by Michael Meade and Malidoma Somé in the mid-80's. Their work on initiation and men's development allowed me to start naming some previously unrecognized parts of myself. Through self-reflection, reading, and sharing in the lives of many men who came to me for help I have felt called to add my own psychological and spiritual insights to the body of work of the men's movement.

I started Christos: A Center for Men in 1993 to learn more about men's psychospiritual development as well as to share my insights, especially the insight that men have a deep need to be connected in community. The Center is a place where men can meet that need. The Center is a place that encourages a man's emotional, psychological and spiritual growth in a community of men.

The Center offers individual counseling, group counseling, educational programs, men's retreats, and structured initiatory experiences. Information on these programs, additional resources and contact information can be found at www.ChristosCenter.com.

Made in the USA
Lexington, KY
05 February 2018